Praise for Jeff Apter

Roy Orbison: King of Hearts

"The look, the voice, the name—all of which seemed to suggest Roy Orbison was a music specter from another galaxy. I'm so proud to have the record on 'Crying,' and so happy for what it did for this really beautiful human being. I'm also proud to call him my friend. Our paths are forever crossed. His music is perfect, like this book."

—Don McLean

"One day, as I was listening to Roy's song 'A Love So Beautiful' back-to-back with Giacomo Puccini's 'Nessun dorma,' I found a small clue to understanding the music of Roy Orbison. His effortless tenor triumphs over life, love, and loss with heartbreaking bravery, as this book attests. The message is timeless: *Vincerò! Vincerò!*"

—Jennifer Warnes, Grammy Award–winning singer-songwriter

"Rockabilly Roy was as good as it gets. His early records are a true inspiration and influence. The image and voice have stood the test of time and will always be part of the rock 'n' roll landscape. Jeff Apter has captured the various dimensions of his life with the utmost respect in this seminal biography of a music legend."

—Slim Jim Phantom of the Stray Cats

"Jeff Apter has done his homework. Roy Orbison emerges from these pages brimming with life. Apter tells a frank and sharply observed story of an American treasure—a recording star in the 1960s and '70s—when music was changing faster than 45 rpms."

—Bob Spitz, *New York Times* bestselling author of *The Beatles: The Biography* and *Led Zeppelin: The Biography*

Carl Perkins: The King of Rockabilly

"This fine biography really does justice to Mr. Blue Suede Shoes!"

—Slim Jim Phantom of the Stray Cats

"As portrayed in Jeff Apter's *Carl Perkins: The King of Rockabilly*, Perkins certainly earns the claim in the book's subtitle. A music writer from Australia, Mr. Apter is an unabashed fan, and his quote-studded account . . . captures the thrills of Perkins's music and his down-to-earth personality. It also serves as a lively primer for the uninitiated and a go-to source of arcana for rockabilly cultists. Mr. Apter gives Perkins his due as the genre's first auteur—songwriter, singer and guitarist's guitarist who influenced generations of musicians, from the Beatles to revivalists like the Stray Cats. Ironically, Perkins's many gifts were often overshadowed by his signature song, 'Blue Suede Shoes,' the rockabilly anthem that became more famous than its creator."

—The Wall Street Journal

"Jeff Apter has succeeded in bringing Carl Perkins to life—not only as a rock and roll pioneer, but as a father, brother, friend, and colleague. In moving prose, Apter tells us about Carl's dirt-poor childhood, his struggle for fame, and his close friendships with Elvis Presley, Roy Orbison and, especially, Johnny Cash. Apter practically brings us to tears as we see the Beatles, Carl's biggest fans, introduce him to a new generation of listeners. This is an essential book for fans of rock and its history."

—Elizabeth J. Rosenthal, author of *His Song: The Musical Journey of Elton John* and *The Master of Drums: Gene Krupa and the Music He Gave the World*

"If Elvis Presley was the voice, Carl Perkins was *the sound*. Not since Nick Tosches's *Hellfire* has a book on rock 'n' roll's wildest ancestors been laid as bare or with as much impassioned scholarship. With a fresh take on the genre's earliest roots, Jeff Apter's chronicle of rockabilly's favorite son is the real deal—blazing, rocking vignettes and firsthand accounts offer us a front-row seat to the life and art of the guitarist who unabashedly shaped the American rock sound and once gave another king a real run for his money. Apter masterfully reminds us that there would be no rock 'n' roll without the blazing guitar of this great innovator. A must for music fans and *crucial* for those whose hearts beat rockabilly. Long live Carl Perkins—the original king!"

—C. M. Kushins, author of *Beast: John Bonham and the Rise of Led Zeppelin*

"If you are a fan of Carl Perkins, of 'Blue Suede Shoes' days, Jeff Apter's new biography, *Carl Perkins: The King of Rockabilly*, is a loving and detailed look at his life, focusing on the deep affection that McCartney, Harrison, and other rock stars had for this gifted and modest man."

—Robert Hilburn, author of *Johnny Cash: The Life*, *Paul Simon: The Life*, and *A Few Words in Defense of Our Country: The Biography of Randy Newman*

"Suited to ardent rockabilly fans."

—Publishers Weekly

"Australian music and popular culture writer Apter adds to his shelf of music biographies with this affectionate look into the life of rockabilly legend Carl Perkins. Apter adopts a fairly strict chronology, from Perkins's childhood days picking cotton in rural Tennessee through his signing with Sun Records, his Million Dollar Quartet sessions, and his rise to international fame while rubbing shoulders and singing or playing guitar with a veritable who's-who of the popular music world. From Johnny Cash to the Beatles, Perkins counted almost all the greats as friends. But he may be best remembered for writing songs covered by others, such as Elvis Presley's rendition of 'Blue Suede Shoes.' Poignant episodes dealing with Perkins's overcoming alcohol-use disorder and family tragedies are juxtaposed with joyful tours in Britain and beyond. Apter also details Perkins's social justice efforts, including establishing a child-abuse prevention center in Jackson, TN. An extensive bibliography and helpful epilogue are included, bringing readers up to date on developments since Perkins's death. Other than Perkins's own 1996 autobiography, little has been published about him, and Apter admirably fills the gap with this detailed and emotionally charged biography."

—Library Journal

"An overdue remembrance of a pioneer of American music."

—Lincoln Journal Star

"Carl Perkins was above all else my friend for over twenty-five years. I'm thankful that he is not forgotten. I very much enjoyed the book, which brought back so many memories."

—Wes Henley, bandmate and friend of Carl Perkins

"Apter's narrative is rich with insider details, exploring not only Perkins' musical achievements but also his personal battles and humanitarian efforts. This biography offers readers a comprehensive look at the man who, as Paul McCartney famously said, played a pivotal role in the birth of rock 'n' roll. For those interested in the history of Rock 'n' Roll Highway 67, *Carl Perkins: The King of Rockabilly* is a must-read. The book's in-depth exploration of Perkins' career and life provides valuable insight into the legacy of a man whose influence helped shape the sound of rock 'n' roll. Perkins' story is not just a tale of music; it's a testament to the enduring spirit of an artist who, despite the odds, left an indelible mark on the world."

—Rock 'n' Roll Highway

"A worthy chronicle of the Sun Records trailblazer. In the absence of your classic arc to glory, perdition and redemption, the author finds virtue instead in Stoic consistency as he pursues a meticulous six-decade chronology of the rockabilly cat's road, every flop album just a pothole en route to, er, another shot of Blue Suede Shoes."

—The Sydney Morning Herald

"The first updated biography in decades of one of rockabilly's most important artists has been unveiled. Boasting a foreword by Stray Cats' Slim Jim Phantom, *Carl Perkins: The King of Rockabilly* promises new details about the star's private battles, humanitarian work and personal inspirations. . . ."

—Vintage Rock

"As a lifelong Beatles fan, reading about Perkins's relationship with the band from his perspective was a delight. Jeff Apter's book captures Perkins's talent, passion, and humility and tells a story that is remarkably American. And it illuminates the world of early rock 'n' roll: the constant touring, the small venues, and the community of musicians that formed as all these different acts shared stages over the years, the radio stations, and the music reviewers at the newspapers. . . . His love for music shines on every page. It's a fun biography for anyone who loves the sound of jangling guitars."

—The Post and Courier

"If there's an old-time music lover on your list, check out *Carl Perkins: The King of Rockabilly*. Like most good biographies, this book takes readers back to Perkins' childhood and his earliest influences, moving through to the start of his career and his pioneering work, as well as the people he played with, onstage and off. This is the book to give someone who remembers the music of the '50s or the one who wasn't 'there' but still loves those tunes."

—The Bookworm Sez

"'Well, it's one for the money, two for the show/three to get ready, now go, cat, go.' That's just what Australian music writer Jeff Apter does in his affectionate, straight-ahead biography *Carl Perkins: The King of Rockabilly*. While 'Blue Suede Shoes' became the hit that propelled Carl Perkins to the top of the charts, selling 250,000 copies just one month after its release in January 1956, and became the song with which he became most associated, Perkins went on to write songs such as 'Daddy Sang Bass,' 'Honcy, Don't,' and 'Dixic Fried' that were cut by many other artists, including Johnny Cash, the Beatles, and Elvis. . . . Will appeal primarily to fans of Perkins, but the book's short and well-paced chapters also serve as a useful introduction to Perkins and his music."

—No Depression

"The most impressive part of Apter's biography is not Perkins' career. It is the revelation that Perkins was a genuinely decent man, a faithful husband, devoted father, and loyal friend. *Carl Perkins: The King of Rockabilly* shows that while nice guys may not always become the biggest stars, they can nevertheless finish first. It is a biography worth reading."

—***Ricochet***

"Where Apter really excels is putting Perkins' music in perspective. . . . Apter succeeds in showing how much more there was to Perkins than 'Blue Suede Shoes.' Perkins is sometimes labeled a one-hit wonder; Apter easily shows the ridiculousness of that opinion. . . . If you want to know about the rock 'n' roll revolution that came storming out of Sun Records in the 1950s, you can't overlook Carl Perkins. His music was as exciting as any of his peers. . . . Apter delivers the quieter story of this under-celebrated musical hero crisply and succinctly, much like a Carl Perkins song."

—***Chapter 16***

"Apter is clearly a Perkins fan and has undertaken an exhaustive exploration of the life of an innovative guitarist, songwriter and singer who learned his craft by working alongside Black sharecroppers who sang blues and rhythm-and-blues in the fields and listening to the spirituals and country music that surrounded him in Tennessee. No one individual did more to bring about the fusion of these elements to form a new music, rock 'n' roll, than Perkins."

—**NOLA.com**

"I've played Carl Perkins in six productions of *Million Dollar Quartet.* I wanted to say a sincere thank-you to Jeff Apter for writing *Carl Perkins: The King of Rockabilly*. Carl means the world to me, and his book was informative, insightful, and truly touching. I learned a lot and will carry the experience of this book with me in all of my future *Million Dollar Quartet* and Carl endeavors."

—**Cason Day, actor, *Million Dollar Quartet***

Keith Urban

"Apter meticulously captures the music industry hurdles Urban overcame on his way to success and gives credit to his 'single-channeled drive and stickability.' Urban's fans will devour this deep dive."

—*Publishers Weekly*

"Keith Urban has done just about everything in country music that anyone could ever imagine. This biography by Jeff Apter reveals the highlights and struggles in getting there. I loved looking at the pictures, not just the celebrations that he's had, but the pictures of his youth really caught my attention. The look in his eyes had the look of destiny. To use one of Keith's quotes, 'Nashville's not my dream. It's my destiny.'"

—Ricky Skaggs, 15-time Grammy Award–winning musician

"Jeff Apter's Keith Urban had dreamed of Nashville stardom ever since he was a young, guitar-pickin' boy from a working class home in Australia. It didn't happen easily or quickly, but came through hard work and tenaciousness. In lively prose, Apter takes us on every happy twist and frustrating turn that Urban faced on his way to the top."

—Elizabeth J. Rosenthal, author of *His Song: The Musical Journey of Elton John* and *The Master of Drums: Gene Krupa and the Music He Gave the World*

"He ain't just that Aussie cowboy with the golden locks and godly good looks who seemingly came out of nowhere in the early 2000s, set the country and pop charts ablaze with his honey-sweet songs, and married a movie star. No, ma'am. There's more than that to Keith Urban—*much* more. From his humble beginnings in blue-collar Brisbane to crooning for swooning swarms in rhinestone-studded Nashville, overcoming addiction, and filling stadiums and tabloid covers around the world, Urban has ridden a long, rocky road to the top, a road full of breathtaking highs, heartbreaking lows, and everything in between. Jeff Apter's long-awaited biography of this beloved modern troubadour is a riveting read that no music fan will want to miss."

—Peter Aaron, author of *The Band FAQ* and co-author of Richie Ramone's autobiography, *I Know Better Now: My Life Before, During and After the Ramones*

"Jeff Apter's perceptive biography is an ideal homage to one of our era's most seminal country musicians. It tells a tale much like the wild and free genre of country music, and the land down under that Keith Urban came from: natural and raw, full of true spirit, and steeped in authenticity."

—Jude Warne, author of *America, the Band: An Authorized Biography* and *Lowdown: The Music of Boz Scaggs*

"A celebratory portrait of Urban's life and career—the perseverance required, even for a natural, as Urban was described early in the piece—while also taking in such key moments as meeting future wife Nicole Kidman at an L.A. bash, whom he described as floating across the room. Informed, engagingly written, this is one for Urban fans—and there's a lot of them out there."

—The Sydney Morning Herald

"A detailed chronicle of the multi-decade, winding path that has made Keith Urban a Nashville superstar and household name . . . A veritable who's who of Australian and international Country music names, specifying those who contributed and collaborated with Keith to ensure his dream was made reality."

—GLAM Adelaide

Roy Orbison
King of Hearts

Books by JEFF APTER

Keith Urban

Carl Perkins: The King of Rockabilly

Roy Orbison: King of Hearts

Lee Gordon Presents . . . How One Man Changed Australian Life Forever

A Pure Drop: The Life of Jeff Buckley

Tragedy: The Ballad of the Bee Gees

Malcolm Young: The Man Who Made AC/DC

High Voltage: The Life of Angus Young

Friday On My Mind: The Life of George Young

Bad Boy Boogie: The True Story of AC/DC Legend Bon Scott

Don't Dream It's Over: The Remarkable Life of Neil Finn

Roy Orbison

King of Hearts

Jeff Apter

CITADEL PRESS
Kensington Publishing Corp.
kensingtonbooks.com

CITADEL PRESS BOOKS are published by

Kensington Publishing Corp.
900 Third Avenue
New York, NY 10022

All Kensington titles, imprints, and distributed lines are available at special quantity discounts for bulk purchases for sales promotions, premiums, fund-raising, educational, or institutional use. Special book excerpts or customized printings can also be created to fit specific needs. For details, write or phone the office of the Kensington sales manager: Kensington Publishing Corp., 900 Third Avenue, New York, NY 10022, attn: Sales Department; phone 1-800-221-2647.

Library of Congress Control Number is available

First hardcover printing: May 2026

ISBN: 978-0-8065-4463-2

ISBN: 978-0-8065-4465-6 (e-book)

10 9 8 7 6 5 4 3 2 1

Printed in the United States of America

The authorized representative in the EU for product safety and compliance

is eucomply OU, Parnu mnt 139b-14, Apt 123

Tallinn, Berlin 11317, hello@eucompliancepartner.com

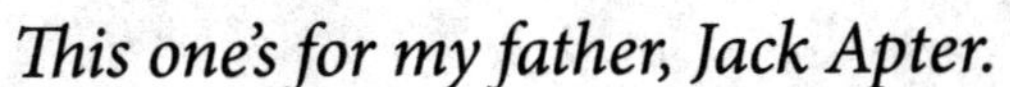

This one's for my father, Jack Apter.

Contents

Foreword

By Slim Jim Phantom of the Stray Cats

There was a steady stream of limos dropping off quite a few recognizable people, as well as a platoon of clipboard-carrying personal assistants on walkie-talkies buzzing around, whisking their clients inside. The whole scene was a beehive of showbiz activity. I was having a good enough time standing at the stage door, smoking and watching the whole thing.

The Stray Cats had been invited to play a song for the 1990 Roy Orbison tribute at Universal Amphitheatre. We had already soundchecked and I was killing time. One particular limo attracted a little more attention and hubbub than the others, and as the door opened, I could see why.

Bob Dylan majestically stepped out and was expertly whisked towards the stage door by a couple of assistants who were brushing aside anyone in the way. He had a perfectly natural and relaxed swagger. I had met him a few times in the past and knew he was 100 percent a rockabilly boy at heart.

As I was waving hello and stepping back to let him through, he handed me a bottle of Old Grand-Dad whiskey and swept me along with him. I was in the right place at the right time. Most of the acts that day had been sharing dressing rooms, but Bob had his own. He pulled me with him as quite a few starstruck performers and crew looked on with a little wonderment and jealousy. We sat in his room for the next few hours, nipped at the bottle, and talked about the original cool factor of rockabilly music and style.

Roy Orbison was a main topic. Bob told me that he had met Roy on his own twenty-first birthday in 1962. It was a pretty cool rockabilly factoid for me.

Today, it is common knowledge that Roy was one of the best singers who ever lived, and the depth of his lush ballads and amazing vocal range are unquestioned. Sometimes though, Rockabilly Roy is overlooked. The rockabilly stuff that he did at Sun Records is as good and rocking as anything. His sweet tenor somehow fit right in with the likes of Elvis, Carl Perkins, Jerry Lee Lewis, Johnny Cash, and the other artists who were signed with one of the coolest and most influential records labels in history.

Sam Phillips, who had instinctive savvy when it came to recognizing talent, signed Roy and the Teen Kings after hearing the Norman Petty-produced demo of "Ooby Dooby" over the phone. A recommendation to Sam from Johnny Cash has also been rumored. Either way, Sam told Roy he was going to be "my new rocker."

The Stray Cats had a Sun Records compilation record that included a few of Roy's early numbers, and we read some early accounts of his beginnings. It was a perfect time capsule of rockabilly history. The songs "Devil Doll," "Go! Go! Go! (Down the Line)," "Domino," and "Rock House" were especially important because they were on one of the earliest records we collectively owned.

I imagined Roy's performances at drive-in theaters playing in between the movies on bills shared with Eddie Cochran and Gene Vincent, with Elvis hanging out at a few of the gigs. Elvis and Roy had become pals. A young rockabilly myself, I was awed by this dream scenario.

With his trademark dark glasses and black suits, Roy was always a mysterious, intriguing, and haunted-looking cat. His top-notch, greasy, high pompadour was approved by all of us. Accounts of the tragic loss of his beautiful wife Claudette and his two young sons soon after were heartbreaking to me even though I had never met the guy.

It was a treat to see Roy get back into the mainstream consciousness with the Traveling Wilburys in 1988. When "Handle with Care" came out, it was an instant classic and a landmark. I believe that Roy was the lynchpin and cementing presence that brought George Harrison, Bob Dylan, Tom Petty, and Jeff Lynne together. The record was so good and drew so much well-deserved positive attention that it made everyone happy. It was also some damn fine listening. I loved how excited George would be when he gave interviews and the subject turned to Roy.

I was, of course, influenced by the Beatles, and that influence inspired me to go deeper and find out who *their* influences were. This search ultimately led me to the original American rock 'n' roll star, namely Rockabilly Roy. There's a mind-blowing Johnny Cash Christmas TV special from 1977 where Carl Perkins, Jerry Lee Lewis, and Roy join Johnny for a tribute to Elvis with a rollicking and stunning version of "This Train." Even among this legendary quartet of singers, Roy shined and everybody knew it. Jerry Lee almost looked annoyed by how good Roy was.

A few years later, when the Stray Cats had spearheaded the return of rockabilly to mainstream commerciality, there were a few TV shows and specials dedicated to these true early rock stars. I was honored to have been asked by Cats' producer Dave Edmunds to do the Carl Perkins special in London in 1985. George was on that one, too, and that was where I first met him and started a nice, long-lasting friendship. I like to think that show helped spark more like it.

Class of '55 was a record released in 1986, produced and recorded by the legendary Chips Moman at Sun Studios, which saw Johnny, Carl, Jerry Lee, and Roy reunite for the album. We were all thrilled to even think that we had a small role to play in bringing our entire beloved genre and its originators back into the spotlight.

A Dick Clark TV special with footage of the original sessions aired in 1989. Dick loved rockabilly and was really into the Stray Cats, so he helped us in any way he could. After an *American Bandstand* performance we did in 1983, Dick had a special compilation tape made for us to watch on the tour bus. It had all the original American rock 'n' rollers, including some footage of Roy that I hadn't seen before. We wore out that tape on the next tour.

The Stray Cats played the Roy Orbison tribute on February 24, 1990. We were contacted by his wife Barbara Orbison and, of course, accepted the invitation. We decided to do "Rock House." This was one of the songs from the Sun compilation that influenced us so much in the early days.

Whoopi Goldberg did the intro. Patrick Swayze and Dean Stockwell were the MCs. The performers included B. B. King, Bonnie Raitt,

Booker T. Jones, Chris Isaak, Dwight Yoakam, Emmylou Harris, Gary Busey, Harry Dean Stanton, Joe Ely, John Fogerty, John Hiatt, John Lee Hooker, k.d. lang, Larry Gatlin, Levon Helm, Michael McDonald, NRBQ, Ricky Skaggs, the Byrds, the TCB Band, and Wendy & Lisa. Everybody was cool. We all knew why we were all there. There were quite a few memorable performances, and k.d. lang's "Crying" has become legendary.

In doing research for this foreword, I went back and watched this historic show, and—if I do say so myself—the Stray Cats were simply awesome. We brought the energy and rockabilly chops that we had developed over the years after getting turned on to this uniquely American style of music. I like to imagine that Roy would have dug what we did with his song. Someone had to represent Rockabilly Roy, and I'm glad it was us.

Mystery Girl was the last album Roy recorded while he was alive, and it was a beautiful send-off. He finished it in November 1988, just a month before he died, and it was released two months after his passing, in February 1989. I remember when I first heard the lead single, "You Got It," my first reaction was that the timpani drums were back on a Roy album!

My second feeling was that Roy had gotten a raw deal. This Jeff Lynne-produced record hearkens back to the full and layered Roy albums from the Sixties but has the right amount of modern sounds, and most importantly, it breathes. The best records all share air. A great record needs space. Think of all your favorite records, and they will all share this quality. Jeff Lynne is one of the all-time top record producers in the history of rock 'n' roll, and he really shines on this one.

The hardest thing in rock 'n' roll is to make a record that uses all the instruments and voices you want but not to have it sound crowded. *Mystery Girl* had all this, plus the Wilburys family for good luck. It should have been Roy's comeback; unfortunately, he didn't stick around long enough to see how much everybody loved this album.

There was a video from the one time Roy ever publicly played "You Got It" at an awards show a few months before. The MTV generation was getting hip to Roy. With this one and *The Traveling Wilburys Vol. 1* album, he was the first deceased artist to have two records in the top

10 for the first time since his rockabilly buddy Elvis accomplished this strange and sad—but still pretty cool—achievement.

I never met Roy but have become very, good friends with his sons Roy Jr. and Alex. I hope they dig what I've got to say about their father.

Thanks to my rocking literary buddy Jeff Apter for writing a super cool book and to James Abbate at Kensington Publishing for asking me to write this foreword.

See you at the Rock House!

PROLOGUE

Revesby Workers Club, Suburban Sydney, Australia, March 11, 1983

Roy Orbison was once described as "more a presence than a person," and I learned why on this night a few decades back. I was barely out of my teens, a suburban kid raised on a steady diet of Aussie rock, Bob Dylan, Lou Reed, and my brother's British Invasion LPs, and yet here I was, in a thousand-seat auditorium in a casino in the western suburbs of Sydney, awaiting the appearance of an enigma from the 1960s. It was the opening show of a three-night stand for the man known as "the Big O"—shows that I later learned came with a hefty payday (Roy earned $12,500 merely for taking the stage). I was a newbie, an Orbison first-timer, having just handed over my $16 at the door.

Like much of my generation, I knew Roy Orbison more through his many greatest hits collections—cassettes and 8-tracks that seemed to be in every car in every Aussie driveway—than from any of his many previous tours of Australia that stretched way back to the early 1960s. And again, like a lot of my peers, my entrée to Roy Orbison had been through the irrepressibly chirpy "Penny Arcade," a monster Australian chart hit in late 1969—and one of the first singles I ever owned—rather than the epic, sweeping ballads I came to discover he'd crafted while with Monument Records. I'd learned Roy Orbison backwards, at least historically speaking.

While I knew enough of the music, it was the man who remained a mystery to me. This American of an indefinable age, who seemed to have been born wearing shades and clad in black from head-to-toe, was an elusive character. You didn't see Roy Orbison videos on the popular TV music show *Countdown*, while in photos he seemed to be avoiding the camera's glare, like rock and roll's very own Greta Garbo. And Roy hadn't bothered the charts since "Penny Arcade." *Who was this guy?*

So, I wasn't sure what to expect when the house lights went down and Roy's band took their places onstage. Then Roy stepped out into the spotlight. "You can't miss him, can you?" one fan said out loud as he began to sing. She wasn't kidding. What ensued left an impression on me that was more permanent than a tattoo.

I'd seen other peers of Roy's play this room, including Del Shannon and Ricky Nelson, and they gave off the strong whiff of nostalgia, acts lost in time, past their prime. (When Jerry Lee Lewis played here, he got into a fistfight with a member of the audience.) And, sure, Roy was a pro, a lifer, who'd been doing this for thirty years, but his connection to the music seemed as profound as ever. Roy wasn't simply going through the emotions tonight; he was *living* these songs.

And these were some songs: He led with "Only the Lonely," where the high notes posed no problems for Roy whatsoever—I gasped, and I swear others in the crowd did the same—and then he delivered "Sweet Dreams," "In Dreams," "Blue Bayou," "Working for the Man," "Oh, Pretty Woman," and many more Big O standards, one after the other, as well as a heartfelt Elvis tribute called "Hound Dog Man." Roy's voice was pristine, his band was right in the groove—and so what if he didn't say much between songs? I mean, what was left to say after "Crying" and "It's Over"?

After a tight hour, Roy and his slick ensemble left the building, another stellar performance delivered. But there was one final surprise. As most of the crowd began filing out of the room, heading for the one-armed-bandits and bars downstairs, I noticed a commotion at an adjacent table. Someone, somehow, had managed to sneak in a boom box without being detected by security, and they'd recorded the entire show, from the instrumental opener all the way through to the final strains of "Running Scared."

"Are we going?" someone asked me as I watched them set up their tape machine and hit *play*. Not a chance, I said; I wasn't going anywhere. Instead, I hung about with these true believers and relived the Orbison show, song by song, thanks to Revesby's very own bootlegger.

As it turned out, it was a wise move, because this was both my first and last memorable encounter with Roy Orbison. Big things were in his immediate future, including an astonishing commercial revival and membership of the most elite of supergroups—and one final tragedy—but Roy Orbison never toured Australia again.

CHAPTER 1

There'll be a stick with mud saying that Roy Orbison came through here

What Roy Kelton Orbison really wanted was a harmonica. The boy, a native of Vernon, Texas, was out walking with his father, Orbie Lee, when talk turned to his upcoming sixth birthday. There was plenty of music in the Orbison household; Orbie knew a few chords on the guitar and sometimes relatives would drop by to play and sing. Charlie, Orbie's brother, also played a little guitar, as did another of Roy's uncles, Kenneth Schultz. Nonetheless, Roy was hell-bent on getting himself a harmonica. Orbie Lee, however, had other ideas.

"Would a guitar be okay, son?" he asked.

Roy thought this through for a minute before replying.

"Sure," he said. "A guitar would be just fine."

Roy was no fool, even at such a young age. Not only would he soon learn that Lefty Frizzell, his earliest musical hero, played the guitar, but owning a six-string had benefits much closer to home. As Roy came to understand, "If I learned to play this guitar and sing fairly well, I got to stay up later than the rest of the kids, and actually be a part of the festivities. It had such a profound effect on my life. That was the foundation of my career."

Like many of his future musical peers, Roy Orbison, who was born midafternoon at Vernon's Christ the King Hospital on Thursday, April 23, 1936, was pure working class. His father, Orbie Lee, was born in 1913 at Olustee in Jackson County, Oklahoma, the youngest of Samuel and Serea Orbison's nine children. The town of Olustee was a dust speck on Highway 6 of less than one square mile, home to about 800 people, many living way below the poverty line. Orbie Lee was his real moniker, not a nickname, as Roy would point out to his friends and, further down the road, to the many curious members of the press. Orbie Lee's best friend was Orbie Harris, who named his son Orbie Jr., who became a friend of Roy. One Orbie in such a small town was rare, but this West Texas backwater was home to several.

Orbie Lee Orbison was a guitar-playing oil worker who shifted the family in 1942 from Vernon to Fort Worth to track down employment in the local defense plants, which were operating at full tilt after the Pearl Harbor disaster of 1941 and America's subsequent involvement in World War II. (Orbie Lee's name had appeared in the draft list of November 1940, but he didn't serve.) Family photos revealed a solidly built man with a serious demeanor. Orbie Lee joined the 30,000 defense workers currently residing in Fort Worth, which comprised about 20 percent of the city's entire population. Roy's mother, Nadine, a diminutive, soft-spoken woman, also worked in the plants. Nadine had been born in Decatur in Wise County, Texas, in 1914; she was the youngest of Royal and Maude Shultz's seven children. Decatur was a small town of about 2,000, the home of Ruby Owens, aka Texas Ruby, a country music pioneer known as "radio's original cowgirl," a Grand Ole Opry favorite. Nadine married Orbie Lee in 1933.

Fort Worth was so significant to the war effort, in fact, that in 1942, President Roosevelt toured the Consolidated assembly site, where B-24 Liberators were built. Employees such as Orbie Lee worked eight-hour shifts at what was known as the "Bomber Plant," which was in operation twenty-four hours a day. When Brigadier General G. C. Brant opened the plant, he declared: "We're digging Hitler's grave here."

Roy's older brother, Grady Lee, had been born at Vernon on July 26, 1933, barely five months after Nadine and Orbie were wed at Tillman County in Oklahoma in late February. The youngest of the three Orbison boys, Samuel Keith, would join the family on June 27, 1946.

The Orbisons' time in Fort Worth would play a huge part in Roy's musical development—even as a kid, he had the feeling that music would play some kind of role in whatever lay ahead. Not only did family and friends often visit to play the guitar and sing, but the Orbison home was the drop-in center for many of the soldiers stationed at the

Fort Worth Army Airfield who were about to ship out to the Pacific or Europe. "They'd sing and drink with such abandon, knowing they might never do it again," Roy told a writer in 1979. "They partied heavy and played heavy." These late nights left a big impression on Roy, particularly what he described as "that sense of do it for all it's worth and do it now—and do it good."

But these get-togethers weren't strictly about music. With all the talk of the war—and Roy could tell that some of their visitors were worried they'd never return—the boy developed what would become a lifelong fascination with history. He also developed an aversion to hard liquor. With Orbie's okay, Roy took his first sip of whiskey: "I was sick for about six days."

Like most kids learning an instrument, Roy kept it simple. Orbie taught him the song "You Are My Sunshine," which in 1941, *Billboard* magazine described as the "tavern and taproom classic of the year," heard pretty much everywhere. It was first recorded by Atlanta's the Pine Ridge Boys and would become one of the official state songs of Louisiana, as well as a go-to number for a very young Roy Orbison. Another song to capture Roy's imagination was called "Darkness on the Delta." Roy had no idea who was the singer; to him, it was simply "the blues . . . performed by unknown colored people."

It was Native American jazz singer, Mildred Bailey, in fact, who popularized "Darkness on the Delta," one of the many songs that seeped into Roy's DNA. Another was the old Tin Pan Alley tune, "In a Shanty in Old Shanty Town," which was also a favorite of a piano-playing teenage wildcat from Ferriday, Louisiana named Jerry Lee Lewis. Then there was Bob Wills's deeply twangy "Dusty Skies," released in 1942, which Roy also learned to play on his guitar. Roy admired the music of Hank Williams and Moon Mullican—a chubby-cheeked Texan dubbed "the king of the hillbilly piano players"—and once looked on wide-eyed as Ernest Tubb, whose large cowboy hat added a few more inches to his lean six-foot frame, sang his hit "Walking the Floor Over You" from the back of a truck as it rolled along the streets of Fort Worth. "There was a lot of music to be heard back then," Roy recalled.

Although he hadn't undergone any formal training—and never would—Roy, a pudgy-faced kid who began wearing glasses at the age of four, was a quick learner. He came up with a technique of loosening the strings of his guitar, inserting a small microphone, and then tightening the strings back up. This way he could play just that bit louder than everybody else in the room. "That was my first amplifier," he said in 1967. "I joined in the fun."

Growing up in Texas, close to the Mexican border, had its advantages. Roy was exposed to what he described as "a mixture of everything: I got some black music, some Mexican music, some country music, some pop music." Roy was shortsighted, literally and colorblind, figuratively. And while he may have been born country, Roy's tastes extended beyond Nashville, although admittedly his musical hero was a country singer, born William Orville Frizzell. "The first singer I heard on the radio who really slayed me was Lefty Frizzell," said Roy. He described Frizzell as "actual country." As far as Roy was concerned, he was the real deal. (Perhaps a little too real; when he was nineteen, Frizzell did a six-month stretch in county jail on a statutory rape charge.) "He had this technique which involved sliding syllables together," said Roy, "that really blew me away."

When Roy was ten and a student at Denver Grade School in Fort Worth, he saw a concert by Lefty, who had been performing on radio in his distinctly plainspoken style since he was barely a teenager. Roy wasn't alone in his admiration. "Without Lefty Frizzell," observed Willie Nelson, yet another native Texan, "a lot of us singers wouldn't have a style." One day, Roy would adopt the nickname "Lefty" as a nod to the man who inspired him.

With the end of World War II, the Orbisons were on the move again. They spent some time back in Vernon before settling in a Texan town called Wink in 1946, when Roy was ten. He enrolled at the Parker Grade School, while the family lived at the Townsend Apartments, located on what passed for Wink's main drag. During the oil boom of the late 1920s and early 1930s, the population of Wink had swollen to almost 5,000, but by the time the Orbisons settled into a duplex about one block away from the site of the former red-light district, the population was barely 1,500. This was nothing like Fort Worth. "They call it Wink," stated reporter Red O'Donnell in the *Nashville Banner*, "because it is so small that if you wink your eye while driving through the town, you'll miss it."

"I expected to see swinging doors and saloons," Roy recalled, "but instead there were all these oil wells and rigs popping up and down, and the people who worked for these oil companies lived in wooden houses. We were a working-class family." He described life in Wink as little more than "football, oil fields, oil, grease, and sand." Not that Roy disliked football; in fact, he became a lifelong fan of the game and played until he was a freshman. ("Just never was big enough," Roy lamented in 1988.) He'd even help manage Wink High's football team. But Roy had larger dreams. He joked with his school friend Leon Thompson, telling him that one day, when he made it big, his statue would reside in what remained of the town square. "There'll be a stick with mud," he declared, "saying that Roy Orbison came through here."

The town offered very little in the way of excitement—only the Rig Theater remained of Wink's four theaters. There was a pool hall, the Day Drugstore, a hardware, the Church of Christ, which Roy and his family attended, and not a lot else. As Roy would quickly discover, "There wasn't much to do except play football and drive sixty miles to get a hamburger." In 1971, now a big star, Roy flashed back to life in Wink when he saw the Peter Bogdanovich film *The Last Picture Show*, with its graphic images of a broken-down locale that was way past its prime. To Roy, that town might as well be Wink. (Some scenes from the 1956 James Dean film *Giant* were filmed in Marfa, two hours south of Wink.)

Wink could be a dangerous place too, with a peculiar sense of justice. "I remember one fellow killed this other fella—dead—and they gave him just a few months in jail," Roy would recall on British TV in 1977. "Then these two boys killed a cow and skinned it and took the meat—and I think they got thirty years each. A very rough town."

Still, Roy had his music. The previous occupants of the duplex where the Orbisons now lived was the Short family. The Short siblings, Jimmy and Leon, became known as the Silver Saddle Ranch Boys, singing cowboys, so the house had some music in its bones. And Roy had begun performing on radio by the time he reached Wink. In 1945, he'd won a contest on KVWC, which broadcast out of Vernon, and started singing on air. "I'd go down every Saturday, to do their jamboree thing, and became a regular," said Roy, who shared the mic with a local DJ known as "Stan the Man." Roy had also taken his first crack at songwriting, coming up with a simple ditty while sitting outside of his grandmother's house strumming his guitar. He called the song "A Vow of Love." It was quite the statement for a plain-looking boy with glasses who hadn't yet hit his teens. A school portrait from the time showed a barefoot Roy, squinting into the sun, hands tucked into the pockets of his jeans, standing slightly apart from his classmates.

Wink was big-sky country and that would have an impact on Roy's music. Fellow Texan Will Jennings, one of his future writing partners, firmly believed this. "[In Wink] you can see [for] 100 miles," Jennings said in 1998. "And you see a little black cloud, and it grows bigger and bigger and gets more and more dramatic, and pretty soon you have thunder and lightning and rain, and you got yourself a big old thunderstorm. And that's how he learned his composition."

In 1946, ten-year-old Roy and a friend checked out a medicine show that rolled into Wink, selling "magic" elixirs and offering peculiar forms of entertainment. "They just set up a bunch of benches in the dirt and strung up lights," recalled Roy, who'd never seen anything like this before. "I didn't know there were such things except in movies." After someone got up and told some jokes and performed a few skits, it was announced that there'd be a talent contest. Roy, with a little encouragement from a buddy who was carrying his guitar, got up and performed "Jolie Blon," a Cajun song ("Pidgin-French-English," according to Roy) that he had learned by slowing down the vinyl record and memorizing the sound of the words. "It made no sense," Roy said. "Absolutely no sense." It didn't matter—Roy was declared the joint winner, sharing the $15 prize with a much older kid. The money didn't last long, but "Jolie Blon" was a keeper: "It was, *is still*," Roy corrected in 1980, "one of my favorite songs."

The medicine show was a rare source of entertainment for the people of Wink. It certainly wasn't a place that touring acts visited regularly, if at all. Roy may have been little more than a kid who'd just earned his first paycheck, but he made a promise to himself: "I said, 'If I ever get popular, I'm gonna play small towns' . . . I think it's unfair if you don't do that."

Wink's lack of distractions meant that kids like Roy needed to create their own entertainment. As a teenager, Roy began attending Wink High and gained a reputation as a practical joker. During one Halloween, Roy helped out at a party that was to be staged in the town's Methodist Church and was asked to run down to the drugstore to buy some gum. On his return, he emptied the stash into a candy dish in the foyer and then handed the dozen empty gum boxes to his classmate, Leon Thompson. "I was shocked to see he had six Chiclets and six Feen-a-mint laxative gum boxes, all empty," Thompson recalled. Looking at the contents of the dish, it was impossible to tell one piece of gum from the other. As Thompson was contemplating this, a group suddenly entered the hall and grabbed the entire contents of the tray, disappearing into the darkness. Neither Roy nor his friend could see who it was.

Come Monday, the hot topic on campus was how the entire Wink football squad had come down with chronic diarrhea over the weekend. Coach Frazier, who looked after the team, was "screaming mad," according to Thompson. "You know," Roy told his friend, "we both should be thankful for no one knowing where all that chewing gum came from."

Thompson was never quite sure whether Roy had acted deliberately.

On another occasion, Roy was on the receiving end of a prank. He'd joined the school band and during a road trip, he opened his lunch box and discovered it contained a ball-peen hammer rather than a snack. Roy had no idea how or when the switch had taken place. The driver turned the bus around and drove to the Wink gas station, where Roy was forced to apologize to the attendant whose hammer had been swiped. When Roy learned that a bandmate named Bobby Blackburn was the culprit, he found his horn and stuffed it with cloth smothered in glue, which Blackburn struggled to remove. Now even, they agreed to a truce.

Despite the pranks, Roy wasn't the type of student to play hooky, although he did once and with good reason. One lunchtime, Roy spotted a senior with the lively name of Ron Slaughter parked outside the school in his aging Studebaker. Roy joined him to smoke a cigarette. "I'm going to Midland to buy some records by the Platters and Tommy Edwards," Slaughter told Roy. "Wanna come?"

The lure of hearing some new music was too much for Roy, who joined Slaughter in the eighty-odd-mile road trip. But he spent much of the next day in fear of being busted. "He couldn't enjoy his one and only time to play hooky," laughed Slaughter.

Roy's friend Leon Thompson lived close to the high school campus (where today, only a few blocks away, stands the Roy Orbison Museum). One afternoon, Thompson saw smoke pouring out of the house and ran home, fearing it was on fire, with the school secretary, Mr. Miller, trailing close behind with a fire extinguisher. "I opened the door," Thompson recalled, "and there stood Roy Orbison." Roy began speaking casually with Thompson as if there was nothing to be concerned about. "He was cooking French fries like he lived there," his friend recalled with a laugh. Thompson was so relieved that he put on a pot of coffee. "Roy and I had a long friendly talk," he said, during which Roy owned up to his love of French fries and T-bone steaks. "But I'd settle for the French fries," Roy said.

Roy also befriended a slightly older Wink local named Bobby Buchanan, who happened to own an Indian motorcycle. They first met in September 1949, when Buchanan returned from a tour of duty with the Army. "Roy loved to ride with me," said Buchanan. Sometimes they'd tear up and down Hendricks Boulevard, Wink's main drag, or head out to the oil derricks that were dotted around the town and burn rubber.

On occasion, Roy and a few other friends would climb aboard Buchanan's bike and head out to the neighboring towns of Kermit and Pyote. "Five teenagers draped over and around one bike," said Buchanan, "hanging on for dear life." Surprisingly, they only had one accident, while Roy was riding. As Buchanan recalled, "The road bent and we didn't." Although Roy slammed on the brakes, passengers and rider were sent sprawling and the bike ended up in a pile of sand. Worried about rattlesnakes—Wink's oil fields were known to be home to some of the biggest rattlers in the state—they quickly dragged the Indian out of the sand and headed home.

"He always liked the sense of freedom that came with the wind in his hair," said Buchanan. Roy agreed. "I like to ride motorcyles," he said. "It clears the air."

When not stuffing horns with glue, burning French fries, or roaring around with Bobby Buchanan, Roy continued his musical evolution at Wink High. The roots of what would become the Wink Westerners, Roy's earliest band, stretched back to late 1949 (or early 1950, depending on whose memory was most reliable). Roy and a Wink High buddy named James Morrow, adept with both the fiddle and mandolin, began jamming at Morrow's family house, which was close to the Wink High campus. "[Roy] was very quiet and shy," said Morrow. "A good person."

Seeking out other players, they dropped by the home of Richard West, another Wink High student, who played the piano. West had an interesting technique, at least during the early days of the band: He only played the black keys. Soon after, they recruited two more school friends—Charles Evans, who joined on bass after taking some lessons from Morrow, and Billy Pat "Spider" Ellis, who played drums for the Wink High band. Having a drummer in their midst was unusual, most likely a first for a West Texan band, given that rock and roll was still a few years off in the future. The band that would eventually be known as the Wink Westerners—a name suggested by their science teacher, Miss Eva Harbin—were accidental trailblazers. Even fellow Texan Johnny Cash didn't hire drummer "Fluke" Holland until 1960.

In the beginning, like a million other high school groups, Roy's outfit was a jukebox act, playing songs that they knew from the radio, sometimes practicing in the band room at Wink High. "We were doing things like 'Lady of Spain' and 'In the Mood,' and pop stuff as well," Roy said in 1979. "Whatever was current in country, we had to do it. As soon as it faded away, we'd drop it." On Roy's urging, they learned "I Love You a Thousand Ways," a 1950 release from his hero Lefty Frizzell, and they also mastered the German march "Under the Double Eagle." When they played the big band tune "Caravan," Roy was able to make his guitar "ring like chimes," West said. A little later, they'd tackle Hank Williams's "Jambalaya," although Roy wasn't a huge Hank fan, at least not yet. ("I found his stuff too Tin Pan Alley–ish for my tastes.") One day, Roy walked into rehearsals with a vinyl record tucked under his arm. "I gotta good'un," he excitedly told the others, and played them Jimmie Dean's "Bummin." That too was soon on their set list.

The quintet began playing in unusual places, such as the Wink pool hall, which was run by a local named Charlie Hoskins. There wasn't a piano in the hall, so on their first visit, West was forced to improvise, tapping out a melody on anything handy. The regulars liked them so much that when they returned, someone had found a piano for West, which had been squeezed into the corner of the poolroom. They got a similar reaction when they played at the Day Drugstore, as James Morrow recalled: "The roughnecks and roustabouts pitched quarters when we played."

Even now, school friends like Leon Thompson sensed that Roy was becoming serious about music. "He used to tinker with the old guitar a lot," said Thompson, "[especially] on those stormy days when the sandstorm blew . . . He kept busy plucking at the strings." Roy's parents, Nadine and Orbie Lee, were right behind him. "Mother and Father encouraged me to further my musical talents," Roy made clear.

Roy knew what he wanted with his music—or didn't want, in the case of horn player Bobby Blackburn, whose stint in the band was short-lived. "No horns," Roy decided, so Blackburn was out. (Bearing no grudge, Blackburn remained close with Roy.) On the surface, Roy looked like a slightly overfed teenager with specs, harmless enough, but he could be tough when required. He once pulled a knife on West's older brother, Grady, when their roughhousing got out of hand. Roy produced the same knife when he got into a scrap with his pal Orbie Harris. Fortunately, Roy never had to use his blade. "Roy was no push-over," said Richard West.

CHAPTER 2

I did nothing at college except play the guitar, really

R.A. Lipscomb was the principal of Wink High and the superintendent of the Wink public schools, and in 1953, he was in the running for the post of Lions Club district governor. He'd heard Roy and his friends play, and with a big Lions Club luncheon coming up, Lipscomb figured that it wouldn't hurt his prospects if he brought some local musical talent with him. Roy and the group were offered $225 for a three-hour engagement. "We'll be there," Roy assured Lipscomb in a heartbeat. It was mad money at a time when the minimum wage was $1 per hour.

To prepare for the gig, they rehearsed at the Wink Community Center, piecing together a set that drew strongly on country and western favorites, but with "In the Mood," the Pied Pipers' silky "Dream," and Louis Armstrong's "Once in a While"—all popular songs, crowd-pleasers—added to the mix. Ron Slaughter, Roy's partner in hooky, agreed to help at the gig. Their performance at the Lions Club in McCamey, Texas, about seventy miles south-east of Wink, went over so well that the audience passed the hat and paid them an extra $35 for an additional hour of music—almost a week's wage in the oil fields. This was much better than picking up quarters from the dusty floor of the Wink pool hall. "[We got paid] for doing what we had been doing for nothing. It was amazing," said Roy.

But what Roy and the band needed was a regular gig and not long after, they were given the perfect opportunity. KERB was a radio station located in Kermit, a town about nine miles' drive from its smaller neighbor, Wink. KERB began broadcasting in 1950, during daytime hours only, servicing the local community. The station hosted a jamboree and in 1953, Roy and the band were hired for what became a weekly gig. "I'd go down every Saturday to do their jamboree thing," Roy recalled in 1979, "and became a regular." Roy and the band—who were now known as the Wink Westerners—shared the bill with Stan the Man, whom Roy had met a few years earlier at Wink.

On air, the Westerners continued to play the favorites: Hank Williams's "Kaw-Liga" and big band numbers like "In the Mood." They'd also mastered "Mexican Joe," a recent number 1 on the country charts for "Gentleman" Jim Reeves, who also got his first big break in radio, working as an announcer on KWKH-AM in Shreveport, Louisiana, the home of the *Louisiana Hayride*.

The ladder-climbing R.A. Lipscomb was still very much in the picture, and in July, he arranged for Roy and the group to take their first lengthy road trip, to Chicago, some 1,300 miles away, where he was to attend the 36th International Lions Club Convention. While Lipscomb schmoozed his fellow Lions, the Westerners set up and played in the front lobby of the Conrad Hilton Hotel. The sprawling complex came as quite the shock for Roy and his friends: The hotel had 3,000 guest rooms, a bowling alley, a twenty-seven-chair barbershop, a 1,200-seat movie theater, and a miniature golf course on the roof. There was nothing like this in Wink.

The more they played gigs such as this, it became apparent to his bandmates that Roy was the best organized Wink Westerner—and probably the most ambitious. Bassist Charles Evans noticed that Roy had begun carrying a little notebook where he would jot down the band's expenses: gas, food, lodging. This was serious business.

Back in Wink, Roy and the band were hired to open for Slim Whitman at the Rig Theater on April 7, 1954. It was a rare appearance in the town by a genuine star—Whitman had reached the country top 10 in 1952 with his rendition of "Love Song of the Waterfall," while his version of "Indian Love Call," a song from the 1920s Broadway musical *Rose-Marie*, performed even better, breaching the top 10 of the pop charts. The lively response to the Westerners' set resonated strongly with their singer and guitarist. "This was a big deal for Roy," said Richard West. "He got a lot of recognition."

Momentum was paramount for a young band like the Wink Westerners, and their opening slot for Whitman—and regular appearances on KERB—led to even more live work. Honky-tonks did a lively trade in postwar America, and West Texas had its share of "tonks," as they were known. They were usually situated on the outskirts of town, for a variety of reasons: There'd be less scrutiny from law enforcement, more room to park cars, and a little breathing space if certain matters needed to be settled in private. These places could get rough.

At the time, Rhinestone Cowboy Glen Campbell was plying his trade in the tonks of New Mexico; he called them the "fightin' and dancin' clubs." Over in Tennessee, Carl Perkins, whom Roy would soon befriend at Sun Records, was serving his apprenticeship in such tonks as the Cotton Boll Club, where locals swilled beer straight from the jug, and the Sand Ditch Tavern, where Carl learned to move while playing to avoid being hit by objects hurled by drunken patrons. "You were on your toes playing those places," said Perkins. "The harder they fought, the louder we played." One night at a tonk called the Hilltop Inn, Carl looked on in horror as a woman shot dead her partner with a .22-caliber pistol.

The tonk that Roy and his fellow Wink Westerners played regularly was the Archway Club in Monahans, a short drive down the TX18 from Wink. Known to its many regulars as the Arch, the tonk promised four key things, as spelled out in its ads: Music. Dancing. Good Company. Ice Cold Beer. Female waitstaff, who were paid $4 per hour, were hired via print ads that asked one thing: "Must be attractive." A crowd of about 1,000 could be sardined into the Arch, which led to a big problem one night in the summer of 1953, around the time Roy and the band began playing there, when someone hurled a tear-gas bomb into the club. A stampede for the exit ensued and about forty people were injured. It was like "something out of a nightmare," in the words of one patron. Two men were charged over the incident.

The Wink Westerners, now clearly led by Roy, drew a younger crowd to the Arch when they played on Saturday nights. None of the band was legal drinking age, but that hardly mattered when the house was full. They arranged a deal with the club's owner: The band got "the gate"—the takings at the door—and the owner pocketed everything that came across the bar. "The band developed a good following," said Wink Westerner Billy Ellis, "and brought in a lot of drinkers to the Arch. [The owner] welcomed the band any time they wanted to play there."

In late June 1953, the Wink Westerners received their first press coverage, a brief mention in the *San Angelo Standard-Times*, who were reporting on yet another Lions Club function of R.A. Lipscomb (now officially Lions district governor). The band and Roy—or "Ray Orbison" as he appeared in print—"provided music for the occasion," the occasion being a gathering of the Lions at Iraan in Pecos County. At yet another Lions-Lipscomb gig, just days before Christmas, this time at Odessa, the Wink Westerners were described by the *Odessa American* as the "Wink Highschool hill-billy band." This was not quite how Roy and the other imagined themselves, musically speaking. "We were maybe country-billy," said bassist Charles Evans. "We were trying to mesh these things together because we didn't want to be classified as country and western."

Roy might have been dreaming of a future beyond the rowdy tonks and local radio jamborees, but he still enjoyed small-town life. His lifelong devotion to cars was in overdrive. He and Richard West, and two other pals—Ray Morgan and Gene Adams—would sometimes drive around Wink, stopping to "serenade the ladies," as West recalled. "We had the best time riding around singing, the four of us." Roy would do something similar with his buddy Ron Slaughter, who still had his old Studebaker. They'd cruise around Wink and neighboring Kermit, occasionally in the company of the high school girls' vocal quartet: Annette Bailey, Priscilla Vinson, and Kay and Diane Roberts. "Packed like sardines in that old car, [we'd] drag the streets making music," Slaughter recalled. They'd hang out and sing at the Bailey drugstore. The Baileys, as Slaughter revealed, "actually thought we were pretty good." It was in yet another car, owned by Bobby Blackburn, that Roy wrote one of his first songs, called "About a Dreamer." It was a cowrite, with Slaughter, which became Roy's preferred writing method.

When not singing, Roy and his friends would play a game they called "ghost-hunting," which involved sitting around a campfire and challenging each other to tell the spookiest ghost story. While hanging out with Leon Thompson on a caper that was known as the Rattlesnake Canyon ghost hunt, Roy suddenly turned serious.

"What if I died?" Roy asked, "and [found out] there is no hell or heaven?"

"Then you better come back and tell me about it fast," Thompson shot back.

This conversation haunted Thompson many years later when he heard that Roy had died.

As Roy's time at Wink High neared its conclusion, he spoke with the editor of the school yearbook, who asked him about his dreams. "To lead a Western band," Roy replied, and the quote would run with his yearbook photo. But an even bigger, bolder future lay ahead for the teenager.

Three-quarters of the Wink Westerners—Roy, Billy Pat Ellis, and Richard West—graduated from Wink High in 1954 and enrolled at North Texas State College in Denton, one of the largest public universities in the state. Roy chose to study geology, figuring that he needed a fall-back plan in the oil business if music didn't work out for him—and to reassure his parents that he was taking care of his future. As Roy explained, "I wanted to get a diploma in case I didn't make it in the music business." But that didn't last long. Roy grew bored during his first year and switched to studying history and English, although the truth was that music had taken over his life. "I did nothing at college except play the guitar, really," Roy confessed, "and learn that [geology] wasn't something I wanted to do." West didn't last long, either; he eventually dropped out and joined the Navy.

The year 1954 proved to be hugely important for Roy, not because of his own musical achievements—the Wink Westerners were pretty much stuck in neutral, apart from running second at the Odessa College's annual variety show in May—but due to a new, wild sound he and millions of other young people heard that emerged out of Memphis, Tennessee. It was the year of Elvis Presley.

A spotty, slightly awkward teenager from Tupelo, Mississippi, Presley had been hanging around the Sun Studio in Memphis since 1953, when—for the grand sum of $3.98—he cut an acetate of two songs popularised by the Ink Spots, "My Happiness" and "That's When Your Heartaches Begin," as a gift for his beloved mother, Gladys. Marion

Keisker, who worked at Sun, asked the kid about his musical influences. "I don't sound like nobody," Presley replied.

Keisker played the tape to her boss, Sam Phillips, who'd gotten his start as a DJ in Alabama in the 1940s. He was intrigued and invited Presley back to the studio. In July 1954, Elvis and his two new bandmates, guitarist Scotty Moore and bassist Bill Black—both recruited by Phillips—recorded juiced-up versions of Arthur Crudup's "That's All Right, Mama," and "Blue Moon of Kentucky," which in its original form was a waltz, written and recorded in 1945 by Grand Ole Opry favorite Bill Monroe and the Blue Grass Boys. Elvis's versions had significantly more muscle than the originals, and influential Southern DJs such as WHBQ's Dewey Phillips and WHHM's John Lepley (aka Sleepy Eyed John) put his first Sun release into high rotation. "I've got a brand-new record," announced WMPS's Bob Neal. "The boy's name is Elvis Presley." Within minutes, the station's phone line was running hot—and within months, Neal would be Elvis's manager. Roy saw Presley play at a Big D Jamboree event in Dallas in the spring of 1955 and was shocked when Elvis spat his gum onto the stage before he sang. "He was this punk kid, just a real raw cat," remembered Roy, "singing like a bird."

When Roy Orbison heard Elvis on record for the first time—on a jukebox—he sensed that a seismic shift was about to take place in pop music. It was unlike anything he'd heard before, and it was a world apart from the schmaltzy crooners who were currently topping the charts. College kids like Roy were very open to what was known as "colored" music, but here it was being performed by a skinny white kid from Tupelo. As Roy observed, "There he was in the flesh, a live, white R&B artist." Jerry Lee Lewis's biographer Nick Tosches called this new sensation "whitefolk rock 'n' roll."

Lefty Frizzell was great, but this was something else entirely—and Roy and his Wink Westerner buddy Billy Ellis became Presley converts. "Roy and I really took to this style and sound of music." Ellis looked on as Roy practiced guitar "for hours to become proficient with Scotty Moore's style." Roy and Ellis even took a class at North Texas State called "stage band music" to help improve their live performances, and Roy began moving around more onstage. Together, they wrote a song that was inspired by Hank Williams's "Kaw-Liga," which they played in the Wink Westerners, but "[we] jazzed it up," as Ellis recalled. They then wrote what Ellis described as "cat talk" lyrics and named their song "Go! Go! Go!"

One evening at North Texas State, Roy looked on as Allen Richard "Dick" Penner and Wade Lee Moore, students and budding musicians, plugged in to play some songs. The duo performed an upbeat original called "Ooby Dooby," which they'd banged out in fifteen minutes while up on the roof of their frat house. Roy couldn't believe what he was hearing. "These two boys stepped out onstage with a guitar and sang 'Ooby Dooby' and they just knocked me flat. I was astounded." Roy wasn't alone; as he looked around him, by his recollection, "people went crazy." The duo had another song, "Wild Women," that Roy also really liked, but he was really drawn to "Ooby Dooby." Roy knew right then that he had to record the song.

Roy craved a recording deal, just like fellow North Texas State student Pat Boone. A fresh-faced young singer—and devout Christian—Boone had been raised in Nashville, but ran off to Texas when he eloped with Shirley Lee Foley, the daughter of country music star Red Foley. (They'd have four children and remain married for sixty-six years.) Boone already had a recording deal with the independent label Republic Records, but was about to sign with another indie called Dot, based in Nashville, where he'd have a breakout hit, a vanilla-flavored cover of Fats Domino's rowdy "Ain't That a Shame," in 1955. Penner and Moore may have written a song that Roy admired, but Boone had something even more tangible: a record deal. "He'd made a record," figured Roy, "so I wanted to make a record."

Years later, Dick Clark would state on camera that Roy "began as Pat Boone's backup singer," which was not correct, but Boone's success did have a big impact on Roy, as did the songs of Penner and Moore. "All these people were doing things I wanted to do," he said.

There was a discernible change when Roy and the Wink Westerners set up to play a New Year's Eve dance at the close of 1954. They ended their set with a take on "Shake, Rattle and Roll," having recently heard Bill Haley's hit cover of the song. This was the first time Roy heard the term "rock and roll," and he decided that it was time for the band to change. It was the end of what he called "the Glenn Miller era, [which] just wasn't lively enough."

It was then that Roy made a life-changing decision: "I said to myself, 'I better get away from school and back to what I know best.'" Music was calling.

Much had changed for Roy by the summer of 1955. Along with band-mates and friends Ellis and Morrow, Roy had switched schools, transferring to Odessa Junior College, which was closer to Wink. He'd also continued playing with the Wink Westerners—now with Jack Kennelley on upright bass and, soon enough, Johnny Wilson on guitar and backing vocals—and had added "Ooby Dooby" to their repertoire. In the fall of 1955, while the band was playing at KMID in Midland, Roy met fourteen-year-old Claudette Frady. They were introduced by Jack Kennelley. Roy was smitten by Claudette straightaway, describing her to the guys in the band as a "queen." He had just met the first great love of his life, the inspiration for some of his signature songs.

Claudette was the daughter of Mr. and Mrs. Chester Frady, and had been born in Odessa, Texas. She had two siblings, Billy Fred and Paulette. Claudette's father "Ches" worked as a dispatcher at the Odessa fire station and belonged to the local arm of the Fraternal Order of Eagles, a nonprofit that did community work. Claudette also had the community spirit; while still in school, she won a competition sponsored by the Odessa Chamber of Commerce to produce a poster advocating fire prevention. As part of her win, Claudette rated a mention in the *Odessa American* newspaper.

As Roy got to know Claudette and they grew close, he thought of her as "my lovely woman child." He always carried a picture of her in his wallet. Roy introduced Claudette to a fellow musician named John Pickering, who described her as "a pretty young brunette in shorts . . . She was a lovely person with a great sense of humor. I could see that Roy Orbison was a very lucky man."

Roy and his band had recently won a talent competition at KMID, a TV station that broadcast out of Midland, which was eighty-odd miles from Wink. The prize was a thirty-minute on-air segment. Roy hadn't seen much TV prior to winning the quest, so this was unexplored territory for him. "Television was very new to West Texas," he said. While "Ooby Dooby" was fast becoming the Westerners' signature song, they also performed "Blue Moon of Kentucky"—playing it the way Elvis did, faster and harder than the original—and Bill Haley's "Rock Around the Clock," which was the number 1 song in the country during July 1955. According to Billy Ellis, the group was "an instant hit with the West Texans, especially the younger set." Roy was correct when he predicted that rock and roll was the new sensation the country was craving. "America needed excitement," he said of the era. "The ten years after the war were fairly dull." Television would also play a big part in this cultural shift.

The group attracted a sponsor from a local business called Pioneer Furniture— "the biggest furniture store in Texas," as Roy recalled—and they were granted a weekly spot, which would be broadcast on KMID-TV on Fridays and KOSA-TV, based in Odessa, on Saturdays. For thirty minutes' work, the group was paid $25. This may have barely covered their expenses, but the segment was the perfect vehicle to promote their regular shows at the Arch and the other venues they were currently playing.

The group had won a new audience and Roy felt that they needed a fresh identity; he wanted to change the band's name. He believed that the Wink Westerners needed something a little more youthful sounding, so they asked their TV audience to send in ideas. Not all the suggestions hit home: "I remember one was Little Roy and the Joy Boys," Roy laughed, "[but] we finally named ourselves the Teen Kings."

CHAPTER 3

That little chicken on the Sun label represented something unique

Throughout much of 1955, Roy looked on enviously as his fellow North Texas State alumnus Pat Boone climbed the national pop chart with his version of "Ain't That a Shame." Boone cracked the top 20 in July. Roy may have had a regular TV spot, a new band name, and a fresh, younger audience, but what he lacked was a record deal. Roy and the Teen Kings had cut two songs, "Ooby Dooby" and "Hey! Miss Fannie," in December 1955 at a studio just outside Dallas, hoping it would get them signed to Columbia Records. However, the label's boss, Don Law, wasn't taken by the Teen Kings and instead handed along the acetate to Sid King and the Five Strings, who cut "Hey! Miss Fannie" for Columbia.

In early 1956, Roy and the Teen Kings began playing a Saturday jamboree at Jal in New Mexico. One night between sets, they met Chester Oliver, who'd struck it rich in the oil business and Weldon Rogers, a country singer, DJ, and record producer who ran a label called Je-Wel. ("[Rogers] had a daughter named Jean, hence the name Je-Wel Records," Roy explained.) Rogers and Oliver liked what they heard and agreed to back Roy and the band to the tune of $1,100 to cut their debut disc. Roy, who wasn't quite twenty, signed his first recording contract.

In June, the Teen Kings packed their gear into the one car and drove to a studio in Clovis, New Mexico. It was an important moment for Roy, marking the official start of his recording career, but significant also for Norman Petty, who owned the studio. "We were the first paying customers," Roy recalled. "It was his first custom session."

(Historians would go on to credit Petty as the creator of the "Clovis Sound"—Roy and the Teen Kings' session would be ground zero.)

Twenty-nine-year-old Petty had been a performer, who, like Roy, got his first break in radio while he was still in high school. After serving in the Air Force, he formed the Norman Petty Trio with his wife Vi and guitarist Jack Vaughn. Petty played piano. They cut a version of Duke Ellington's "Mood Indigo," which was a breakout hit in 1954. *Cashbox* magazine crowned the trio the "Most Promising Instrumental Group" of the year.

Petty turned his attention to production, building a studio in his hometown of Clovis, a rural spot that was home to the Cannon Air Force Base. Roy admitted that recording at Petty's studio was simply a matter of convenience, as it would be for other artists from the region. "It was just the closest place to where Buddy Knox, Buddy Holly, and myself lived," he said. Clovis was roughly 250 miles from Wink—a near neighbor by Texan terms. Roy's one problem was that he'd recently had his favorite guitar stolen from his car, which was parked outside the Scott Theater in Odessa, a crime that rated a mention in the pages of the *Odessa American*. A local named Carrol R. Pyle was charged with the theft and released on $1,000 bond. (Roy's electric guitar was valued at $250.)

Armed with a new guitar, Roy and the Teen Kings cut several tracks at Petty's studio in early March 1956, including "Ooby Dooby" and a ballad titled "Trying to Get to You." The latter was first recorded by an R&B group called the Eagles a couple of years prior, and was a favorite of Roy's girlfriend Claudette. Upon playback in the studio, Roy sized up what they'd recorded in a peculiar way, as if he were a fan listening in, rather than the performer. "I didn't criticize [my] voice in a way most people might," Roy later said. "It just hit me that if I heard that person sing again, I would know that I had heard that person before. In that I was very lucky." "Ooby Dooby" was a rocker, not a style completely suited to his voice, but Roy felt that he had something unique to work with.

Roy was impressed enough with the session to recommend Petty's studio to a fellow Texan he'd met on the road named Buddy Holly. When Holly played a show in Odessa, Roy took the opportunity to introduce himself. "I'm a fan," Roy told him, "and I also play." Roy was particularly struck by what Holly could do with his Fender Stratocaster. "[He] played the loudest guitar I've ever heard." Soon after, Roy and the Teen Kings gigged at Lubbock and noticed Holly looking on from the audience.

Roy learned that he and Holly (born Charles Hardin Holley) shared much more than poor eyesight and good manners. They were born just a few months apart and had grown up within 100 miles of each other—Holly's hometown was Lubbock, home to the Reese Air Force Base. Roy and Buddy shared a lot of the same musical heroes, including Moon Mullican and Jimmie Rodgers. And both were at the beginning of their recording careers: In April 1956, Decca released Holly's debut single, "Blue Days, Black Nights," not long after the release of "Ooby Dooby."

They became friends and boosters of each other's career as their stars began to rise—whenever Holly played Odessa, he would tell the audience, "It's good to back in Orbison land." Holly also had Roy to thank for connecting him with Norman Petty, because together they'd achieve remarkable things.

Roy and the Teen Kings may have cut their debut single, but they had no real idea how to get it heard. Je-Wel was only a small regional label, operating out of Odessa and "Ooby Dooby" was their first release—the distinct yellow label displayed the catalog number JE-101-B. Fact-checking was not the label's strength: On some pressings, the B-side was incorrectly listed as "Trying to Get You," rather than "Trying to Get to You," while Roy's surname was misspelled as "Oribson." And Je-Wel had none of the reach of Memphis's Sun Records, a label that was currently doing big business in the South and beyond, with early releases from Elvis Presley—whom Roy met at a gig in Memphis—Johnny Cash, and most recently, Carl Perkins, the son of a sharecropper from Tiptonville, Tennessee, whose "Blue Suede Shoes" was poised to become the label's first million-seller. In 1955, Sun's Sam Phillips had sold Presley's contract to RCA Victor for a hefty sum—one day, Roy took the opportunity to ask Phillips why he'd done that. "For Carl Perkins and $40,000," Phillips told him with a grin.

"Sun was a very tiny label," said Roy, "but [its reach was] a lot bigger than just West Texas."

Roy was a big fan of Sun Records. He didn't just like the music that was coming out of the shoebox-size studio on Memphis's Union Avenue. Roy was also impressed by something else—the Sun logo. "That little chicken on the Sun label," he said, "represented something unique."

Over the ensuing years, Roy would provide different versions of what next occurred. What was indisputable was that he had met Cash, who had been recording for Sam Phillips's label since September 1954, when he cut "Hey, Porter!", and sought his advice.

"How do you get on Sun?" Roy asked Johnny Cash.

"Call Sam Phillips," Cash replied. "Tell him I recommended you."

This didn't play out quite as Roy hoped.

"Johnny and the boys said you might be interested in me recording on your label," Roy said when he got Phillips on the phone.

"Johnny Cash doesn't run my record company," snapped Phillips. Then the producer hung up.

Roy was frustrated: "I couldn't make any headway," he said. "No contact." Seeking further guidance, Roy met with Cecil "Pop" Holifield, who ran record shops in Odessa and Midland, and had promoted local shows by Elvis Presley and Johnny Cash. "Pop was the only record man I knew," Roy confessed. Holifield had enough traction with Phillips to get him on the phone, and he played the producer "Ooby Dooby," telling him that the record was in high demand in his store.

"Can you get this guy to Memphis in three days' time?" Phillips asked Holifield, forgetting all about his recent hang-up on Roy. "The damn thing intrigued me," Phillips said of "Ooby Dooby." "It was so nonsensical, and yet it had a type of beat that just hit."

Roy was thrilled when he got the news from Holifield, but at the same time knew that he was still under contract to Je-Wel. He spoke with his father: Should he go ahead and rerecord the song with Phillips? "This is the chance of a lifetime," Orbie Lee told him. "To be on Sun means you're going to be a recording star." That was all the justification Roy needed, and to his relief, getting released from the Je-Wel deal proved relatively easy, because Roy and the band were not yet twenty-one when they signed the contract.

Roy and the Teen Kings promptly arrived on the doorstep of Sun Studio just seventy-two hours after Phillips's call, as the producer had requested. Roy's world was about to be turned upside down.

Roy rerecorded "Ooby Dooby" with Phillips in Memphis on March 19, but he didn't think there was a vast difference between that and the original that he'd recorded with Norman Petty at Clovis. "Maybe the Sun version is a little more intense, has a little more drive," Roy figured. And while Phillips knew it was a novelty song, he sensed that "Ooby Dooby" had genuine commercial potential. "I was very impressed with the inflection Roy brought to it. In fact, I think I was more impressed than Roy."

And Roy did have a peculiar attitude toward "Ooby Dooby." When musician John Pickering told Roy that he liked it, he was surprised by his reaction. "It seemed to embarrass him . . . I was not at all sure that he was particularly proud of the song." Later in his career, Roy would explain that if a song was a hit, "I have to be prepared to sing it for the rest of my days." It seemed that was a lesson he learned the hard way with "Ooby Dooby."

During the session, Roy pushed Phillips. He wanted "Trying to Get to You" to be the B-side of "Ooby Dooby," but the producer wasn't interested. Roy was unaware that Elvis Presley had recorded the song, first at Sun and more recently for his debut LP at RCA Victor, until Phillips explained that Presley had a lock on the song. "You can't record it," Phillips told Roy firmly. (Roy did cut it while at Sun, but only as a demo.) Instead, he cut "Go! Go! Go! (Down the Line)," the song that he had written with Billy Ellis, as the B-side. This also gave Phillips one copyright on the release. "I guess he had a contract to fill," Roy said with a shrug, when asked about "Trying to Get to You."

Sun 242—"Ooby Dooby" backed with "Go! Go! Go! (Down the Line)"—was released in May 1956. On May 20, beneath the headline TEEN KINGS FORESEE NATIONWIDE SUCCESS, Roy and the band, along with "their sponsor" Cecil Holifield, received several columns of coverage in the *Odessa American*. Tellingly, Roy was credited as the group's "leader." As Holifield told reporter Tracy Byers, "There's more unknown great singers than there are known. I knew the boys could make a hit if given a chance." He made it clear that "Ooby Dooby" was already selling "like wildfire" in West Texas.

A photographer snapped a beaming Roy and the band—which now included Johnny Wilson, as well as Jack Kennelley, Billy Pat Ellis, and James Morrow—while the *Odessa American* predicted that "Ooby Dooby" was a "surefire hit record . . . it looks like money-in-the-bank for all the boys, especially Orbison." And within days, the Teen Kings had even more influential publications praising their new release.

Music trade magazine *Billboard* gave the Teen Kings their "Spotlight of the Week" slot, declaring that "Orbison's spectacular untamed singing quality spells big action for both sides." Their writer also spotted chart potential in "Go! Go! Go!", describing "Ooby Dooby" and "Go! Go! Go!" as "wild swinging country blues." The editors of *Cashbox* felt likewise, heaping praise on the Teen Kings' debut, stating: "These are two powerhouse entries in the race for nationwide popularity."

Roy and the Teen Kings celebrated by playing a street dance to mark Odessa's seventieth anniversary celebrations before hitting the road. Traveling in two cars, a '55 Oldsmobile borrowed from Roy's father Orbie Lee, and a '55 Chevy Bel Air owned by guitarist Johnny Wilson, they set out on a tour of eight Southern states, beginning on May 27. To Roy, tours such as this were a big advantage of being signed to Sun. "What they had was something that no other company had. [Sun acts would] go out and hit the road, and there was a whole network of country music promoters." As far as Roy was concerned, "It was the best promotion in the world." Being the lesser-known act on the bill—their Southern tour was in the company of Carl "Mr. Blue Suede Shoes" Perkins, Johnny Cash, and Johnny Horton—meant that Roy was frequently delegated to speak with DJs of small local stations when they rolled into a new town. But he discovered that it had its benefits. "After you met all these people," Roy explained, "they got to know you and saw that you were sincere about your business. [That] early groundwork . . . proved very beneficial."

At some shows on this tour, Roy and the Teen Kings would perform at drive-ins between movies, targeting a younger audience. They would set up on the flat roof of concession stands and their music would be pumped through the speakers that hung in the windows of the parked cars. "[These were] very frantic, hectic shows," recalled Roy.

"We were trying to make stage shows out of one hit record, which is very difficult." As their single continued to sell and he and the band rolled into Birmingham, Roy was billed in the local press as "the 'Ooby Dooby' boy himself."

Roy and the band added a performance piece to their set that they called "the bug." As Roy explained, "We had an imaginary bug we would throw to each other. When it hit you, you had to shake." But they didn't really need to ham it up onstage, because the Teen Kings had a genuine hit on their hands with "Ooby Dooby." On June 7, *Billboard* again praised the band and singled out "Ooby Dooby" as their "buy of the week," reporting TEEN KINGS CHALKING UP NEW SUCCESS. "'Ooby Dooby' has now caught on in sales over the North, as well as the South." By mid-June 1956, their debut single hit a peak of number 59 on the *Billboard* Hot 100 and was fast-tracking its way to sales of 200,000 copies. And all this despite Roy's candid admission: "I didn't really like the song, [but] I do like what it did for me."

When his first royalty payment arrived for "Ooby Dooby," Roy proudly posed for an *Odessa American* photographer holding his check. The next day's headline read: THE CASH ROLLS IN. This check enabled Roy to fulfill three long-held wishes. First up, he bought a white Cadillac, which he drove to Lansky Bros. in Memphis, a favorite clothing store of Elvis Presley. "They had all this wild gear," said Roy. "All the rockabillies got their clothes there." At Lansky Bros., Roy selected a few lace shirts to match his new gold shoes, which were a gift from fellow Sun artist, Jimmy Williams. Roy also bought a diamond ring—"I've always fancied them as a symbol of success." But it proved to be a bit of a letdown. "You can't do anything but wear them," Roy told a reporter.

Despite her boy's success, Roy's mother Nadine was always the voice of reason. "[She] warned me of the pitfalls of being rich," Roy said. His first trip to Las Vegas proved that Nadine might be onto something. "I lost more than I'd care to admit," Roy said afterwards, and he swore that he'd never gamble on cards again.

CHAPTER 4

They were bombs

On June 1 1956, Roy's tour reached Memphis for a show at the Overton Park Shell, an open-air amphitheater with a capacity of around 5,000. It was the "first big popular music show of the summer," announced Memphis daily *The Commercial Appeal* and the largest gig yet for Roy and the Teen Kings. The concert was promoted by Memphis DJ Bob Neal. He booked shows for Roy, Carl Perkins, and many of their fellow Sun artists under the Stars, Inc. banner, which he ran out of the Sterick Building, a Gothic pile known to locals as "the queen of Memphis." *The Commercial Appeal* described Neal as "the Ziegfeld of the bluejean brigade," who had brought to his Memphis hometown an event that would "pay homage to the cult of tight trousers and gaudy guitars." Rock and roll, in other words.

Even though Elvis Presley wasn't on the bill at the Overton Park Shell gig, his presence was unavoidable. ("Yep, he showed up," confirmed *The Commercial Appeal.*) At the end of the concert, after Roy and the various other acts had played to a lively response, it was Elvis who was called up onstage by the crowd, having spent the concert in the wings looking on. He took a couple of bows while he "demurely fluttered his eyelashes into a blinding spotlight," reported *The Commercial Appeal.* Presley also posed for a photo with Roy, which was the closest he ever came to sharing a bill with "Elvis the Pelvis." There was a reason for this, as Roy explained: "He said, 'You were just that good that I'll never appear onstage with you.'" In a fine piece of understatement, Roy admitted that "it was a nice compliment."

The next day, the morning edition of the Memphis newspaper

described Roy and the Teen Kings' act as resembling "eels in advanced epilepsy." Clearly, they hadn't yet ditched "the bug."

Roy admired Elvis and his music, but he developed a stronger bond with such Sun labelmates as Carl Perkins. They would sometimes go out driving in Roy's new Cadillac and from behind the wheel, he would sing parts of songs he was writing. "Do you think I should go up another octave?" Roy would ask Perkins, who couldn't believe what he was hearing. "How high can you go?" he'd ask. "You're just about through the car roof now."

Roy and Johnny Cash, who further along would become neighbors, also grew close. "We became brothers right from the start," Cash would write. "I really loved Roy. He was a very kind, considerate man." Roy would dazzle Cash with his crystal-clear memory, as the Man in Black would relate in his memoir. "Around Roy, you didn't dare tell a story about something in which he'd been involved without asking, 'Is that the way it was, Roy?'"

Roy helped other fledgling artists that he met on the road. During the summer of 1956, with "Ooby Dooby" still lodged in the *Billboard* Hot 100, a newcomer was added to the bill when Roy's tour was booked to play the Family Drive-In at Dexter in Missouri. Narvel Felts was a seventeen-year-old singer from Keiser in Arkansas, who'd been discovered at a school talent show. He performed as part of the Jerry Mercer Band. The sight of Roy and the band rolling up to the gig in his shiny new Cadillac left a deep impression on the teenager, but he quickly learned that Roy's personality wasn't quite as flashy as his ride. "I found him to be a soft-spoken, friendly person," said Felts. A few days after the Dexter show, Felts got a call from his manager, Calvin Richardson, who had big news. "Orbison is going to help me get an audition for you with Sun." It was a hell of a gesture from Roy, who'd only had one release for the label.

As the long, hot summer rolled on, Roy and the Teen Kings headlined a "gala variety music show" at the football stadium in Grenada, Missouri on July 5. "["Ooby Dooby"] is being hummed by adults as well from coast to coast," reported the *Enterprise-Tocsin* newspaper. A few days later they played the Armory in Huntsville and the *Huntsville*

Times described Roy as "the hottest new Rock and Roll artist in the business." When the roadshow reached Arkansas, Roy's surname may have been misspelled as "Oberison" in the *Hope Star* newspaper, but the hype was heavy: He was again described as the "hottest new artist in the business."

"The young fellow with the appearance of the average high school kid seems to be off to the big time," noted the *Hope Star*'s reporter. "Onstage, he's a teen-king with real zing, and he's a hit with all the boppin' fans everywhere." It was mentioned that Roy was currently "unmarried and with no 'steady,'" and that he enjoyed "dating, drawing and, of course, his music." The suggestion that Roy was a man without a steady would have come as a shock to Claudette, who was becoming a big part of his life.

Roy knew enough about the music biz to understand that one minor hit single didn't constitute a career. In the fall, he returned to the Sun studio to cut a song called "Rock House." It had been written by Harold Jenkins, a twenty-three-year-old rockabilly rebel from Friars Point, Mississippi (who'd soon change his stage name to Conway Twitty). He'd composed it as a theme song for his own group, the Rockhousers, although it was officially credited to "Orbison/Jenkins" upon release in late September. The B-side was Johnny Cash's "You're My Baby"—originally titled "Little Wooly Booger"—a song that Cash later admitted was "the worst thing I ever conceived in any field." Regardless, in October, *Billboard* predicted success for this new Sun release. They even cooked up a new term to describe Roy's music: They called it "rockabilly beat."

In mid-November, Roy and the band played what was described as a "rock and roll dance party" at the Malco in Memphis, along with Carl Perkins and Warren Smith. "This show is strictly for the younger generation," reported *The Commercial Appeal*. The matinee concert on November 15, however, was sparsely attended. "Those there, though, got a kick out of it—although it apparently did not send them into screaming hysterics," observed the Memphis daily.

Perhaps it was a portent of what was to come for Roy, because his new release, "Rock House," was not a hit. Roy dismissed this and his future Sun recordings. "They were bombs."

In January 1957, Narvel Felts, whom Roy had befriended the previous summer, was given his shot at a Sun record deal, proof that Roy was as good as his word. The ever-supportive Roy was already in the studio when Felts and the others in the Jerry Mercer Band reached Memphis for their audition. Also looking on was Johnny Cash, as well as the studio's resident engineer, Jack Clements, plus a new Sun signing by the name of Jerry Lee Lewis, and Harold Jenkins, who was also on the hunt for a record deal.

During a break in the session, Roy pulled Jenkins and Felts aside.

"Guys, if I were you," he advised them, "I'd look elsewhere for a label."

He explained that Sam Phillips wasn't interested in either of them; as far as Roy could tell from recent experience, he had no interest in him or Carl Perkins, who'd both had hits with the label. "He's only interested in Cash and this new kid, Jerry Lee Lewis," Roy said. (Roy's suspicions were correct and both Felts and Twitty eventually signed to Mercury Records.)

Roy's sense that he'd lost Phillips's support had been eating away at him ever since the early success of "Ooby Dooby." He felt that in the wake of Presley's departure to RCA Victor, Phillips had been trying his mold his acts to become the "new Elvis," hence his fascination with rocker Jerry Lee Lewis. Carl Perkins felt the same about Phillips; he believed he'd been losing his backing ever since "Blue Suede Shoes." Roy may have still been searching for a style to claim as his own, but he knew that hip swivelling and sexual innuendos weren't his thing—he'd tried a heavy-breathing vocal on "Go! Go! Go!", the flip side of "Ooby Dooby," and it wasn't convincing.

"First of all, Sam didn't really know what he was doing," Roy later said of Phillips. "He was a kind man, in that if he put you on his label, he'd done you a big favor and you were indebted to him, automatically." But there was a problem: Phillips tried to do for Roy what he had done for Elvis and introduced him to black artists and records, such as Arthur Crudup's "That's All Right, Mama" and "Mystery Train" and suggested, strongly, that he try and re-create the same emotion and feeling.

"Sing just like that," Phillips told him.

But it simply didn't work for Roy in the same way it had for

Presley. "He wasn't talking my language," Roy said. "I never felt comfortable doing rock 'n' roll or rhythm and blues. I was more interested in ballads."

Roy, however, would credit the development of his distinctive voice to his time at Sun, because the studio was so small that he learned to sing "over" the top of the drums. "Elvis, Jerry Lee Lewis, Johnny Cash, and I developed strong voices in that studio. We would just go into the studio and do it without overdubbing or four-tracking or anything." While at Sun, Roy also learned how to record quickly, a trait he maintained throughout his career. "Since I wrote my songs, I knew them well, so we'd get a bunch of guys together and just go in and do it."

But a follow-up hit continued to elude Roy. His next release for Sun, in early 1957, "Sweet and Easy to Love," was also a flop, despite the stellar backing vocals of the Roses, a West Texan trio who'd also worked with Buddy Holly. (The record was credited to "ROY ORBISON and The Roses.") Roy was becoming disillusioned with the music industry—and being as good as broke, he was forced to return his prized Cadillac (for a time) and end his association with the Teen Kings. Drummer Billy Pat Ellis knew it was only a matter of time: "Roy had the vision, he would write the songs and get the gigs," he said in 1999. "We always knew the talent was there in Roy." But their split was not amicable, according to Sam Phillips's biographer Peter Guralnick. After a disagreement over credits, the band left Roy in the studio during a session and never returned. "They . . . just walked out, loading up the Cadillac that was the symbol of their success." From now on, Roy would be going it alone.

His fallout with the Teen Kings hit Roy hard, and he spent the next month staying with Phillips at his home in Memphis, trying to figure out his next move.

One afternoon, Roy asked a favor of the producer: "Can Claudette come visit?"

"Roy," Phillips replied, trying to keep a straight face, "you can bring her in if she's good looking." Roy, as Phillips recounted, went on to explain "that he really loved her and she was his college sweetheart." Claudette left a deep impression on Phillips's son, Knox, who described her as "the most beautiful thing that ever walked around this vicinity."

While Claudette was staying at the Phillips house, Sam was

surprised when she and Roy agreed to sleep in separate rooms. "He had so much damn innocence about him," chuckled Phillips. "And he never really changed from that."

Roy and Claudette were married on June 21, 1957 at a ceremony at the Church of Christ in Kermit. By this time, Roy had returned to West Texas, having spent much of the previous year either on the road or in Memphis. Roy was so inspired by the new Mrs. Orbison that he sat down and wrote a song in her honor, which he simply called "Claudette." "It was based on experiences I recall," Roy said a little mysteriously when asked about the lyric.

Roy occasionally dropped in to Norman Petty's studio in New Mexico, where he'd first recorded "Ooby Dooby" back in 1955. The studio had since become a hot spot for local artists: Buddy Holly and the Crickets had recorded a demo for "That'll Be the Day" there with Petty—the song would become a US and UK number 1 and a million-seller in 1957—while another act known as the Five Bops cut a song with Petty called "Jitterbuggin,'" which became a regional hit. The Five Bops also cut a track about a man who drowned while trying to save a child called "Borne on the Wind," which caught the attention of Roy.

One of the Five Bops was eighteen-year-old Bill Dees, a native Texan like Roy, who was born in Electra and raised in Borger. And Dees had trod a similar path to Roy—he had been taught music basics by a family member, his mother, who showed him how to play the ukelele and piano and sang harmonies with Bill and his brothers. Dees had also gotten his start in radio, in Amarillo.

Dees had looked on as Roy played a show in his hometown of Electra and walked away a convert: "His voice was so loud and clear and piercing. [Onstage] he was as immobile as a statue, just his right leg would move." Dees also saw Roy perform at a high school auditorium in Clovis around the time of "Ooby Dooby," and got to meet him soon after. "[I] found out what a sincere, mild-mannered person he was."

In due course, Bill Dees would play a big part in Roy's career resurrection.

Roy had cowritten a plaintive ballad called "An Empty Cup (And a Broken Date)," and he recorded a demo of the track while at Petty's studio in August 1957. Looking on was John Pickering, the twenty-four-year-old lead singer for a vocal group called the Picks, who'd recently sang on Buddy Holly's "Oh, Boy!", which would reach number 10 on the US charts. Pickering was mesmerized by Roy.

"It was the first time I had ever really heard *the voice* on a ballad," he later wrote. "I was not prepared for this from an unassuming, definitely homely, product of Wink, Texas. Suddenly he was Rock Hudson, Mario Lanza, and Tarzan all wrapped into one. I had goosebumps all the way to my toenails."

But Roy was still struggling with Sam Phillips, who was savoring the huge success of Jerry Lee Lewis's "Whole Lotta Shakin' Goin' On," a number 3 mainstream hit. Phillips was not inclined to release an Orbison ballad on his label. Sun's engineer, Jack Clements, had gone so far as to advise Roy, point-blank, against singing anything other than upbeat material. "Stay away from those ballads, Orby," he told him. "I didn't see what a great singer he would become," Clements later confessed.

However, Roy's luck would change when one afternoon he bid farewell to Claudette and drove off to play a gig with the Everly Brothers in Gary, Indiana.

It had been a stellar year for Don and Phil Everly, coal miners' sons who'd been raised in Shenandoah, Iowa. Both had recently finished high school in Nashville, and thanks to an introduction from country music kingmaker Chet Atkins, signed a deal with Wesley Rose of Acuff-Rose music publishers and Archie Bleyer, a former bandleader who ran the Cadence Records label. "Bye Bye Love," a heavy-hearted valentine written by husband-and-wife team Felice and Boudleaux Bryant, had been rejected by thirty acts before the Everlys recorded it in early March 1957. It reached number 2 on the *Billboard* pop chart, topped the *Cashbox* chart, and launched a stellar career for the siblings.

The Everly Brothers were red-hot when Roy met with them in Gary, Indiana for one of the few gigs he played in 1957. ("I'd just about stopped performing," he said of this bleak period.) As Roy left the dressing room, the siblings pulled him aside.

"Roy, do you have any new material?" they asked. "We've got a session coming up in Nashville."

"I do have this one thing," Roy replied. He was thinking about "Claudette," the song he'd written as a tribute to his wife. Perhaps, Roy thought, the Everlys could do it justice. He sang it to them in the hallway outside the dressing room, accompanying himself on guitar.

"We'd love to cut it," the brothers agreed.

Roy had one problem: He didn't have a tape of the song with him, so he found a piece of cardboard and scribbled down the lyrics. Don and Phil thanked him, pocketed Roy's notes, and took the song with them to Nashville. Back in Texas, having been forced to move in with his parents in Wink, a very broke Roy and Claudette crossed their fingers and awaited the record's release.

Another friend of Roy's whose career was on the upswing was Buddy Holly. During September 1957, Roy was in Nashville when he reconnected with Holly, who'd just scored his first UK chart-topper with "That'll Be the Day." "He had a [record] chart under his arm, he was real proud," said Roy, "and showed us where his record was number 1 in England." Roy liked his fellow Texan a whole lot, but couldn't help but have mixed feelings. "Sometimes I felt jealous and proud to know him at the same time," he admitted.

Holly had tapped into a whole new frontier for American musicians of the era. Wesley Rose, the Everly Brothers' manager—who'd in time work with Roy—had told Don and Phil that there was an eager audience awaiting them on the other side of the Atlantic. "If you toured England," Rose firmly believed, "you'd have number ones." Holly's "That'll Be the Day" was the proof, likewise Elvis's "All Shook Up," which became his debut British number 1 in July 1957.

There was also a potential new audience for Roy in the UK. In early October, he received his first British press coverage, a big splash in *Disc Parade* magazine. London Records had a distribution deal with Sun and they'd released an EP of Roy's work called—a little inaccurately—*Hillbilly Rock*. The four tracks were "Ooby Dooby," "Rock House," "Go! Go! Go!", and "You're My Baby." Big things were predicted by *Disc*

Parade: "Watch out for rockin' Roy. It could be that Roy Orbison, from Texas, is set for a really big future—the Presley way."

It would be a few more years before he first took the trip, but the UK would one day provide a lifeline for Roy.

CHAPTER 5

I was poverty stricken

Before Roy could explore new horizons in the UK, he had to contend with his ongoing problems with Sam Phillips and Sun. "Things went downhill," Roy said, "because of what I wanted to do and what Sam *wanted* me to do." Roy had continued writing ballads, but didn't bother playing them to Phillips, because he knew they'd be rejected. As for Roy's peers, they'd been faring much better than him in 1957: Johnny Cash had big hits on the country and western chart with "Home of the Blues" and "Big River," which had also broken into the top 20 of the pop charts. "Great Balls of Fire," meanwhile, had been a runaway smash for Phillips and his artist most likely, Jerry Lee Lewis, reaching number 2 on the *Billboard* Hot 100 in late '57 and selling more than a million copies within ten days of its release. It also topped the UK singles chart.

As for Roy, still stuck in Wink, he wasn't so much treading water as drowning. In December 1957, he cut a new single at Sun, a novelty track with the unfortunate name of "Chicken Hearted." It was written by Bill Justis, who'd recently hit the jackpot with the instrumental "Raunchy," released on Phillips International Records, a subsidiary of Sun. "Raunchy" was a smash, hitting number 2 on the *Billboard* Hot 100—and it also did good business in the UK, where it helped connect a fifteen-year-old British kid named George Harrison, who'd mastered the song's riff, with members of a new group called the Quarrymen. Roy's "Chicken Hearted" wouldn't have such historical significance; it came and went with barely a murmur. It was best summed up by writer Colin Escott in his liner notes for *Roy Orbison: The Sun Years*, where he described "Chicken Hearted" as "the quintessential nerd's lament, almost a backing track for a Charles Atlas commercial." Roy hated the song. According to the BBC documentary, *One of the Lonely Ones*, he felt that "it was one of the worst recordings in the history of the world."

It seemed that Roy's future might be in songwriting, because a variety of acts cut his songs during 1957 and 1958. Johnny Cash recorded Roy's "You Tell Me," even though it was a track that the composer didn't care for. "[It] wasn't much of a song," Roy said, "but John had to sing it and I always kid him about it."

Cash, like Roy, had become disillusioned with Sam Phillips and Sun, and only recorded the song after being advised—by letter, not in person—that in order to sign with Columbia, where he'd been offered a higher royalty rate and better terms, he had to record several tracks for Sun. Among them was "You Tell Me," which didn't emerge until September 1959 and failed to chart.

"I was quite seriously annoyed," Cash wrote, "but did as I was told." He left Sun in early 1958 and Carl Perkins did likewise not long after. Both signed with Columbia.

Before leaving Sun, Cash offered his friend some free advice: "You know, Roy, you need to do two things: change your name and lower your voice." Cash later wrote about this, stating, drolly, "That was fairly typical of my commercial judgment." He'd also suggested that Jerry Lee Lewis cut Jack Clements's "It'll Be Me," rather than "Whole Lotta Shakin' Going On," which became his first million-seller. Johnny Cash, by his own admission, wasn't the best guy to ask for career guidance.

Elsewhere, Sun's Warren Smith had recorded Roy's very Hank Williams–like "So Long, I'm Gone," which reached number 74 on the Hot 100, while Ken Cook, a friend of Roy's from Odessa, cut "I Fell in Love" for Sun, with Roy helping on harmonies. Roy also did his bit for fellow musician Johnny Wilson, who recorded for the Brunswick label—he and Claudette were attendants at his wedding at the Wink Church of Christ in January 1958.

But Roy's biggest chance of success was the Everly Brothers' recording of "Claudette," which they'd chosen as the B-side of "All I Have to Do is Dream," another Boudleaux Bryant track. It was released in April—and by May, it was breaking all kinds of records, becoming the first single to top numerous *Billboard* charts at the same time. It remained number 1 for three weeks and charted for five months, much of that camped inside the top 10. Former Wink Westerner Richard West first heard "Claudette" on a Navy jukebox and wasn't surprised that his former buddy and bandmate had hit the big time. "Roy always had his own style," said West.

Roy was back on the road while the Everly Brothers took over the charts, playing shows with Johnny Cash and a twenty-nine-year-old singer from Newport, Arkansas, who performed as Sonny Burgess and the Pacers. (He'd cut "Red Headed Woman" for Sun in 1956.) By the time the tour reached Albuquerque, Burgess's Cadillac had broken down and he rode with Cash and Roy. As Roy recalled, Burgess was quite a sight for the working folk of rural America: "Sonny had dyed his hair red, had a red Fender guitar, and wore red shoes." After the Albuquerque show, Burgess told Roy, "They'll always remember us . . . as the Wink Wildcat and the Red Clown."

While on the road, Roy also encountered Ronnie "the Hawk" Hawkins, another larger-than-life character. They shared a bill at the University of Arkansas and sat together in a car and talked shop after the show. "I sure do want to get into the business," the twenty-three-year-old Hawkins, a former bootlegger, said to Roy. "Can you recommend a song I should record?"

Roy played him a snippet of "Mary Lou," written by Obediah Jessie (aka Young Jessie), which Hawkins went on to record in August 1959 with the musicians that would become known as the Band. "Mary Lou" hit the Canadian top 10 and reached number 26 on the *Billboard* Hot 100.

Roy may have helped set yet another career in motion, but despite the success of "Claudette," he drifted away from the music business, spending much of 1958 in Wink with his wife and family. The Orbisons' first child, a boy they named Roy Dewayne, was born in Wink on April 18. "I was poverty stricken," Roy told Covey Bean from the *Odessa American*. Yet he hadn't given up on music. "I kinda felt like I'd make it someday, so I just kept hoping and stuck around."

It seemed as though Roy was caught in the past. When he did play shows, he was either promoted as "Mr. Ooby Dooby" or "Roy Orbison: Teen-age Rock 'n' Roller," which seemed a little odd for a guy in his early twenties no longer fronting the Teen Kings. Yet this was Roy's tag when he shared a bill with Patsy Cline, Bob Wills and His Texas Playboys, and Carl Perkins at Pershing, Nebraska in early May 1958.

Roy decided to make his first proper move to separate himself from Sun and began sending demos of his new songs to Wesley Rose of Acuff-Rose Music, who represented the Everly Brothers. The music publisher Acuff-Rose was a Nashville powerhouse that had been established in 1942 by Rose's father, Fred, and Roy Acuff, an influential figure known as "the king of country music," who'd gotten his start in the same type of medicine show (Dr. Hauer's Medicine Show, in Acuff's case) that Roy witnessed as a kid in Wink.

Wesley Rose, who was born in Chicago, had trained as an accountant before joining his father's company in 1945, when he was twenty-seven. He soon became Roy's manager, booking through Acuff-Rose Artists the few gigs that he did play, and pitching his songs to different singers. But Roy always worked best with a collaborator, and he soon reconnected with someone who'd become his next writing partner.

The "Claudette" royalties had enabled Roy to move to Nashville, where he, his wife, and their baby son Roy Dewayne were now living in a cramped apartment at 766 Roycroft Place. To write in peace, Roy would go for a drive and compose in his car—or sometimes *on* his car. "I'd jump on the fender," recalled Roy, "and play the guitar and sing." This was how Roy came to befriend Joe Melson.

They'd actually met before, back when Roy and the Wink Westerners had a regular spot on KOSA-TV in Odessa. Melson and his band, the Cavaliers, had a similar segment on KOSA-TV's neighbor, KMID-TV. Melson, like Roy, was a Texan, the son of a sharecropper (just like Roy's friend Carl Perkins). The impressively pompadoured Melson, who'd studied at Odessa Junior College, was a trained singer, songwriter, and guitarist. He was also a sharp dresser, as a former classmate recalled: "He would get off the bus wearing a sports coat with jeans and high-topped leather shoes and a guitar slung over his shoulder."

One day, Melson spotted Roy sitting in his Caddy, trying to write. It was "a long, green Cadillac," as Melson remembered during an interview on Real Oldies radio. Melson tapped on the window and he and Roy got reacquainted. "You know," Roy told him, "you write a pretty good song. And I write a pretty good song. Together we'd have a dynamite song." It was the first time they'd really talked about business. "Sometimes good things just happen by accident," Melson figured.

Both Joe Melson and Wesley Rose would become important players in the Roy Orbison story, but first Roy needed to sever his ties with Sam Phillips.

The situation between Roy and Phillips reached boiling point by the end of September 1958, when Roy cut a song for RCA and Phillips filed a lawsuit challenging this. Phillips phoned Roy, who was at Johnny Cash's house, and as Cash recalled, "really let him have it." By Cash's recollection, Phillips told Roy: "You can't sing! I had to cram the microphone down your throat just to pick you up, your voice is so weak."

Roy managed to laugh it off—he knew Phillips's accusation wasn't true—but he needed to make a concession in order to leave Sun, so he agreed to sign over the copyrights of the original material he'd recorded for the label. During his time with Sun, Roy had numerous problems with Phillips, but at the core was his concern about money: "We were being paid less than most artists . . . that's why we all left," he said of himself and Cash and Carl Perkins, among others, who only received a 3-percent royalty on record sales. "I don't think Elvis made any money at Sun. I didn't make much."

Yet on the upside, there were friendships Roy made while he recorded for Sun, especially with Johnny Cash and Carl Perkins, which would never fade. There was a spirit of camaraderie between the Sun acts, most of whom were raised in poverty. They'd often play on each other's sessions, sometimes without formal credit. Roy, for instance, helped a rockabilly cat named Rudy Grayzell on his release "I Think of You," while Jerry Lee Lewis recorded Roy and the Teen Kings' "Go! Go! Go!", rechristened "Down the Line," as the B-side of his 1958 single, "Breathless." "We all helped each other out back when we started," Roy said. "It was everybody wanting to hear the feel of the music; people really wanted to be involved in music."

Lewis had played piano on Carl Perkins's single "Matchbox," although after a couple of big hits, Jerry Lee balked when Roy asked him to play on one of his sessions. "No, I don't do that anymore," Lewis advised him. That wasn't out of character for the volatile piano man from Ferriday, Louisiana, whose appraisal of Roy, as he told a writer from *Rolling Stone*, was equally blunt: "He minded his business, stayed in his place. He might come by just to say hello, hug your neck real nice, and get out of your hair. He was that kind of person."

Unfortunately for Roy, while RCA's Chet Atkins was a huge supporter, working with him didn't pan out a whole lot better than his efforts at Sun. Of his numerous sessions for the label over the course of the next year, only two singles were deemed worthy of a release: "Seems to Me" and its B-side "Sweet and Innocent," in late September 1958, and the up-tempo "Almost Eighteen," which Roy wrote, backed with "Jolie," a breezy number with a French twist, penned by the Bryant husband and wife team, which was released in December 1958. The songs were catchy enough but emotionally insubstantial, more suited to songbird Connie Francis than the man who'd made waves with "Ooby Dooby" a few years earlier.

"Seems to Me" was reviewed favorably enough by *The Philadelphia Inquirer* in late October 1958. "The shuffle rhythm has always been ear-catching and susceptible for dancing. On this waxing, Roy Orbison utilizes this beat and 'Sweet and Innocent' has that delightful country-folk flavor for over all appeal." But the record didn't chart nationally, at least not for Roy, although toothy family outfit the Osmonds turned "Sweet and Innocent" into a million- seller in 1971.

Roy had hit another dead end. "After the second record," Roy told Australian writer Glenn A. Baker, "Chet [Atkins] felt that he didn't have the power within the structure of RCA to do for me what needed to be done. He said, 'I just don't have the clout.'"

During what proved to be Roy's final session for RCA, a bass player named Bob Moore told him that he was buying a stake in a start-up called Monument Records. Roy had never heard of the label, but this didn't stop Moore placing a call to Fred Foster, who ran Monument, advising him that Roy was about to be cut loose by RCA. "He's a free agent," said Moore.

North Carolina native Foster, who'd learned the trade in the sales and promotion departments of Mercury Records and ABC-Paramount, had established Monument in early 1958 with just $1,200 in the bank, and two young children at home. Foster named the label in honor of the Washington Monument, which, after several trips to the capital—which became his adopted hometown—he'd noticed was the dominant feature of the city's skyline. The label was part of the London Group, which distributed records worldwide for various independents, including Monument and Memphis's Hi Records.

Foster's first big splash was a folk song called "Gotta Travel On," recorded by a former toolmaker named Billy Grammer and released in October 1958. It sold 900,000 copies and crossed over into both country and pop charts and even spawned a dance craze known as "the Shag." Foster set up camp at Old Hickory Lake, near Nashville, living in the same neighborhood as songwriter Boudleaux Bryant. He hired a Baltimore attorney named Franklin Goldstein and an accountant named Gunther Borris, also from Baltimore, whose belief in Monument was so strong that they worked pro bono for the first year—and ended up staying with the company for more than a decade. Various influential people willingly supported Foster, including his neighbor Bryant, as well as Chet Akins, Wesley Rose, and Anita Kerr, a highly regarded singer, arranger, and composer, who'd worked with Jim Reeves and Patsy Cline and helped develop the silky style known as the "Nashville Sound."

It wasn't long after Roy's disheartening discussion with Chet Atkins that he got a call from his manager Rose.

"How would you like to be on Monument Records?"

"What's Monument Records?" Roy replied.

Rose told Roy to meet him at the Acuff-Rose office in Nashville. When Roy arrived, Rose told him that he had a session in progress.

"What session?" asked Roy, clearly confused.

"Yours, Roy," he was informed.

Roy and Rose took a taxi to a studio where a session was indeed in progress. "Only," as Roy recalled, "I wasn't there." He was duly rushed into the booth to record the same songs he'd recorded for RCA, "Sweet and Innocent" and "Almost Eighteen," which he was now recording for Monument. To make matters just that little bit stranger, the session was taking place in Studio B, owned by Roy's former label, RCA.

That night, over dinner, Roy finally met Fred Foster. If the session he'd just attended wasn't confusing enough, there was a bigger misunderstanding in store: He'd later be told that Foster agreed to meet him purely by accident. Foster was a big fan of "Rock 'n' Roll Ruby," a record by Sun's Warren Smith, and having confused it with Roy's "Ooby Dooby," agreed straightaway when Rose approached him regarding a deal for his client. He'd signed the wrong guy—or at least that was what Roy was told.

Foster, not surprisingly, would come to deny this story, insisting that he signed Roy despite warnings he'd received from others in the industry that the man from Wink wasn't going to make it, that he was "too ugly." Roy may have looked nothing like Fabian or Frankie Avalon, but Foster knew better. "Man, I thought, is that superficial or what," he said during the BBC documentary *One of the Lonely Ones*. He firmly believed that Roy was his guy.

As far as Roy was concerned, signing with Acuff-Rose and Monument was his biggest break yet. He described it as "a heavenly move." A bold new phase of Roy's musical journey had begun.

CHAPTER 6

I don't care if a song with the same name is a smash now, or yesterday, it don't make any difference

Roy didn't strike pay dirt immediately with Monument—in fact, he only earned $1,710 during the entire year of 1959, barely enough to feed his family. Neither "Sweet and Innocent" or "Almost Eighteen" were released, while his first official single for the label, "Paper Boy," backed by "With the Bug," was not a hit upon its limited release in September 1959. It sold only a few thousand copies and was little more than a promotional single for DJs. But stylistically, Roy changed things up with "Paper Boy"—it was reminiscent of Buddy Holly's September 1957 smash "Everyday," with its subtle use of strings and horns. Roy was very clearly moving in a different musical direction.

Through a mutual friend named Ray Rush, a member of vocal group the Roses, Roy reconnected with Joe Melson, whom Rush was trying to help get a record deal. Rush arranged for Melson to visit Roy at home where he sang his song "Raindrops" to the Orbisons. Melson said that Claudette turned to her husband and told him, "That's the prettiest song I've ever heard, Roy." (Roy recorded it in 1961 for his *Lonely and Blue* LP.) Roy hadn't forgotten his comment to Melson—"together we'd have a dynamite song"—and they began collaborating.

They had very different personalities, according to Fred Foster: "Joe was the instigator, [whereas] Roy was kind of like laid-back and shy." But creative sparks flew between the pair.

The two men struck upon an unusual writing method, which, in typical Roy fashion, involved a motor car. They'd drive around in Roy's Cadillac, listening to the radio, "and play the pop stations and try to write," as Melson would recall. One of their first cowrites was called "I'm in a Blue, Blue Mood," which was recorded by the singer whom Roy had steered away from Sun Records, now known as Conway Twitty. He had a huge global smash under his belt, 1958's "It's Only Make Believe," which Twitty recorded for MGM Records. "I'm in a Blue, Blue Mood" wasn't a hit, but its unmistakably melancholic aura hinted strongly at the direction Roy was heading.

Roy and Melson's breakthrough came while they were staying in a motel in Odessa. As Melson recalled, "I hit on a melody line on the guitar and Roy really liked it." Roy said to Melson, "That's a real uptown melody." The pair exchanged knowing looks, quickly reached for their notepads, and a song was born. "We wrote 'Uptown' that night," said Melson.

Melson was in the RCA studio in Nashville in late summer 1959 when Roy recorded his vocal. "When Roy sang 'Uptown' for the first time, it had magic. [And] when Roy sailed into falsetto, it gave the song the punch it needed." Roy wanted to work with strings, real strings, rather than the fiddles typically heard in Nashville productions, and asked Fred Foster if they could do this with "Uptown." (In fact, Roy said that Foster took some persuading and he had to "plead" for the use of strings.) Foster contacted Anita Kerr, who came into the studio with three string players, and their contribution melded beautifully with the tenor sax of Boots Randolph and a chorus led by Kerr and Melson.

Also working on "Uptown" was engineer Bill Porter, the son of a pro ball player, who was at the starting point of a remarkable career that would feature credits on forty-nine top 10 singles. Porter performed a quick act of improvisation to achieve proper "separation" for Roy's vocals on "Uptown." He set Roy up behind a coatrack, which functioned as an impromptu isolation booth. "Few people know this, but Orbison's voice initially was very thin-sounding," Porter said when asked about the session. "It didn't have much body to it." Porter used a tape loop to "thicken" Roy's vocals.

The result was Roy's first truly original song, created with the help of what would become his dream team: Fred Foster and Bill Porter behind the studio glass, plus cowriter Melson and arranger Anita Kerr, as well as Nashville studio "cats" Buddy Harman on drums, Harold Bradley on rhythm guitar, and bassist Bob Moore. "When we listened to the playbacks," said Melson, "we looked at each other and almost wept because the strings were so pretty." The song also had more swing than anything Roy had recorded before; there was an unmistakable groove. It was "Uptown" by name and by nature.

"Uptown," however, wasn't a smash. On its release in September 1959, it didn't get beyond number 72 on the *Billboard* Hot 100 and only sold about 75,000 copies. But Roy had not only joined forces with the right people, he'd also edged closer to what would become his classic sound.

Roy and Melson often put in long nights writing; sometimes they'd fall asleep with their guitars still slung around their necks. But there was a method behind their marathons. Upon waking, they'd play back what they completed the night before and see if it stood up to review. As Melson pointed out to a reporter, "Our philosophy was, if it sounds good in the broad daylight, think what it will sound like when those people are lonely at night." And "lonely" was the key word when it came to the next Orbison-Melson collaboration.

Roy had a studio session booked in Nashville during April 1960 and spent the week prior sorting through potential material with Fred Foster. Roy previewed a new song called "Come Back to Me (My Love)," but Foster felt it was a little too like "Teen Angel," a recent number 1 for pop singer Mark Dinning, an Acuff-Rose cut that was recorded in Nashville. But there was something about Roy's vocal that Foster liked. Roy then sang him another new song he'd written with Melson over a series of months, which they'd called "Only the Lonely." The introduction was very similar to "Come Back to Me." Both Foster and Roy liked this new track and deemed it studio-worthy.

Foster, however, had some concerns about the title. Pat Boone, Roy's acquaintance from Texas State, had a recent hit called "Gee, But It's Lonely," while another "Only the Lonely" had been the opening track of the 1958 LP *Frank Sinatra Sings for Only the Lonely*. Foster worried that there might be some confusion, but Roy felt differently.

"Fred, I don't care if a song with the same name is a smash now, or yesterday, it don't make any difference," Roy told his producer prior to the session. "This is what it's called, 'Only the Lonely.'" (Although by way of compromise, he agreed to add the subtitle "Know the Way

I Feel.") Roy had a vision and a plan—and there was no way that he was changing the name of the track. Harold Bradley, who'd play on the session, noted later that Roy "was so organized and so headstrong." He knew what he wanted.

But Roy, at least for a moment, did have someone else in mind for "Only the Lonely." In spring 1960, on the way to the studio in Nashville, Roy, driving a borrowed truck, stopped to see Elvis Presley, who had just a few weeks earlier finished his two-year stint in the Army. Roy intended to play him the song in the hope he might record it. Roy reached Elvis's Memphis home, Graceland, at about 6 a.m., and handed the guard at the gate a note, which he then passed to Elvis in the main house. A message soon came back from Elvis, advising Roy that there was a crowd of people inside, asleep "all over the place," and that they'd catch up in Nashville instead. "I'll see you there," Presley wrote.

Roy felt slighted; he sensed that he had a hit on his hands and Presley should have at least made the effort to hear the track. When Roy reached the studio in Nashville, he bumped into Phil Everly, whom he hadn't seen since the success of "Claudette." Roy sang a little of "Only the Lonely" to Everly, but Phil stopped him halfway through and commenced to play a song that he was working on. It seemed that "Only the Lonely" didn't impress Phil Everly, either. Two big players had missed an opportunity to cut Roy's best song yet.

Then there was another problem: Presley had booked the RCA studio solid for the next three days, around the clock. "When is it unbooked?" Roy asked Wesley Rose. "You're not making any sense."

Another seventy-two hours passed before Roy finally got to work on "Only the Lonely." "I was ready," he said with characteristic understatement. He worked with the same team from "Uptown"—Fred Foster and engineer Bill Porter, and Joe Melson, who sang the "dum-dum-dum-be-do-wah" backing vocals with Anita Kerr, who hired the Nashville Symphony Orchestra for the session. The studio was almost overflowing with players, as Roy would recall: "There were thirty people crowded in . . . I was backed up against a coatrack singing."

Finally, Roy was provided with the opportunity to explore what Sun's Jack Clements called the "big production sounds" he craved, sounds that he simply couldn't achieve while at Sun. "We just didn't have the personnel or studio to deliver that," said Clements. But now Roy could reach for the sky, thanks to his growing confidence and the help of the best players Monument's money could buy. And by singing in the first person, Roy personalized his sorrow, helping listeners connect with what he was feeling. He may have been raised in macho Texas, but deep down, Roy Orbison had a sensitive side. Here was the proof. As Fred Foster told the BBC, "Roy had the guts to put into words what everybody was thinking but couldn't admit openly." (Many years later, Roy discovered that the nineteenth-century German writer Goethe had used the line "only the lonely know the way that I feel." He said he was "astounded" when he found out.)

Roy turned twenty-four during April, as he and his team readied "Only the Lonely" for release, and he felt that his birthday was a good omen. He hoped, quietly, that "Only the Lonely" would make the top 20, but he chose not to tell anyone for fear of bringing on bad luck.

One of the first responses Roy got for "Only the Lonely" wasn't especially positive: "You can't dance to that, it's not in meter," he was told on its release in May 1960. "You'd be dancing with one foot off the floor." "I don't care," Roy replied, "if people dance or they don't. I never wanted to dance to any of my songs." Fans, however, quickly warmed to the song. "As far as us teenagers are concerned," one Maurice M. Sponcler Jr. advised the *Atlanta Constitution* in a letter, "Roy Orbison's 'Only the Lonely' is really the coolest. It is a song with a good beat that is expertly sung."

Roy even rated a mention in *Seventeen* magazine, the domain of pretty boy "dreamboats" such as Fabian and Frankie Avalon. "This boy has a tremendous voice and he proved it with 'Only the Lonely,'" *Seventeen*'s editor-publisher Enid A. Haupt declared. Roy proved to be an uneasy fit, though, because he was profiled alongside Elvis Presley, whose "main hobby" was listed as "collecting teddy bears." As for Roy, his hobbies of "model airplanes, drawing, and sketching" just weren't quite as cute. Still, the magazine had huge reach among those too young to vote, yet old enough to buy records.

Following the record's release, Roy and Wesley Rose flew to New York for a promotional tour. New York wasn't Roy's favorite city—"you have to be well versed in how to get along in the world," he said of the Big Apple—but this was a trip he'd remember for the rest of his life. They were killing time in a Manhattan movie theater when Rose suggested they go "check the charts." This wasn't something Roy liked to do, but in this instance, he agreed. They went downstairs to what Roy remembered as "a beautifully appointed men's room," and Rose made the call, checking the progress of "Only the Lonely" on the two key trade charts, *Billboard* and *Cashbox*.

Rose returned with a broad grin: "It's number 88 and number 71, first week in," he told Roy. They went back to their seats, but within minutes, Roy turned to Rose and said, "I don't want to watch the movie anymore." Rose agreed. Roy's mind was racing: "I thought Top 20 for sure."

May 1960 was a red-letter month for new releases—the Everlys had "Cathy's Clown" high in the charts (followed by "When Will I Be Loved?"), Elvis released "Stuck on You," Etta James dropped "All I Could Do Was Cry," while Brenda Lee sang "I'm Sorry"—but Roy's "Only the Lonely" was an equally hot property.

One reporter noted that it was climbing the charts "at supersonic speed," and by mid-June, "Only the Lonely" was doing just that: It was number 31 and rising fast. The following week, it reached number 23, and by the time Roy made his debut on *American Bandstand* in late July, a show seen by an audience of around twenty million, it was number 4. "Only the Lonely" had also started to make inroads into the Australian pop charts, where it would hit a peak of number 6 and chart for three months. It was the first of twenty top 20 hits that Roy achieved in Australia, which in time became one of his key markets. In the UK, meanwhile, it was fast-tracking its way to number 1, while across the border in Canada, it reached number 2. It also hit various top 10s throughout Europe. Elvis Presley was so impressed when he finally heard "Only the Lonely" that he bought dozens of copies of the record and handed them out to his Memphis buddies.

With "Only the Lonely," Roy Orbison had finally found his sound—and a new title. When he left Nashville in July to play a show at the Birmingham Armory with Hank Locklin and Charlie Rich, he was billed simply as "Roy Orbison 'Only the Lonely.'"

Momentum was everything in the pop world, something Roy knew only too well. While "Only the Lonely" was still high in the charts, he got back to work with Joe Melson, whose wife had just given birth to their second child, a girl. Duly inspired, Melson was working on a track he called "Blue Angel," which he played over the phone to Roy. "It sounds like a hit," Roy said, and on August 8, they returned to the studio. Melson was now writing with Roy's vocal very much front of mind. "We pieced each song together phrase-by-phrase, step-by-step, all molded around his voice."

Roy was also finding his groove in the studio with Fred Foster. "I had everything I wanted," he said in 1980 when asked about their partnership. "[Foster] was smart enough to get out of the way at the right time. He didn't put his foot in his mouth by suggesting I sound like this or that. He just liked what sounded good to him, which is the best producer you could have. It was fantastic." Foster returned the compliment. "Roy and I sparked each other so much," he said in 1978, "that when we got to the studio, we'd both be so psyched up there was no way we'd miss."

Chart response to "Blue Angel," which was released in August, was immediate, but some critics weren't convinced that it matched "Only the Lonely" (which was fair enough; the sugary-sweet confection lacked the melodramatic oomph of its predecessor). Jack Curtis from the *Arizona Republic* wasn't sold on Orbison's vocal: "[It's] almost too well planned to be very effective. He slurs many of his words and phrases, though not because he feels the song that way. It's as if that's what he must do to impart a style."

Once again, none of this really mattered to Roy's fans. As he hit the road through September and October, playing to full houses at the Riverside Ballroom in Phoenix, the Civic Auditorium in Albuquerque, and Amarillo's Municipal Auditorium, Roy was in the enviable position of having two singles charting simultaneously. In November, "Blue Angel" reached the top 20, alongside hits from Ray Charles ("Georgia on My Mind"), Bobby Vee ("Devil or Angel"), Paul Anka ("Summer's Gone"), and the Drifters' "Save the Last Dance for Me," while "Only the Lonely" was still in the top 100. "Blue Angel" eventually peaked at number 9 on the *Billboard* Hot 100 and number 11 on the UK Record Retailers' Top

50. In this peculiar era of pop, wedged between the first wave of rock and roll and the coming of the Beatles, Roy was top of the pile.

In late November, Roy headlined a bill at the City Auditorium in Wichita Falls, Texas, supported by Mark Dinning and Johnny Tillotson. The show was advertised, simply enough, as the night of "Million Selling Artists." Roy had every intention of living up to this billing, because he was soon writing his next hit single with Joe Melson. Its title, "I'm Hurtin,'" made it abundantly clear that Roy and Melson had struck upon a winning formula, songs about heartache and loneliness, which they'd first tapped into with "Only the Lonely."

Roy previewed "I'm Hurtin'" on air in Phoenix with KRUX's popular morning DJ Lucky Lawrence during December 1960. Subsequent reviews of the song remarked upon a discernible trend in Roy's music. "Again Orbison goes into musical orbit," noted the music critic at the *Niagara Falls Review*. "The song is another hard luck tale—please pity poor Roy." The B-side, a cover of the forlorn, "I Can't Stop Loving You," was a nod to one of Roy's musical heroes, Don Gibson, a master of brokenhearted ballads. (Ray Charles would hit number 1 with his version in 1962.) Roy's manager, Wesley Rose, had worked with Gibson, and Roy was already considering the idea of an entire album of Gibson numbers.

Despite another fine vocal from Roy—and smooth backing vocals from Wade Moore, the cowriter of "Ooby Dooby"— "I'm Hurtin,'" like "Blue Angel," felt a little too generic, too familiar, to be great. Perhaps there were a few too many "dum de dum de dum ooh yeah yeahs" for one track—although a surging orchestral passage hinted at bigger things to come. Still, "I'm Hurtin'" made it to number 27 on the *Billboard* Hot 100, becoming Roy's fourth charting single in a row.

In a year's end record wrap in the *Kingston* (Ontario) *Whig-Standard*, critic Ray Shank made a prediction: "In our mind, the loveliest 1960 recording was that by a newcomer called Roy Orbison. 'Only the Lonely' was a tremendous effort and if this fellow doesn't become a big name star, just call us MUD." Roy had every reason to argue that he'd been around a long time for a newcomer, but it had been a hell of a year. Somehow, he'd even found the time to champion other artists, helping a doo-wop outfit from Odessa named the Velvets get a deal with Monument.

Yet somehow, 1961 would be even bigger for Roy. Soon enough he'd own the charts.

CHAPTER 7

When I heard it played back, I knew that was going straight to number one

Real magic happened when Roy next stepped up to the microphone in RCA's Studio B in Nashville. It was late February 1961, not long after the release of his debut LP for Monument, *Lonely and Blue*. Roy was once again working with Joe Melson, Fred Foster, and Bill Porter, on a new song with a title—"Running Scared"—that he'd lifted from a newspaper headline he read while on a flight to New York.

As Roy prepared to cut his vocal, Foster pulled him aside. He felt that Roy shouldn't sing in falsetto, which was his intention, but in a more natural tone.

"Roy," he said, "it's just not going to make it unless you can hit it full voice."

"Man," Roy replied, "I don't think I can hit that—it'll be terrible."

Foster was insistent. "Well, if it is," he told Roy, "you'll be the only one who'll ever hear it, 'cause we'll erase it."

Roy thought this through and said, "All right. I'll try it. Why not?"

Roy returned to the booth and sang the closing lines of "Running Scared" one more time. The result was so remarkable, virtually operatic, that an astonished Porter turned to Foster and said that he sure hoped he captured the results on tape. "If you didn't, it's all over for you."

In fact, Roy's third and final take was such a powerful, heart-wrenching vocal that the musicians in the studio stopped playing and looked at each other, totally shocked. They'd all worked with great singers, but no one had ever heard anything like this before. "It just seemed like a magical take as it began," Foster recalled. "From that time on, he hit all the high notes." Roy knew it was a great track, perhaps his best yet, despite no recognizable chorus. "When I heard it played back, I knew that was going straight to number 1."

For all its pathos, Roy felt that "Running Scared" was "a happy song." He said that while most people assumed it was the outpouring of a man with a broken heart—which it was, to some extent—it ended positively. "[The narrator] is very sure of getting the girl when he first sees her," Roy explained, "and then he's not so sure, and then he gets desperate, and then he says, 'Forget it.' *And then she comes back*." As for his career-making vocal, Roy admitted that he did what he did intuitively, instinctively. "For a baritone to sing as high as I do is ridiculous," he said. "It only comes from the fact I don't know what I'm doing."

While in the studio, Roy also recorded "Love Hurts," another aching-hearted ballad written by Boudleaux Bryant, recently cut by the Everly Brothers. Fred Foster liked "Love Hurts" so much that he wanted it as the A-side, which led to an argument with Roy, who was sold on "Running Scared." To resolve the conflict with his star client, Rose decided to testdrive the record. He traveled to Chicago, where he struck up a deal with a friendly DJ who played both sides of the single, then did the same thirty minutes later, and so on for the next couple of hours. The DJ then asked listeners to nominate their favorite track. After several "trial spins," hundreds of fans called in and voted "Running Scared" the winner. "I had told him that 'Running Scared' was the A-side," said Roy.

Critical reaction to "Running Scared" was uniformly positive; the record was a hit. "[It] is an emotional ballad with a powerful and insistent backing," stated an early review. "The effect he creates is just the sort that will put any record onto millions of record players throughout the country." "Roy sings the lyrics [of "Running Scared"] as if he were afraid of them," wrote Charles J. Schreiber in Montreal's *The Gazette*, "but this produces an intriguing sound."

"Running Scared" was released in March 1961, a time when the charts and airwaves were filled with Elvis's "Surrender," the Everly Brothers' "Walk Right Back," and Del Shannon's "Runaway," along with more saccharine fare such as Connie Francis's "Where the Boys Are" and the pure Muzak of "Wheels" by the String-A-Longs. There was also a flurry of doo-wop hits like the Marcels' "Blue Moon" and the

Tokens' "Tonight I Fell in Love," but that wasn't Roy's style, as noted by the *Muskogee Daily Phoenix* in their review of "Running Scared": "[It] does not contain one Doo-Wah, Doo-Wah. (How about that!)."

By early May, "Running Scared" had cracked the *Billboard* Top 30, and by the middle of the month, was battling it out with Shannon's "Runaway" for number 1. Ricky Nelson's "Travelin' Man" was also in the top 10, along with Gene McDaniels's "A Hundred Pounds of Clay," but "Running Scared," for its sheer dramatic impact and musical vision, towered over all of them. It was a great moment in time for Monument Records, because the Velvets, whom Roy had helped get signed to the label, were also climbing the charts with what would be their biggest hit, "Tonight (Could Be the Night)." (They'd follow it up with an Orbison-Melson track called "Laugh.")

On June 5, 1961, "Running Scared" topped the *Billboard* Hot 100. It was Roy's first number 1 and would remain on the chart for a staggering seventeen weeks. Roy was on his way to selling four million records during the year, remarkable numbers. "The only one [Roy] should be scared of," chuckled Charles Schreiber in *The Buffalo News*, "is the tax collector."

As for the "Running Scared" UK release, it was greeted with the usual fanfare—England loved Roy Orbison. "No need to be scared, Roy," Pete Murray wrote about "Running Scared" in the *Manchester Evening News*, "it's running right up the Hit Parade." It would hit number 9 in the UK. There'd already been a rumor that Roy might play shows in England with Sheb Wooley, a star of TV's *Rawhide* and creator of the novelty number 1 "The Purple People Eater." Another rumor hinted at Roy touring England backed by the Webs, a group from Dothan, Alabama, whose members included a guitarist named Bobby Goldsboro, but nothing had been confirmed.

As it turned out, Fred Foster did have a point, because the B-side, "Love Hurts," became a hit in Australia, where both "Love Hurts" and "Running Scared" reached the top 10 during June 1961. "Roy practically sobs his way through this sad and mournful tune," noted the wonderfully named Sandy Lee Funk in the April 21 edition of the *Richmond* (Virginia) *News Leader*. ("Love Hurts" had staying power; it would be covered around 100 times, most notably by Emmylou Harris and Gram Parsons, and became a hit for rock band Nazareth in 1974 and Jim Capaldi the year after.)

By the time Roy returned to the live circuit, he was a bona fide star. "He is referred to throughout America as 'the big new excitement,'" announced a journalist prior to a show by Roy in late June '61. "His capacity knows no end for seldom is a writer of music a singer, but Orbison attains the miraculous by also being a terrific performer and stylist." Roy was invited to the Cotton Bowl in Dallas, where, along with TV actor Dwayne Hickman (CBS's *Dobie Gillis*), and fellow singers Bobby Vee and Bobby Rydell, they shared the enviable job of crowning Miss Teenage America.

While in Texas, on a rare day off, Roy visited Wink, his old hometown of "football, oil fields, oil, grease, and sand," as he'd once described it. A hell of a lot had happened to Roy since his days at Wink High. Life was good.

Roy enjoyed his salad days, buying a Ford Thunderbird to park alongside his Cadillac, and indulging his lifelong passion for model airplanes—his first model had been a Battle of Britain Spitfire replica, which he'd had since he was a kid. He also purchased a speedboat, which he christened *Claudette*, of course, and began thinking about having a new home built for his wife and their son, ideally by the water. When asked by a reporter about life away from music, Roy said that he enjoyed "nighttimes, automobiles, good food, and handicrafts" and disliked "haughty entertainers" and "insincere people." His personal ambition was "continual happiness," and as for his professional ambition, well, that was simple: "To better my career," Roy stated.

Bettering his career may have seemed like a very tall order, given the runaway success of "Only the Lonely" and "Running Scared," because between them they charted on the *Billboard* Hot 100 for thirty-eight weeks. But Roy's next single, another ballad, came pretty damned close to topping even those hits, despite breaking an unwritten rule of the pop world. There was a belief that you didn't release two ballads back-to-back, that it was commercial suicide—after all, how much sorrow could listeners take? But Roy was currently operating purely on instinct, so common wisdom meant nothing. "Musical guidance I really didn't have," he said. "I just did whatever I felt like doing. Nothing was design . . . [at least] nothing that was successful."

Roy's latest collaboration with Joe Melson was an emotionally charged slow burner called "Crying," although its working title had been "Once Again," based around a refrain—"I'm crying / Once again I'm crying"—that had stuck in Melson's head while they were writing. Roy's contribution to the lyric was drawn from what he somewhat vaguely referred to as "a past experience, the retelling of a thing with a girlfriend I had." When pushed, Roy said he remembered breaking up with a partner, whom he spotted across the street while he was in town getting a haircut. As he confessed to a reporter, "I wanted to go over and say, 'Let's forget about what happened and carry on.'" But Roy didn't try and reconnect. Instead, he paid for his trim and drove away, distraught, telling himself, "Boy, you really made a mistake." The lovestruck lyric just about wrote itself.

Roy had earmarked the song for Don Gibson, but wisely changed his mind and recorded it for himself, again at his happy hunting ground of RCA Studio B, in late June 1961. When the session was done, Roy looked at Fred Foster, who had an inscrutable look on his face. "What's wrong with it?" Roy asked him.

"Just one thing," Foster replied, who was now smiling. "It's not out yet."

"I thought it was a good song," Roy surmised. "It went straight to number 1, so there was no bother there."

While in the studio, Roy also recorded "Candy Man," a co-write from Beverly Ross and a twenty-five-year-old Brill Building songwriter named Fred Neil. It was among an assortment of demos that Fred Foster had brought into the Nashville studio and thrown onto a table, stating, "There's a hit among these." Roy recorded an up-tempo demo of "Candy Man," in a manner he described as "Ray Charles-style-fast." Roy liked "Candy Man" so much he thought it might make it an A-side—thereby adhering to the "never release two ballads in a row" philosophy—but was outvoted by Fred Foster and his manager Wesley Rose.

Yet, just as there'd been with "Running Scared" and "Love Hurts," there was some confusion about what song actually *was* the A-side. Roy had preferred "Candy Man," and a problem at the pressing plant resulted in acetates of "Candy Man" being sent to DJs in the Washington area, rather than "Crying." "It may be his biggest seller yet," the *Montreal Star*'s Tony Temple predicted of "Candy Man" in his "Rhythm 'n' News" column on August 19, 1961. "On this side Orbison switches his style and croons a very fine blues—and he really knows how to do it." "Candy Man" quickly became a favorite and even entered the *Billboard* chart in early August, hitting a peak of number 25 before being withdrawn in preference to "Crying." "Somebody tried to pull a fast one," Wesley Rose told the press when asked about the confusion, "but he outsmarted himself." Rose, however, didn't disclose who that "somebody" was.

It said multitudes about the commercial potential of the material Roy was being pitched, let alone the material he was writing with Joe Melson, that a song mistakenly issued as a single was an accidental hit. However, a very humble Roy played this down: "All I wanted to do," he admitted, "was hear my records on a jukebox—that was all I wanted."

"Many adjectives have been used to describe the vocal style of Roy Orbison," stated the *Yuma* (Arizona) *Daily Sun*'s Gary Todd, in his review of "Crying," in mid-August. "For my money, POWERFUL and DRIVING [his caps] are the most appropriate. All indications are that 'Crying' will prove a successful follow-up to the last Orbison great, 'Running Scared.'" "Roy sings one of his own compositions that has a great deal of depth," observed *The Buffalo News*'s Charles Schreiber in his critique of "Crying": "A smart, ear-catching arrangement . . . leads into a lush and melodic ballad. This should be another big one for Roy."

It now seemed almost inevitable that every Roy Orbison release of 1961 was a smash, and "Crying" continued the trend. In early October, "Crying" topped the *Cashbox* chart for a week, and only a speed bump in the shape of Ray Charles's "Hit the Road Jack" prevented it from topping the *Billboard* Hot 100. It peaked at number 2 on October 9 and stuck to the chart like glue for sixteen weeks. Its many American fans included a young Michigan kid named Willard Mitt Romney, who'd cite it as among his ten all-time favorite songs when he one day ran for US president. "Crying" also became Roy's first Australian number 1, charting for almost five months, and hit number 3 in Canada. Even without leaving America—not yet, anyway—Roy was breaking out all over the planet.

Barry Gibb, the eldest brother of a fledgling trio working in Australia called the Bee Gees, had a powerful reaction when he heard "Crying." "To me," he admitted, "it was the voice of God."

In what was a sensational year for Roy, his drawing power as a live act grew in tandem with his domination of the charts. In early October, "Monument Recording Star" Roy filled the Nor-Dan Center in Danville, Virginia, and then a few days later, when he packed out the New Dominion Barn Dance at the stately 1,800-seat Lyric Theater in Richmond, he was promoted as "The Nation's No. 1 Singer with the No. 1 Song, 'Crying.'" Soon after, the "Fabulous Roy Orbison" played the Municipal Auditorium at Bradenton in Florida.

Roy's star seemingly couldn't rise any higher, although on a personal level, sharing bills with Don Gibson, as Roy did on November 2 at Ardmore in Oklahoma, and then again two days later at the 2,700-capacity Memorial Auditorium in Wichita Falls, was probably a bigger thrill. "Roy Orbison is happy and smiling these days," Jeanne Harrison wrote in the *Redding Record Searchlight*. "His hit, 'Crying,' hit the number one spot in the nation's top ten tunes last week."

The Roy Orbison road show—with his songwriting partner Joe Melson on the bill—then headed to Texas, first for a concert at the Club Rendezvous in Lubbock, the hometown of his late pal Buddy Holly, on November 30. Roy had caught up with Holly only weeks before he died in February 1959. "I just realized I play guitar just exactly the way you do!" Holly told him. Roy said afterwards that it was the "greatest compliment."

The press engaged overdrive when Roy filled the Sportatorium in Vernon weeks later, noting how this "former Thalia boy," now a "Recording star for Monument and Decca Records" had sold "6 million records in 1961." And then in mid-December, just as Claudette learned that she was pregnant with their second child, Roy played a student dance at his old alma mater, Odessa Junior College. As part of a daylong celebration, Roy also crowned the homecoming queen at a ceremony staged in the college gym. The winner, seventeen-year-old sophomore Brenda Slough, flashed a toothy grin when she posed for a photo with Roy that appeared in the following day's edition of the *Odessa American*.

While in town, Roy took the time to speak with Covey Bean, a staff writer from the paper. "I was poverty stricken," Roy said when asked about his time at Odessa Junior College when he was supposedly studying geology. "A mere three years later," noted Bean, "Orbison is the hottest thing around in the record business . . . whose annual income now runs in six figures." Bean's timeline may have been askew—Roy left college well before 1958—but his point was well made. As Roy chatted with the reporter, a waitress approached their table. "Are you *the* Roy Orbison?" she asked. "I am," Roy replied warmly.

Roy's homecoming was made even sweeter still when he learned that *Billboard* had declared "Crying" the fourth most popular song of 1961, outranked only by Bobby Lewis's "Tossin' and Turnin,'" Patsy Cline's "I Fall to Pieces"—a brokenhearted ballad to equal Roy's best—and "Michael, Row the Boat Ashore" by East Coast folkies the Highwaymen. "Running Scared" made it to number 13 on the *Billboard* list.

But despite all of Roy's success, there was some trouble behind the scenes. Sam Phillips had watched with dismay as Roy, Johnny Cash, and Warren Smith all enjoyed considerable success since leaving Sun. Not the kind of guy to let an opportunity slip by, Phillips had dug into the tape vaults and released music from former Sun artists Carl Perkins and Cash, to the chagrin of the acts themselves. Cash's cover of Don Gibson's "Oh, Lonesome Me," released by Sun in 1960, had been a top 20 hit on the country charts at a time when Cash was recording for Columbia Records. And in the wake of Roy's monumental success, Phillips had sifted through old studio tapes, fixed a few errors, and packaged his findings into a twelve-track album titled *At the Rock House*. Phillips released the LP on Sun in late 1961.

"Ooby Dooby," Roy's only hit with the label, was a standout of *At the Rock House*, along with "This Kind of Love," which could have been mistaken for an Everly Brothers outtake. A slightly tweaked "Devil Doll" was released as a single. Trade mag *Billboard* reviewed the album generously in its December 11 issue, alongside new LPs from Bill Black's Combo, who'd recently opened for Roy at a show in Pensacola, Florida, and Nina Simone's *Nina at the Village Gate*. *Billboard* noted that *At the Rock House* was "likely to generate plenty of additional counter action" and was a collection of material "done in the familiar and exciting rocking dramatic style of Orbison." Yet the review failed to mention that, at least technically speaking, it wasn't new material at all.

At the Rock House, however, wasn't a hit. It was at best a historical document, capturing a moment in time, when, as music historian Colin Escott accurately stated, "Sam Phillips had kept Roy Orbison on a steady diet of rock & roll," and "Orbison knew that his talent was being wasted at Sun." Roy was incensed when he learned about the album, even though Phillips was doing nothing illegal, Roy having signed away the rights to his music in order to leave the label. Roy drove to Memphis, where he confronted Phillips and demanded that he hand over the tapes of any unissued music left in the Sun vaults. Phillips gave him some, but not all, of the material and, as Roy would tell the story, smiled wryly as he did so.

"You'll be back," Phillips said.

Also in the studio was Jud Phillips, a skilled promoter who helped his brother Sam keep Sun Records afloat. Jud looked first at Roy, and then at Sam, and shook his head.

"The hell he will!" he told his sibling, as Roy headed out the door.

CHAPTER 8

I have to say I was the one who was really responsible for that sound

Roy saw in the new year in much the same way he'd kicked off 1961. He was back in Nashville's Studio B on January 9, surrounded by the familiar faces of the Nashville A-Team: Boots Randolph on sax, guitarists Fred Carter Jr. and Grady Martin, drummer Buddy Harman, and Bob Moore on bass. Guitar maestro Chet Atkins also sat in on the session. Looking around him, Roy's producer Fred Foster knew his artist was in good hands: "With that bunch of [studio] guys, you have no problem."

Roy felt likewise. "I kinda feel at home here," he said of Nashville, "and I don't know how easily I could adapt myself to any other studios."

Yet Roy's latest Monument session came with a twist, because the key song they were working on, "Dream Baby (How Long Must I Dream)," wasn't an Orbison-Melson original. The career of its creator Cindy Walker was, in the words of Bill C. Malone, the author of *Country Music USA*, "a product of luck, pluck, and talent." The daughter of a cotton broker, raised on her grandparents' farm near Mart, Texas, she'd gotten her start aged twenty-two in 1940, while on a trip to Los Angeles with her family. Acting purely on impulse, she asked her father to stop the car outside the Sunset Boulevard office of Larry Crosby, the manager of his famous sibling. "You're squirrely, girl," her father said, "Bing Crosby's not in that building." Undeterred, Walker went inside and played Larry a song she'd written specifically for Bing called "Lone Star Trail."

It became a top 10 hit for Crosby and led to an extended stay on the West Coast for Walker, as well as a fruitful partnership with singing cowboy and film star Bob Wills, best heard in the Western swing classics "Dusty Skies" and "Cherokee Maiden." Despite having the blond good looks of a solo star, Walker became a tunesmith in demand, whose songs were also cut by Gene Autry, Ernest Tubb, and Hank Snow. Like Roy, she'd worked with the Nashville Symphony, who'd performed her song, "I Was Just Walking Out the Door," in 1961.

Now back in Texas, Walker wasn't the biggest fan of "Dream Baby (How Long Must I Dream)." "I thought it was monotonous," Walker said of her song. "You know, 'Dream baby, doo doo doo do doo.'" She didn't even know that Roy was recording the track until she got a call from Fred Foster in mid-January 1962.

"How's the weather down there?" he asked.

"Well, pretty cold," Walker replied.

"Let me play something over the phone that'll warm the cockles of your heart," Foster said, and he proceeded to play her "Dream Baby (How Long Must I Dream)."

Walker was beyond impressed: "Roy did such a great job, I nearly fainted."

Roy played a string of dates as he awaited the February 10 release of "Dream Baby (How Long Must I Dream)." He filled the Fort Homer Hesterly Armory in Tampa on February 4, a show sponsored by the Fraternal Order of Police. The marquee outside the venue displaying Roy's image didn't pull any punches. It read: 7 HITS IN 21 MONTHS.

Next up, Roy was the "featured singer" at a dance staged at the Municipal Auditorium in Clearwater, Florida, hosted by the Clearwater Parks and Recreation Dept. and local radio station WLCY. On March 1, Roy appeared "in person," this time in Austin, Texas, as part of the "Twisterama of 1962." Dance craze "The Twist," driven by Chubby Checker's stream of hits (his latest was "Slow Twistin'"), was not Roy's domain, even though he topped the bill at Austin. Lee Dorsey and the Champs, known for performing the "Tequila Twist," were also on the card. But a gig was a gig, and each show helped push Roy's latest record higher up the chart—by this time, "Dream Baby (How Long Must I Dream)" had fairly raced into the *Billboard* Hot 100, heading for a peak of number 4.

Roy was now a bona fide star in America, although some members of the foreign press still weren't sure what to make of him. "He looks more like an insurance agent than a pop star," Melvyn David observed with some justification in UK newspaper *The Heywood Advertiser*, "and though his hair is nicely waved he bears none of the usual pop star characteristics. Who, then, is this man and what sort of power does he possess to make fans go wild every time they hear him sing? What makes him a star?" Ultimately, David decided quite rightly that it was all about Roy's voice, "probably the most dramatic on record."

Roy's team of Fred Foster and Wesley Rose began to focus more attention offshore, in the lead-up to Roy's first UK tour. By mid-1962, Roy had made serious inroads across the Atlantic: He'd already scored his first UK number 1 with "Only the Lonely" and "Dream Baby (How Long Must I Dream)" had hit number 2, while "Crying," "Running Scared," and "Blue Angel" all charted strongly. But very few of Roy's current chart peers had played concerts in England, aside from the Everly Brothers, who visited in 1960. For Roy, Ricky Nelson, Del Shannon, and Elvis Presley, among many others, it remained unexplored territory, where a young, postwar audience was hungry for new sounds from America.

And England loved Roy's music—the local media heaped praise on "Dream Baby (How Long Must I Dream)." In the *Liverpool Echo*'s "Off the Record" column, it was described as the "type of musical infection that could easily build into a chart epidemic." On March 7, a week before "Dream Baby (How Long Must I Dream)" entered the UK singles chart (destined to reach number 2), a four-piece outfit named the Beatles, also from Liverpool, plugged in for a live set at the BBC radio program *Teenager's Turn—Here We Go*. This was the Beatles' first BBC radio session, and when it was broadcast the following day, among the songs they performed was Roy's "Dream Baby (How Long Must I Dream)."

"We were in awe of him," admitted their guitarist, George Harrison. Roy had no idea who or what these Beatles were, but like much of the Western world, he would find out pretty quickly.

In early June 1962, Roy—whose second child was due later in the month—visited London for a promotional visit, having sailed from New York on board the USS *France*. "Dream Baby (How Long Must

I Dream)" was still in the UK charts, sitting at number 23 after sixteen weeks. He traveled with Fred Foster and fellow recording artist and songwriter John D. Loudermilk, who'd written the Everly Brothers' big 1961 hit, "Ebony Eyes." (Roy would record Loudermilk's songs "I'll Never Tell" and "Break My Mind.") It was Foster who did much of the talking with the local music press, making it very clear that "the British market is too important to overlook." The *New Musical Express* (*NME*), in return, said Foster was "the uncrowned king of Nashville." When asked about Roy's latest release, Foster boasted that "Dream Baby (How Long Must I Dream)" was recorded "in twenty minutes flat," which he believed said plenty about the people with whom his star client was working. "[They're] a clique of musicians who know exactly what they're doing."

Interestingly, despite the inroads that Roy had made into the UK charts, Foster felt he could achieve more. "Roy's success over here has been good," Foster conceded, "he's had good material. But it could have been better." Foster even made a wager—if Roy's next single, a track called "The Crowd," wasn't a hit in the UK, "I am prepared to bring Roy over here to record. If an American sound is no longer required for the British market, then we'll give you an English one."

The trio left the UK with handshakes and good feelings all around, and the *NME*'s Derek Johnson was given an assurance that Roy was considering a British tour later in 1962. As for his latest, "The Crowd," Johnson was a convert: "It's a fantastic record in many respects—a real raver of a disc . . . I have a strong suspicion that this is going to be a big, big hit for Mr. Orbison."

"The Crowd" was given the royal treatment by press back home upon its release in May. "Roy Orbison, who wails like a country and western Jackie Wilson with a hot-foot," crowed New Jersey reporter Bill McLaughlin in his "Platter Chatter" column, "has out a belting new release which should rival 'Running Scared' in its vocal intensity. [It's] a toughie tagged 'The Crowd.'" "The Orbison disk is typical of practically all his tremendous smashes," figured Long Beach journalist Ted Plonas in the *Press-Telegram*, "in that it starts off quiet, then subtly sneaks up on you, building to a musically dramatic climax." Yet there was the odd dissenting voice, such as Charles Schreiber, critic for *The Buffalo News*, who felt Roy's latest was more style than substance. "Roy sings as if he were interested in becoming the successor to the late Mario Lanza, and the orchestra is right in there pitching with him . . . all the stops have been pulled out for dramatic effect."

And while it wasn't short of pathos—as well as soaring strings and heavenly voices—"The Crowd" didn't live up to commercial expectations. The latest Orbison-Melson cowrite only made number 26 on the *Billboard* Hot 100 and barely reached number 40 in the UK. In Australia, it stalled at number 23. Perhaps he was too busy at home to promote the record properly, because a second son, Anthony King Orbison, was born to Roy and Claudette on June 29.

Regardless, Roy was in good spirits when he played at the Oil Show in Midland, where he went over a storm and was encored several times. After the concert, Roy spoke with reporters and was signing autographs when he was told that some of his old friends from Wink were outside, including Ron Slaughter and his wife. According to Slaughter, Roy "dropped his pencil" and rushed over to greet them. Roy introduced Slaughter to the press and said, "You know what I remember most about this guy?" He proceeded to relate the story about playing hooky from school for the first and only time with Slaughter, who was on his way to Midland to go record shopping.

"That was a heck of a thing to be remembered for," laughed Slaughter.

Undaunted by the hiccup in his chart numbers, Roy got back to work in late summer 1962. Roy never forgot that he came from solid Texan working-class stock, and back when he was trying to get his music career rolling, he'd worked briefly for El Paso Natural Gas, "cutting up steel and loading it into trucks and chopping weeds and painting water towers," as Roy recalled. He'd come home from a shift and then play a gig; by the end of another long day, he'd be too exhausted to eat or even undress. "I'd lay down and wouldn't even turn over." Then he'd get up the next day and do it all over again. All this came back to Roy as he composed a song called "Working for the Man"—perhaps his memory was also jogged by a headline in the *Atlanta Journal* promoting his upcoming gig that read, OIL DRILLER HITS IT RICH IN SHOW BIZ.

Roy revealed that "the man" he mentioned in his lyric was his boss at El Paso, a hard-ass named Mr. Rose. As Roy remembered clearly, "He wouldn't cut me any slack." Joe Melson too had done hard time as a laborer, picking cotton on the family farm near Rayburn, Texas. "One day I walked out of that cotton field and said I would never pick cotton again," he told Phil Sullivan from *The Nashville Tennessean*. But despite their similar experiences, Roy didn't call on Melson to help with his latest cut. He wrote it by himself.

Recorded in August and released in early September 1962, "Working for the Man" fared better for Roy overseas than it did at home in America, where it only reached number 33 in the Hot 100. In Australia, it was a smash hit, his second number 1, and it clung to the charts for almost six months. Australia's biggest recording star, Frank Ifield, who currently had a UK number 1 with "I Remember You," was name-checking Roy as his biggest influence, which made perfect sense: Ifield had a similarly silky voice. (Some time later, he'd record Roy's "Crawling Back.")

When Roy was asked why "Working for the Man" hadn't sold so well in America, he blamed his lyric. "It was too complicated," he believed. It certainly didn't harm his live popularity, because when Roy played a gig on Pontchartrain Beach in New Orleans at the time of the record's release, he drew a record crowd of 60,000 mainly teenage fans.

"Working for the Man" was significant for another reason, because it marked the end of Roy's working relationship with Joe Melson, at least for the time being. It had been a remarkably productive time for the pair—they'd generated eight charting singles in three years, including five US top 10s, selling millions of records along the way. It was a run of hits to rival the best songwriters of their generation, something that Roy would never again experience. Such cuts as "Only the Lonely," "Crying," and "Running Scared" had become classics, fan favorites that Roy would perform for the rest of his life. They'd also be mandatory inclusions on the numerous Roy Orbison best-ofs and greatest hits compilations that would be released over the ensuing decades. The first, August 1962's *Roy Orbison's Greatest Hits*, contained eight cowrites with Melson, from "Uptown" to "Blue Angel," and "I'm Hurtin'" to "The Crowd." *Greatest Hits* became Roy's first gold album.

Joe Melson's role in the rise of Roy Orbison was significant, undeniable. As he told writer Colin Escott, "I'd helped him establish the artistry and style. We each had our own style and we put those styles together and it became greater than both of us. I'm on every one of the major records. Even Roy admitted the fame wasn't divided equally."

Roy said very little publicly about moving on from Joe Melson. But Bill Dees, the former member of the Five Bops who'd become his next writing partner—Roy always worked best with a collaborator—had a theory as to why the Orbison-Melson partnership ended: Roy had set his sights on the big screen. He hoped to emulate Elvis Presley. "He wanted to be a film star. [Roy] lost contact with people who cared about his music and could give him good advice." Melson was more diplomatic and didn't speak publicly about his split with Roy until 1965, when he simply told a reporter: "Roy and I don't work together anymore because our schedules won't coincide."

Joe Melson continued writing for Acuff-Rose and recording for their country label Hickory Records. In July 1962, Melson released a single, "Dance," which he'd cowritten with Roy. It wasn't a hit.

By early 1963, it seemed that Roy's hot streak might be over. He was no longer writing with Melson, and his most recent singles hadn't hit the lofty heights of "Only the Lonely" and "Running Scared"—at least Stateside. His relationship with Fred Foster was also nearing an end. Roy was now flexing a lot of muscle when working on new music in RCA Studio B. As far as Roy was concerned, he was in charge, not his producer; clearly, he'd come a long way since his first session with Monument.

Roy was usually serene when dealing with the press, very much a Texan gentleman, but he'd downplay the significant role that Foster had played in his career and would express it in a very un-Orbison like manner. "Fred Foster never wrote an arrangement in his life," Roy wrote in a letter to the *NME*, reflecting on his time with Monument. "He didn't know an A chord from a B chord." Roy insisted that he picked the players used in his sessions, not Foster. "I have to say I was the one who was really responsible for that sound," Roy wrote bluntly.

Before they parted ways, however, Roy and Foster would conjure up a little more magic.

CHAPTER 9

What is this crap? What is a Beatle anyway?

America's musical mood had started to change by 1963. White-bread folk acts including Peter, Paul and Mary and the Kingston Trio were fast taking over from the clean-cut pop stars of recent years. Such acts as Pat Boone, Bobby Rydell, and Frankie Avalon were now out of time, yesterday's heroes. Revolution was in the air, as empowering but radio-friendly strums like "If I Had a Hammer," as sung by Peter, Paul and Mary, dominated the charts, airwaves, and the odd protest march. It would reach number 10 in the late summer of 1962, the second of ten charting hits for the thoroughly wholesome trio.

Early in 1963, Roy had been pitched a Bob Dylan song called "Don't Think Twice, It's All Right," which, if he recorded it, might have helped him crack the folk market. But Roy passed and instead Peter, Paul and Mary—who'd already had hits with Dylan numbers—cut a version that climbed to number 9 on the *Billboard* Hot 100. "It was a great song," Roy admitted, "[but] I'd just written 'In Dreams' and we didn't have any place for it."

"In Dreams" came to Roy after a dream in which he imagined Elvis singing a new hit number, "something about gold," as Roy would recall. "It was just beautiful, and I said, 'Well, ol' Elvis has another smash.' Then I woke up and realized Elvis couldn't have sung it; I was dreaming." A few days later, the words Roy had heard in his dream came back to him, which he quickly jotted down. They became the lyrics for "In Dreams." Recorded during the first week of the new year and released soon after, "In Dreams" was no ordinary pop song—it was more like a dark lullaby.

Backed with a peculiar piece of exotica titled "Shahdaroba"—written by Cindy Walker, who'd composed "Dream Baby (How Long Must I Dream)"—Roy's latest was given the big thumbs-up by *Cashbox* magazine in late January '63. "Orbison, who has a solid hit way with the two-siders, comes up with another pairing that has the hit ingredients notched into every groove." The magazine described "In Dreams" as a "cha cha beat opus," which was as good a description as any of a song that sounded like nothing else at the time. When compared with the current US number 1, Steve Lawrence's vanilla-flavored "Go Away Little Girl," Roy's "In Dreams" was more like a fever dream, occupying another universe entirely. Easy listening it was not.

"In Dreams" hit the *Billboard* Hot 100 on February 9 and within weeks, it was on its way to number 7, selling almost 500,000 copies, by which time Roy was packing his bags for his first international sortie. Finally, the specifics of his UK tour had been set in place: the first of his twenty-one dates (in twenty-two days) would take place on May 18 at the Adelphi venue in Slough. One of the tour's three promoters was Tito Burns, an impresario who'd discovered Dusty Springfield and would promote Bob Dylan's first UK concerts. The other acts on the bill would include Gerry and the Pacemakers—who were topping the UK charts with "How Do You Do It"—David MacBeth, Louise Cordet ("the lovely film and recording star"), the Terry Young Six, and the Beatles. The latter were currently the hottest young group in the UK, who'd one day celebrate in song the very same Blackburn, Lancashire where Roy would close his tour on June 9 with a show at King George's Hall.

While the money on offer was good, another big persuader was the UK success of fellow American Del Shannon, who'd toured England in September 1962. Shannon added Roy's "Running Scared" and "Crying" to his sets, and as Roy learned, "The songs went over incredibly well. I got to thinking that maybe if he did that well with my songs, I might do as well if I came over." (During the 1960s, Shannon cut his own versions of Roy's "Running Scared," "Crying," and "Oh, Pretty Woman." He was a huge fan.) But the biggest factor of all was instrumentalist Duane Eddy, who'd been the first pick for the tour, but when the promoter learned that he was unavailable, "they figured they'd get me," said Roy.

Roy's touring band, known as the Webs, comprised Bobby

Goldsboro and John Rainey Adkins on guitars, Bill Gilmore on bass, drummer Robert Nix, and pianist Bobby Peterson. Goldsboro, who was from Dothan in Alabama, was also a budding solo artist, who'd scored a regional hit with a weepy called "Molly." His personal manager and high school friend, Perry "Buddy" Buie, doubled as Roy's tour manager.

Goldsboro met Roy when he had been booked for a gig in Ozark—"He was nearly the hottest thing going," said Goldsboro, "yet his price was real reasonable"—and needed a backing band, having just fired his latest ensemble. Buie recommended the Webs and Roy was so impressed that he hired them to back him for all his upcoming gigs. Goldsboro promptly dropped out of college, undertook a crash course in Roy's music, "and it worked out surprisingly well." (They'd play together for the next two years and grew close: "Roy became one of the guys, telling stories, telling jokes, being funny," said Goldsboro. They'd often go to the movies together on rare days off, Roy being a big movie buff.) The only downside for Goldsboro and the Webs was that Roy flew between gigs, while they traveled by road and shared one room.

In April, just prior to his departure for London, Roy spoke with June Harris from the British magazine *Disc*. Roy was in the process of completing a new LP, which he'd christen *In Dreams*. "I've written five of the titles," he told Harris. In his scarce downtime, Roy said that he enjoyed his model airplanes: "I've got twelve now," he said, including a British Spitfire with six-foot wings. "I build 'em, you know." He also had a cabin cruiser moored on Old Hickory Lake, at Hendersonville, which was where the palatial Orbison "dream home," currently being built, would be located. As for his upcoming tour, Roy was still deliberating over his set list. "I guess I'll just have to find out what hits I've had in England before I plan my stage act," Roy admitted. "I don't even know which of my records has sold over there."

This wasn't entirely true, at least according to Janet Martin, a twenty-year-old British woman who had met Fred Foster in mid-1962 when he visited the UK. She was running Roy's British fan club, but Foster persuaded her to relocate to the States and work at Monument. Now, with Roy's tour in the works, she was back in the UK ensuring everything was in order. Martin believed that Roy was "terribly conscious of the British market." As for Roy the performer, Martin told

Roy Kelton Orbison,
aged 6, in 1942.
*ARCHIVIO GBB/
Alamy Stock Photo.*

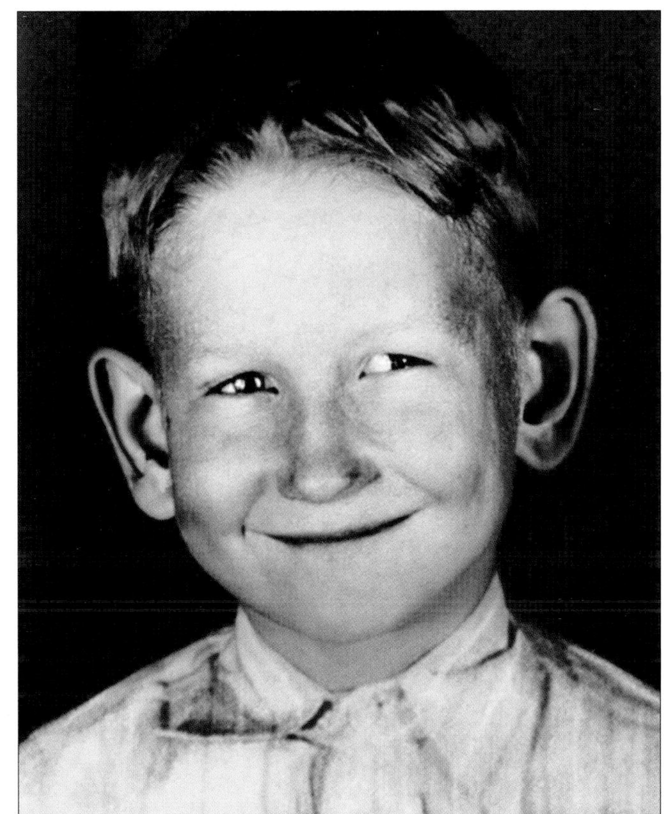

(second from left)
his band the Teen Kings,
ı 1950s.
*ett Collection Inc/
ny Stock Photo.*

John Lennon feeds Roy birthday cake, while Roy’s wife, Claudette, Ringo Sta and Roy Jr look on. London, April 1964. *Smith Archive/ Alamy Stock Photo.*

Roy in Germany, March 1965. *Jack de Nijs/Anefo/ Wikimedia Commons.*

Roy with Australian rocker Johnny O’Keefe, Sydney, 1964. *Philip Morris.*

Roy with Mimie Methorst (aka Miss Holland) and a gold record for "Oh, Pretty Woman." Holland, March 1965. *Jack de Nijs/Anefo/ Wikimedia Commons.*

just before fracturing
nkle at Hawkstone Park, UK,
ch 1966.
ity Mirror/Mirrorpix/
ny Stock Photo.

Roy interviews nanny candidates in 1967, in the wake of Claudette's death. *Trinity Mirror/Mirrorpix/ Alamy Stock Photo.*

Roy on the set of *The Fastest Guitar Alive*, which was released in 1967. *Pictorial Press Ltd/Alamy Stock Photo.*

ROY ORBISON
. . . "I couldn't put the guitar down."

and movies. He has written more than a half dozen songs which he'll sing in "Fastest Guitar."

Roy learned to play guitar

"Then I couldn't put the guitar down. I did set it in the closet for football, but I always went back to it. It was a comfort to hold a guitar and

An illustration of Roy from the *Twin City Sentinel*, June 1966. *Courtesy of Lee Enterprises.*

Roy and his second wife, Barbara, with Wesley Orbison, 1970.
Trinity Mirror/Mirrorpix/ Alamy Stock Photo.

Roy on stage at the Cincinnati Gardens, April 1976.
David Shoenfelt/Wikimedia Commons; creativecommons. org/licenses/by-sa/3.0/deed.en.

Roy with (left to right) Carl Perkins, Johnny Cas and Jerry Lee Lewis, November 1977. *CBS Television/ Wikimedia Commons.*

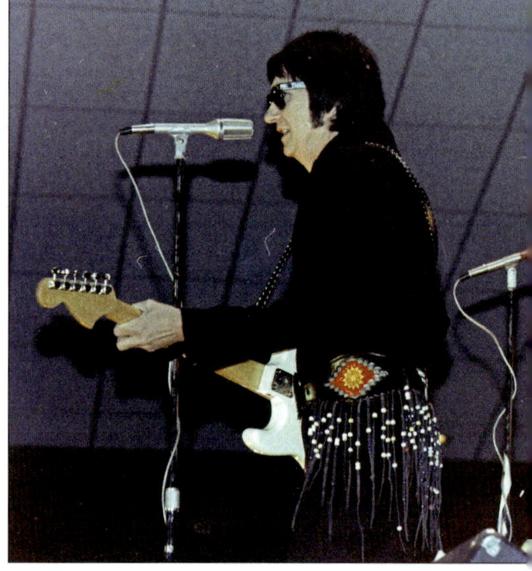

Roy performing at Nigro, Albany in 1984. *Bruce Tuten/Wikimedia Commons; /creativecommons.org/licenses/by/2.0/deed.en.*

Roy during the shoot for *Roy Orbison and Friends: A Black and White Night*, with (left to right) Ronnie Tutt, Bruce Springsteen, Tom Waits, Elvis Costello, and T Bone Burnett, Los Angeles, September 1987. *Everett Collection Inc/ Alamy Stock Photo.*

Roy with his fellow Traveling Wilburys (left to right):
Bob Dylan, Jeff Lynne, Tom Petty, and George Harrison, 1988.
Wikimedia Commons.

The Roy Orbison Museum in his old hometown of Wink, Texas.
The Lyda Hill Texas Collection of Photographs in Carol M. Highsmith's America Project, Library of Congress, Prints and Photographs Division/Wikimedia Commons.

Roy's star on Hollywood Boulevard.
Dietmar Rabich/ Wikimedia Commons; creativecommons.org/licenses/by-sa/4.0/deed.en.

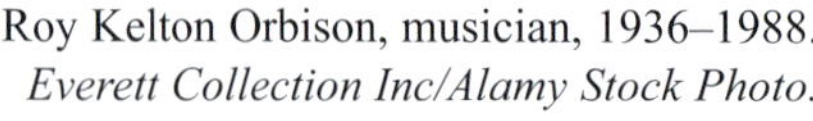

Roy Kelton Orbison, musician, 1936–1988.
Everett Collection Inc/Alamy Stock Photo.

the *NME*'s Ian Dove that his British fans should expect "no gimmicks." "Roy is a performer who relies a lot on putting a song across. Roy doesn't get screams—but he gets . . . tremendous applause."

While speaking with the *NME*, Janet Martin made it known that Roy liked the simple things—he was a genuine family man. "He gets all the excitement he wants just shopping for groceries with his wife." She said that Roy was happy strumming his guitar or "watching TV"—he was usually watching football—and was devoted to his kids, who were still very young. Roy Dewayne, now four years old, could sing "Crying," "and he knocks his dad out."

Days before leaving the country, Roy played a show in Alabama. Roy flew to the gig in a private plane and inadvertently forgot his prescription glasses when he disembarked, leaving him with just his tinted Faosa shades. "That evening," Roy recalled, "I put the dark glasses on. Then I flew to England for the [Beatles] tour." Roy wasn't thrilled: "Only an idiot wears shades at night, indoors, but it was the only way to go." Purely by accident, a key component of the Roy Orbison mystique had been created.

"It proved to be the best mistake I ever made," Roy chuckled.

Roy, still wearing his dark glasses, maintained that he knew nothing of the Beatles until he reached the Adelphi in Slough for the opening night of the tour. But the Beatles certainly knew about Roy. When they were recording their recent hit single, "Please Please Me," in late 1962, their producer George Martin asked them to speed up the tempo. He got the distinct sense they were trying to sound a little too much like Roy. John Lennon would admit as much: "It was my attempt at writing a Roy Orbison song, would you believe it?" He'd just heard "Only the Lonely," and the impact was undeniable. "Orbison had that fantastic voice," said Lennon.

At the Adelphi, on the afternoon of the first show, Roy stood outside the venue and looked long and hard at the marquee. Roy was billed as THE DYNAMIC AMERICAN RECORDING STAR, but he couldn't help but notice that another act featured prominently.

"What is this crap?" Roy asked out loud. "*What is a Beatle anyway?*"

"I'm one," sheepishly replied John Lennon, who was nearby.

Roy felt just terrible—he had no idea that a Beatle was standing there.

Before the concert, Roy was asked by the Beatles if they could play last at the Adelphi show. (Roy's recollection was that they said to him, "Since you're making most of the money"—Roy was earning more than double the Beatles' fee—"let us close the show.") Roy felt that their request was cheeky, given that he was the featured international act on the bill, and his current single, "In Dreams," was lodged firmly in the UK top 10. "Let me think about it," said Roy. He told them he'd make up his mind after final rehearsals.

Roy's set was heavy with such slow burners as "Only the Lonely," "Blue Angel," "Running Scared," and "In Dreams," epic songs he delivered while barely moving onstage, whereas he discovered in rehearsal that the Beatles' set was vastly different. It was packed with up-tempo numbers, *very up-tempo numbers*, including "Long Tall Sally" and "Twist and Shout," ravers performed with enough energy to light a small city. "It didn't make sense to me to go on after all this rocking music and do ballads," figured Roy, so he agreed to their request.

But as the Fab Four learned on opening night, Roy Orbison was a hard act to follow. The 2,000-capacity Adelphi was packed; it was so full, in fact, that the trio of promoters couldn't find a seat and were forced to stand at the back of the hall to watch the show. Roy and his band took the stage and kicked off with "Only the Lonely," and immediately he had the audience under his spell. Roy's set was short, only six songs, but the impact was enough to create big problems for the night's final act.

George Harrison spoke about the Adelphi show during *The Beatles Anthology* project. He explained that he and the other Beatles were behind the curtains, getting ready for their set while Roy was still onstage. "Roy would be out there and at the end he'd be singing, 'She's walking back to me, do do do do da do do-do.' And the audience would go wild. We'd be waiting there and he'd do another big encore and we'd be thinking, 'How are we going to follow this?' It was really serious stuff."

Roy's version of opening night was that after he played his closer "In Dreams," he was encored "fourteen times" (maybe even seventeen, as he once told radio's Wolfman Jack) and a concerned group of Beatles turned to him before they went on and mouthed, "Yankee, go home!" *Disc*'s June Harris reviewed the show and believed that Roy was encored three times and was "an outstanding success" while the Beatles "were a knockout." At the midway point of their eight-song set, Gerry Marsden from Gerry and the Pacemakers walked out onstage and presented the Beatles with a silver disc for sales of their latest hit, "From Me to You." The young audience, of course, went wild.

Roy quickly grasped why everyone inside the Adelphi seemed to be screaming at the Beatles. "They impressed me very much like Elvis Presley did," he said in 1980, when asked about the tour. "They were not as professional or polished . . . as they became a couple of years later, [but] as boys they were terrific, they just sparkled, they were really exciting." The entire band, smiling broadly, eagerly agreed to be photographed backstage with Roy, who was still wearing his tinted specs. After all, Roy was one of their idols.

But there was also no shortage of excitement from English audiences toward Roy. Paul Garrison, Roy's drummer for the tour, recalled that one night there was a mad rush for the stage during his set; a potential invasion was only circumvented when the stage crew dropped the iron fire curtain. A newspaper headline read, ROY ORBISON TAKES AUDIENCE BY STORM, although on that night, it had almost been the opposite. "After the shows, we were captives in the theaters," Garrison said. "Many times we had to disguise ourselves to get out."

After Slough, the tour moved on to Hanley, Southampton, Ipswich, and Nottingham—all sellouts—before reaching the Beatles' hometown of Liverpool on May 26 to play to yet another full house at the 2,300-seat Empire Theatre.

After the show, Lennon and Paul McCartney spoke with Roy. "What about America for us?" they asked, explaining that the few releases they'd had in the States, on independent label Vee-Jay Records, hadn't connected with a big audience.

"If you come to America," advised Roy, "and you're seen on national television—preferably *The* [Ed] *Sullivan Show*—and you let people know you're from England, it will be just as big in America as it is here." Roy also recommended that they keep their hair long and don't alter their wardrobe. His advice would prove to be incredibly prophetic.

On May 30, the Orbison-Beatles road show reached Manchester for a performance at the Odeon Cinema. In the audience was a sharply dressed thirty-one-year-old *Daily Express* journalist named Derek Taylor. He'd been instructed by his editor to write about the Beatles—harshly, if required—and try to make sense of why they'd become such big stars in the UK. Although he'd never heard of Roy Orbison, Taylor's journalistic curiosity was piqued as he watched the American "stroll up to the microphone to a hushed, almost reverent reception," as he'd later write. Taylor was astonished; he couldn't get over the fact that Roy looked nothing like most of the shaggy-haired acts currently making waves. Roy's appearance, Taylor noted, "was, not to put too fine a point on it, unconventional for a pop star . . . that smooth white face was surrounded by a halo of lacquered hair. Also, he was plump. There is no 'sex image' in his personality and no antics onstage."

This didn't mean, however, that Taylor wasn't impressed. He was won over by "the man's enormous skill with a song and repose at the microphone." When Roy finished his set, Taylor was struck by how the audience "applauded him as if he were the top-of-the-bill act"—which, of course, Roy was, but no matter. He'd won over another influential convert, because Taylor would soon become the Beatles' press agent.

Taylor wasn't operating in isolation, because the English press was mad for Roy. In the opinion of *Record Mirror*, he was "one of the few performers who sells discs purely on the sound and not on the person . . . [he's] a bespectacled un-hip looking gent in his thirties." Nonetheless, Roy was a must-see live act: "He's one of the most captivating and entertaining performers that have come from the States."

As for the Beatles, a couple of weeks into the tour and they were still getting used to playing after the enigmatic American with the operatic voice. "It was terrible following Roy," Ringo Starr confessed. "He'd slay them and they'd scream for more." In the back of the tour bus, as they traveled between cities, Roy would sit with his acoustic guitar, working on new material. Sometimes he'd play snippets to the others.

"Oh, it's great, Roy," Paul McCartney said to him one night. "Have you just written that?" McCartney later revealed what he was really thinking: "We have to have something as good." "All My Loving" was one of the songs McCartney worked on during their three-week road trip, and Roy's influence on its harmonies and melody was undeniable.

On June 7, while in Glasgow, Roy took the opportunity to fulfill a lifelong dream. As a kid, whenever he played cowboys with his friends, Roy asked to be the bad guy, mainly because they dressed in black—there was just something about the image that he admired. Roy had made a promise to himself, when he finally had some money, that he'd indulge in what he called the "all-black clothing thing." In Glasgow, before playing at the Odeon, Roy met with a tailor named Bob Fletcher, who was recommended by the Beatles, and stocked up on black shirts, buying twenty-seven in all. (When not singing or shopping, Roy caught some episodes of iTV's *Coronation Street* and become a fan of the soap.)

As the tour rolled on and press coverage intensified, Roy had to deal with a conundrum: He was wearing his dark glasses in the many photos taken onstage, backstage, and elsewhere, which he felt was a bit embarrassing. "But," as he came to accept, "these photographs went around the world, and I was stuck with them." When teamed with his all-black wardrobe and dyed hair, a whole new Roy Orbison look—his signature style—was born.

Roy's tour with the Beatles was a critical and financial success. *Record Mirror* described it as "fabulously successful . . . more loot was mopped up than for a long time."

"I waited two years to make this trip," Roy said as he boarded a flight back to the US after the final show in Blackburn, "and it was all worthwhile." Roy's UK popularity was so strong that he'd return for another tour within three months. He'd found a whole new audience.

CHAPTER 10

If you don't sing sincerely, people can tell and they won't buy your records

Over the course of two weeks in February 1964, the Orbisons finally moved into their dream home on the banks of Hendersonville's Old Hickory Lake, at Caudill Drive. Roy's UK agent, Peter Walsh, told the press that the property "just takes your breath away" and cost "thousands of dollars to build." (A report in the *Nashville Banner* estimated $75,000.) It was a multilevel house, deceptively modest from a distance, which seemed to grow larger as you approached the property. Seven bedrooms were spread over 8,000 square feet of space; Roy's ever-expanding collection of cars filled the property's numerous garages.

Roy planned for an indoor pool, but instead ended up with two—one for him and Claudette, the other for his boys. The living room, said Walsh, was "gigantic"; its main feature was an eight-foot-wide open fireplace. Two waterfalls trickled down each side of the main staircase—Roy said that he liked the "pretty sound" of running water. There was an electric elevator in the house, a sizable kitchen and dinette, and six bathrooms. Claudette even had her own beauty salon. While relaxing in the master bedroom, Roy would press a switch and a TV set—one of five in the property—would descend from the ceiling, as if by magic.

Roy could take a short stroll to the lake, where his speedboat was moored, on the way admiring the built-in barbecue on the outside deck. Roy had set up a music room in the basement, where he wrote and recorded demos. The wall was lined with gold and silver discs. In the corner was a space where he stored his model planes. "It's a real gas," Walsh said of Chez Orbison.

Johnny Cash, Roy's friend from his Sun Records days, would move in next door with his family. Although Roy liked his privacy, he made an exception for Cash, and they'd see a lot of each other—when their schedules allowed—and sometimes ate breakfast together. "It was a particularly close friendship," Cash wrote.

The Orbisons' spread, nicknamed the Fortress, was designed by local architect Braxton Dixon, who'd created a similarly grand estate for Fred Foster, which also fronted Old Hickory Lake. Dixon himself lived with his wife Anna and their four children in a Hendersonville property known to locals as "the round house," which Dixon liked to describe as a "modern day castle."

Family, as Roy told a writer from England's *Record Mirror*, was paramount, and his new home provided the perfect base for the Orbison clan. Roy's parents Orbie Lee and Nadine loved to visit and check in on their grandkids—eventually they'd move in nearby. "[Family] keeps everything in balance," Roy said, "and makes you aware of who you are personally." Roy was a very protective parent; he didn't allow the press to take photos of his children, and when day-trippers learned where the Orbisons lived, he had a seven-foot-high fence erected around the Fortress.

The only problem for Roy—other than nosy day-trippers—was finding the time to enjoy his new home, because his past few months had been as crazy as any time in his career. Dark glasses firmly in place, he'd returned to the UK in September 1963, this time with Claudette by his side. She looked on as her husband was mobbed at the airport upon their arrival by "about 100 hysterical girls," according to one onlooker. In between tours, Roy's UK presence had been maintained by his latest single, "Falling," which had hit a peak of number 9—in the US it only reached position 22.

Roy's second UK tour was as hectic as his first. His first show was on September 14, and he stayed on the road until October 6, playing dozens of concerts across England, with a quick trip to Scotland for two nights at the Odeon Theatre in Glasgow. This time around, Roy toured with Freddie and the Dreamers—whose singer, Freddie Garrity, was big fan of Roy—as well as Brian Poole and the Tremeloes and the Searchers. His buddies the Beatles were occupied elsewhere, busy readying their latest number 1 smash, "She Loves You," while being toasted by the UK press and preparing for an American onslaught early in the new year.

Roy's run of dates began at the 3,000-seat Walthamstow Granada, which was, as reported in *Disc* magazine, "packed to the rafters" for both Saturday night shows. The audience began screaming for Roy as the other artists on the bill played, "a long time before his act was announced," wrote *Disc*'s June Harris. But backstage, Roy had some throat problems; he was worried he couldn't manage the high notes in "Running Scared." He needn't have been concerned—as Harris noted, when he hit the note, "everyone breathed in relief." "Mean Woman Blues," Roy's latest single (a double A-side with "Blue Bayou," headed for number 3 on the UK charts) went over so well that one female fan at the front of the stage burst into tears as he sang.

Afterwards, Roy admitted that he had been worried about his throat—"it felt a little shaky"—but figured that the only way to test it out was by singing "Running Scared." "You weren't the only one who was relieved when I made it, I can tell you," he told June Harris.

"Mean Woman Blues" presented a different, raunchier side of Roy, a man who, in the opinion of *Record Mirror*, "has had more changes of style than probably any other pop singer." The song was written by Claude Demetrius, who'd gotten his start with jazz great Louis Armstrong, and had originally been cut by Elvis Presley for the soundtrack of his 1957 film *Loving You*. (It was also the B-side of Jerry Lee Lewis's "Great Balls of Fire.")

Roy's version was released in August 1963. On the flip side was "Blue Bayou," which Roy had written with Joe Melson prior to their split. Roy revealed that the dreamy, wistful "Blue Bayou" was all about being on the road, nothing more. He insisted that it was a happy song, unlike many of his biggest hits. "The fellow's bound and determined to get back to where you sleep all day and the catfish play and the girls and all that stuff," Roy explained. "It's a beautiful thought." The single fared even better in Australia than it did the UK and became his fourth Australian number 1 during October 1963.

Upon his return to the States, Roy barely stopped to take a breath, releasing his version of Willie Nelson's sweetly sentimental "Pretty Paper" in time for Christmas (it reached number 15 in the US and number 6 in the UK and Australia). The recording was used as part of a Canadian PSA that Roy recorded to support underprivileged kids. "Christmas is a very special time for children," stated Roy, "but many Edmonton children will only experience unhappiness Christmas morning unless you care. This is Roy Orbison asking you to buy a new toy for a boy or girl and bring it to any of the Santa Anonymous depots in the city."

As the Orbisons settled into the Fortress, their palace by the lake in Hendersonville, it seemed that Roy had it all: sold-out international tours, hits in several different countries, even a Christmas message for the downtrodden. Could his life get any better?

Roy's Australian fan base had been crying out for him to tour since 1960's "Only the Lonely," and he duly obliged during January 1964, filling concert halls in Sydney, Melbourne, Brisbane, Adelaide, and Hobart. (These were the first of 120 shows he'd play, in five countries, during a year spent constantly in motion.) The tour was staged by Pan-Pacific Promotions, a company run by Harry M. Miller, a young impresario who was hustling his way to becoming one of the leading promoters in the region. The Beach Boys toured with Roy for shows awkwardly promoted as "Surfside '64." ("They were absolutely terrible," observed a fan who saw the Beach Boys play in Melbourne. "They sounded nothing like their records.")

Roy spent some time with Brian Wilson, the emotionally fragile key songwriter and creative force of the Beach Boys, who told him a secret. "I'm not going to tour again," Brian said, explaining that he'd prefer to stay in California and write. He also had a question for Roy: "What are the Beatles like?" Roy's response required a great deal of tact. "I explained to him the best I could, tried to tell him that the Beatles would be the biggest group in the world. I had to do it very tender and very nicely because the Beach Boys were number 1 then."

Early on in his visit, Roy sat down with *The Sydney Morning Herald*'s Jock Veitch, who asked about the secret of his success. "Sincerity," Roy replied with admirable precision. "If you don't sing sincerely, people can tell and they won't buy your records." Roy knew of what he spoke; "Pretty Paper," which was currently riding high in the local charts, was his eleventh hit in Australia in four years, including four number 1s.

Roy chuckled when asked about his accent, which he explained was no longer "pure Texas. It's now mixed up with a bit of Tennessee . . . and I've got a bit of a British accent, too." Talk turned to money and Roy said that the past year had been one of his best financially. "I probably made about 300,000 dollars." When asked about his overall worth, Roy estimated it to be "about 700,000 dollars." He was inching ever closer to one of his life goals—to be a millionaire by the time he turned thirty, in two years' time.

"It looks like I'll make it," said Roy, smiling, "but I don't care about it as much as I used to."

While Roy agreed that the money was great, he maintained that his family was his priority, not his bank balance. "They're more important for a start." As if to prove his point, he had a weeklong Hawaiian holiday booked with Claudette for the end of the tour. Also important for Roy was the way in which he treated those around him: "I think I've managed not to let success go to my head . . . I always try to be nice to people."

Roy may have been one of pop music's good guys, but he had a little trouble with overzealous Australian audiences. A few days earlier, while playing in Brisbane, he'd been mobbed after the show and a fan ran off with his dark prescription glasses. Thankfully, security was quick to react and retrieve his specs. "My eyes are weak," Roy said. "I wouldn't have been able to do the tour without them." His father Orbie Lee accompanied him on the tour and was so struck by the country that he said to Roy, "If I was ten years younger, I'd stay here and never come back." Roy loved the place too. "I'm crazy about Australia."

On his return to the States, Roy got back to the serious business of hit-making. It had been seven years since Roy's path crossed with that of Bill Dees, the former Five Bop, who now had a deal with Acuff-Rose Publishing. In early 1964, Roy cut one of Dees's songs, called "Borne on the Wind," which would be co-credited to Roy and Dees. It was a top 10 hit in Australia and made it to number 15 in the UK, although it failed to chart in America. Dees didn't know that Roy had recorded the song or that it became a hit overseas, until he read about it in *Billboard*. "The record company never told us," he said.

Dees got the chance to collaborate properly with Roy in March 1964, just before he left for yet another UK tour. The call to meet with Roy in Hendersonville couldn't have come at a better time: "I was out of work," Dees admitted. The Dees family—Bill, his wife Mona, and their four young children—had recently moved to Nashville from Texas and times were tough. Dees was playing solo shows at night and pulling some shifts at a warehouse during the day.

Dees had a song called "It's Over At Last," and Roy wanted to use a specific lyric of the song—"It's over"—repeated three times. As Dees recalled, "We then wrote the whole thing from scratch, but he did most of the writing . . . he knew exactly where he wanted to go." Soon after, Dees was in Fred Foster's Nashville studio, which Foster had recently bought from Sam Phillips, looking on while the song was recorded. It was unlike anything he'd witnessed before. "It was the biggest [session] there had ever been in Nashville to that time," said Dees, who recalled that there were thirty-six players in the orchestra alone. Coincidentally, that was the same amount of takes it took Roy to nail the vocal.

"It's Over" marked Roy's return to the operatic-style ballad that had been so successful for him with "Crying" and "In Dreams." He definitely hadn't lost his touch. When a fourteen-year-old Jersey Shore loner named Bruce Springsteen first heard "It's Over," he was so overcome that he made a vow. When Roy hit what Springsteen described as "the note where it sounds like the world's going to end" during the song's finale, the fledgling rocker told himself that he might never speak with another woman again. It would be just too painful. Roy's song was the proof.

Many years later, while making a keynote address at the South by Southwest Festival, Springsteen remained smitten. "Roy was the coolest, uncool loser you'd ever seen," he explained. "With his Coke-bottle black glasses, his three-octave range, he seemed to take joy sticking his knife deep into the hot belly of your teenage insecurities."

Roy was often asked about the powerful emotions in his best-known songs. Surely, he was writing about real-life situations. Roy typically distanced himself, insisting that just like all of us, he'd suffered loss and heartache, but he wasn't writing about specific events in his life. And he never wrote while in the midst of emotional turmoil.

It just didn't work that way for him. Roy said that when he was hurting, "I can't sleep, I can't think, I can't eat. So how you gonna write a song? All the songs that I wrote that were successful were written when I was in a contented state of mind." Loneliness, Roy told a reporter, was "the worst thing in the world" (a line he'd repeat in a track called, appropriately, "Loneliness"), but his songs were works of imagination, not acts of musical vérité.

However, it may have been a different situation with "It's Over," albeit inadvertently. Many years down the line, Barbara, Roy's second wife, revealed that she'd been told how Fred Foster walked out of the studio while Roy cut his vocal for "It's Over," tears in his eyes. Foster had heard whispers that Roy's wife Claudette had cheated on him, and while Roy wasn't apparently aware of this—at least not yet—the lyric was way too close to the bone for Foster, who had to leave the session. Perhaps he feared he might have told Roy if he'd stayed.

The trade response on the song's release in April 1964 was glowing. *Cashbox* reported that "It's Over" packed "a throbbing, martial beat-like lover's lament that once again builds to a big finish." Roy's latest also appeared in *Billboard*'s "Hot Pop Spotlights" column, alongside new music from the Four Seasons, Neil Sedaka, and Rufus Thomas. "The drama-ballad king scores again with pathos and chorus and strings that build, build, build," stated *Billboard*'s reviewer. "It's Over" reached number 9 in America, and on July 1, hit the top of the British chart, where it remained for two weeks, and charted for a total of eighteen. Roy was back on top.

Roy reconnected with three of the Beatles—Paul McCartney was elsewhere—when he celebrated his twenty-eighth birthday during his third visit to England, in late April 1964. A smiling Claudette, who was traveling with Roy, spoon-fed John Lennon cake at Roy's birthday party at London's on-trend La Dolce Vita restaurant, as a press photographer snapped away.

Roy's latest UK tour began in the same venue, the Adelphi Cinema in Slough, where the year before the Beatles had mouthed "Yankee, go home!" when Roy was encored time and time again. But a lot had changed in less than twelve months. The Beatles were in the midst of shooting *A Hard Day's Night*, their first foray into a lucrative side of showbiz—feature films—that Roy was keen to explore. (Roy visited the set and was photographed chatting with George Harrison.) And two months earlier, as Roy predicted, they had broken through Stateside when they appeared on *The Ed Sullivan Show*. More than seventy million viewers saw the band from Liverpool perform on February 9 and overnight, their world exploded.

The front cover of the April 4 issue of *Billboard*, the same edition where Roy's "It's Over" was reviewed in glowing terms, carried what seemed like a warning: "Chart Crawls with Beatles." Roy's buddies from Liverpool currently had twelve songs in the magazine's Hot 100 and the two top albums on the US LPs chart: *Meet the Beatles!* and *Introducing… The Beatles*. "Everyone's tired of the Beatles," joked *Billboard*'s Jack Maher and Tom Noonan, "except the listening and buying public." The musical mood of America was changing yet again. Roy admired their success, but knew that he needed to watch his back. "I coulda been swamped by the Beatles," he admitted.

Roy had found a comfortable groove when he spoke with the UK press, who couldn't get enough of the amiable Texan. In May 1964, Roy sat down for a lengthy interview with David Griffiths of *Record Mirror* and waxed lyrical about topics as varied as the local food ("the vegetables are fantastic") and English women ("[they] seem to be more interesting than American women—they are sort of lively and project more personality than American girls"). He cited London as just about his "favorite place" in the world, second only to Nashville—and just ahead of Hawaii. ("If it wasn't so remote, I could live there.") And no, Roy insisted, he wasn't pandering when it came to London. "I'm not just saying that to please fans," he said. "I love it." Roy had even warmed to the silky instrumentals of Acker Bilk, a Brit best known for the hit "Stranger on the Shore," who seemed way out of step in this era of the Beatles and the British Invasion groups. Nonetheless, Roy admitted that he "loved his records."

Roy was still in the dark about certain things, though, such as "mod clothes." "I'm not really hip enough to know what they are," he told Griffiths. Roy was happy to stick with his black ensemble and what were now his trademark shades. He had his own look, his own thing.

CHAPTER 11

I've gotta go home and love on that sweet woman

In August 1964, Roy visited his friend Carl Perkins at his home in Jackson, Tennessee. Roy hadn't seen a lot of Carl since the days they'd gone out driving, and Roy would sing material that he was working on, seeking out Carl's opinion. Over the years, Carl's estimation of Roy never wavered. As far as Mr. Blue Suede Shoes was concerned, "He's the kind of man you would like to have living next door so you could lay some tomatoes on the fence for him." Having just cut his latest record with Fred Foster in Nashville, Roy was so eager to play it to Carl that he drove the 130 miles to Jackson, non-stop, in his maroon 1963 Cadillac, with the reel-to-reel tape sitting on the passenger seat. The song was called "Oh, Pretty Woman." Carl, of course, loved what he heard.

The song had come to life while Roy and Bill Dees were at Roy's house working together in July. Dees had a Spanish-flavored melody that he described as "a simple thing [which] we hadn't figured out how to use." Claudette was heading out to go shopping and in a flirtatious manner, she said to Roy, "Give me some money, honey."

"What for?" Roy asked.

"I need to go to the store," replied Claudette.

Dees, who was looking on, said to Roy, "A pretty woman don't need no money," and almost as soon as Claudette left, the pair began singing what would become the track's key lyric—"pretty woman/ walking down the street." As Dees recalled, "By the time Claudette came back, we had the song." It took all of forty minutes. (They titled it "Oh, Pretty Woman," to avoid confusion with another song Roy had cowritten called, "Pretty Woman.") As the song came together, Dees realized they'd hit on something special: "I could hear the [woman's] heels clicking on the pavement, the pretty woman walking down the street."

The growl that Roy used during the song was his nod to Bob Hope, who used it to great comic effect in the movie *Son of Paleface*. It took some work to perfect, as Roy discovered: "I had to practice and rehearse a bit." (The trick was not letting his throat get dry.) As for Roy's use of the word "mercy," he may have overheard Dees, who tended to use the term "when I see a pretty woman or eat good food." But Dees accepted that Roy pulled it off much better on record: "I couldn't do it like he did it."

"Oh, Pretty Woman" came together in record time: Roy and Dees wrote in on a Friday, Roy recorded it on the following Friday, August 2, and it was in stores two weeks later. "It was the fastest thing I ever saw," said Dees. There may have been a commercial necessity for the single's rushed release, as Rees explained: "The Beatles were hot"—their "A Hard Day's Night" was the current US number 1—"and Fred Foster felt that Monument had to release it quickly." Dees sensed that the "yeah yeah" lyric in the song was Roy's nod to his buddies in the Fab Four.

Roy agreed to shoot a film clip for "Oh, Pretty Woman," which wasn't common practice for pop singers at the time. It was shot in mid-October '64, when he was next in the UK, and directed by expat South African Stanley Dorfman, the cocreator of the hit UK music show *Top of the Pops*. Filmed on the rooftop garden of London's Derry & Toms department store, Dorfman's camera followed Roy, looking sharp in a dark, collarless jacket, his jet-black pompadour swept high, as he fixated on a pretty woman's legs. Roy did his best to resemble the coolest dude currently on the music scene, rather than a stalker.

While the clip was a handy promotion for the song and would be aired twice on *Top of the Pops*, it offered no evidence that Roy could switch smoothly between music and film like his former Sun labelmate Elvis Presley. Roy seemed stiff in front of a camera, very aware of its presence, and he had none of Elvis's swagger. That didn't really matter—at least not now—because by the time Roy shot the film clip, Fred Foster had issued a press release advising that "Oh, Pretty Woman" had just passed the million sales mark in America and had sold a further 400,000 copies in the UK. The song was a monster hit, eventually reaching number 1 in the US, the UK, Australia, and ten other countries. (In *Billboard*'s year-end poll for 1964, it was ranked number 4, outsold by only the Beatles' "She Loves You" and "I Want to Hold Your Hand," and Louis Armstrong's "Hello, Dolly!')

When Roy performed "Oh, Pretty Woman" on ABC's *Shindig!* in mid-October, he seemed taken aback by the screams of the audience. Every now and again, he'd flash a slightly awkward grin for the camera. It was as though he was asking, "Are you sure that's for me?" And he definitely didn't know what to make of the team of young women—the *Shindig!* girls—that "invaded" the stage when he returned later in the program to perform Ray Charles's "What'd I Say" (which had been the B-side of Roy's "Borne on the Wind"). Roy seemed more at ease when the Everly Brothers joined him at the microphone to close out the song, and the show.

A few weeks later, CBS host Ed Sullivan addressed his huge viewing audience in his idiosyncratic shuffling, mumbling style. "Ladies and gentlemen," he announced, "record polls on both sides of the Atlantic have been all churned up here, because a fella out of Odessa, Texas, Roy Orbison, is leading the list with his number. So here is the bespectacled number one king, Roy Orbison." Roy, looking as dapper as ever, was surrounded by his band as they rocked "Oh, Pretty Woman" on a set that might have borrowed from the land of the giants, dotted with mock-ups of oversize speakers and amplifiers. Some seventy million Americans looked on.

On the Monday after *The Ed Sullivan Show*, Fred Foster received an order for a further 100,000 copies of "Oh, Pretty Woman." The same happened again the following day and continued every day for more than a week. "Oh, Pretty Woman" ensured that Roy earned his first million before he turned thirty. But, as Roy pointed out to an Australian reporter, "That's [a million] on paper. They haven't given me the money yet."

Money was becoming an issue for Roy's collaborator, Bill Dees. "Oh, Pretty Woman" may have been Roy's biggest song yet, but for Dees—at least on paper—it was just another recording session. Dees was paid the standard rate of $80 for his studio work (he contributed vocals to the track) and later, when he asked Monument about a gold record for his efforts, Dees was told he'd have to pay for it.

Although Dees would earn substantial sums from his cowrites with Roy, money was proving to be the source of some conflict with Roy. Dees was also playing in Roy's latest touring band, the Candymen, along with Barry Booth on piano, drummer Paul Garrison, bassist Bill Gilmore, and guitarists John Rainey Adkins and Billy Sanford. Roy would typically play six nights a week, paying each musician $50 per show. The money was good, but as Dees told Roy, they should be paid $350 for their week's work, because they'd usually be "in a strange town on the seventh night" and were unlikely to find a one-night gig anywhere on such short notice.

Roy balked at the idea. He told Dees: "Nobody works seven days a week."

Drummer Paul Garrison exacted his revenge. Roy had a few standard jokes that he shared during concerts—"I just flew in, and boy, are my arms tired"—and one night Garrison set up his drums early and told all of Roy's usual gags to the audience ahead of the show. "Roy wondered why nobody would laugh," Bill Dees recalled. When Roy found out about Garrison's stunt, he was furious. "He almost fired him," said Dees.

When Roy was back at Hendersonville in the fall, he received a phone call, telling him that his wife Claudette had been "stepping out" with Braxton Dixon, the architect who designed their house. Roy was no choirboy; he was guilty of the occasional dalliance while on tour. Brit singer Marianne Faithfull had a close encounter with him in her hotel room late one night, although they didn't sleep together. ("It's possible that he was making a pass," she accepted.) And after a show in Clearwater, Florida, a reporter looked on as Roy was approached by "two babes with back-combed bouffants . . . wearing dresses a hand's width above their knee knobs." "We loved your white suit, Roy," they shrieked before hugging him tightly. In the audience that night watching Roy was a female fan who wore slacks so tight, "it looked as if she had dipped herself in a tub of latex," according to the same reporter. But while temptations like this were commonplace on the road, Roy demanded fidelity from his wife. As Claudette's Aunt Patty stated, "Whatever he'd done with the girls overseas, he expected Claudette to remain faithful, barefoot, and pregnant." When it came to marriage, Roy was old-fashioned at best, a chauvinist at worst.

Roy confronted Claudette about the affair, and she confirmed that yes, it was true. He then called Dixon, who insisted that it wasn't serious. Roy thought otherwise—he was livid—and fired Dixon, who still had work to complete on the Fortress. He then advised his lawyer Ward Hudgins to petition for an annulment, which was granted on October 14. Roy did, however, agree that Claudette could live with her parents in Pasadena, Texas and raise their boys while he was out on the road, which was now most of the time. Roy's writing partner Bill Dees was one of many who were shocked when they heard the news. "When he and Claudette split up, 'It's Over' was like a slap in the face," he said. "I could hardly see how he could go on stage and sing it."

It was also a difficult time for many of Roy's contemporaries. Carl Perkins was in the midst of a long fallow period after the success of "Blue Suede Shoes" and was struggling with alcoholism. Johnny Cash was currently in a tug-of-love between his first wife, Vivian Liberto, and June Carter, while Elvis Presley, stuck on a Hollywood treadmill of mediocre rom-coms, was gradually disappearing into the twilight zone behind the gates of Graceland. Jerry Lee Lewis, still reeling from the huge controversy surrounding his marriage to his teenage cousin, Myra Gale Brown, had left Sun Records in 1963 and was now completely absent from the radio or the charts.

Back in the UK during October, Roy spoke about the split with reporter Chris Hutchins. He later said that "Roy told me he was heartbroken." As Hutchins pointed out, "it was Claudette who persuaded Roy to persevere with his songwriting and singing" when his career was in a slump, and "they cared deeply for each other." Claudette wasn't just the mother of Roy's children—she was his rock. Hutchins believed that "it was obvious that they would soon be together again." Roy made his feelings for Claudette very clear, according to his former writing partner Joe Melson, because sometimes he'd stop their writing sessions and announce: "I've gotta go home and love on that sweet woman."

"She was his first love," said Melson. "He was always ready to get back to Claudette." The potential of a reunion between Roy and Claudette improved when she learned that she was pregnant. Their third child was due in May 1965.

Before any reconciliation could occur, however, Roy had business issues to deal with. In January 1965, Roy renewed his publishing deal with Acuff-Rose, which guaranteed him a twenty-year royalty payment of $10,000 per annum. But Roy admitted that he was "severely depressed;" he was still dealing with the emotional fallout of his divorce from Claudette. It was hardly the ideal time to be negotiating any kind of business deal. Roy said that Wesley Rose told him to not bother reading the contracts, advising him "that they were standard agreements," which he duly signed. This would come back to haunt him in the years to come.

In what would become a pattern whenever Roy's personal life was in turmoil, he hit the road in the new year, returning for his second Australian tour, playing shows with the Rolling Stones. (It was the first of nine countries Roy would perform in during 1965.) Roy was bemused when informed about the bill: "The balance of that show didn't make a lot of sense to me," he said. "People who came to see me wouldn't come to see the Rolling Stones."

But Roy did strike up a solid rapport with the blues-loving Englishmen, who were making their Australian debut. They spent a fair bit of the tour traveling together in armored vans, which would collect the musicians at each city's airport and deliver them to their hotel, shielding them from overzealous fans who stalked the Stones at every turn. Mick Jagger, Keith Richards, and the other Stones addressed Roy as "Mr. Orbison." Clearly, they were thrilled to be keeping the company of such a big name. (Yet Roy was barely six months older than Stones bassist, Bill Wyman.) When both acts appeared on the Australian TV special *Big Beat '65*, Roy played "Oh, Pretty Woman" and then introduced the Stones, describing them as "the trendsetters in the international big beat."

As the tour rolled on through Sydney, Melbourne, Adelaide, Brisbane, and Hobart across two weeks in January, a challenge was agreed upon by the two headliners: Whoever would play their least favorite song would win a prize. Roy stepped up one night and played "Ooby Dooby," a number he'd long outgrown, but the Stones backed out, reneging on their arrangement. Instead, they gave Roy a gift—a cigarette case, which they'd had inscribed: "To Mr. Ooby Dooby from the Rolling Stones."

When the road show crossed the Tasman in February for a week of concerts in New Zealand, Roy joined the Stones on a trip to the famous springs in Rotorua, on the North Island. Mick Jagger had a camera with him and took a candid snap that he has kept to this day. It was a photo of Roy, "sitting in these hot springs, his glasses still on," Jagger recalled in 1989. "A fine figure of a man in the hot springs, he was."

After Australia, Roy headed to the UK and Europe, where he'd play shows through late March, and was joined by a very pregnant Claudette. On his return to the States, it seemed that every new track Roy recorded carried at the very least a hint of his domestic situation. The first of these had actually appeared in February 1965. Titled "Goodnight," it sounded like the postmortem of a breakup. When Roy sang about "the way things used to be" and how much he missed hearing the words *good night*, his voice almost breaking, those close to him understood what was on his mind.

Bill Dees firmly believed that the song was inspired by Claudette, particularly the line "my lovely woman child." "Roy thought of Claudette like that," said Dees, who was now also living in Hendersonville. He named his twenty-four-foot pontoon, moored at the rear of his property, *Oh, Pretty Woman*, a tangible product of his successful writing partnership with Roy.

But "Goodnight" didn't perform well, selling less than 200,000 copies, although it did reach number 4 in Australia. "The low sales were astonishing," said Fred Foster. "Believe me, I worked that record because I wanted to sell as many as possible." The more up-tempo "(Say) You're My Girl," which followed not long after, again hinted very strongly at what Roy was going through, with its talk of makeups, breakups, and cheating. But outside of Australia, where it hit the top 10, it fared even worse than "Goodnight," and sold less than 100,000 copies, barely making it to number 39 on the *Billboard* Hot 100.

Wesley Kelton Orbison was born on May 13, 1965 in Jacinto City, just east of Houston, close to the home of Claudette's parents. Roy was with Claudette during their third child's birth, as the tension between them gradually eased. Just prior to Wesley's birth, Roy had been in the audience at *The Ed Sullivan Show* in New York, looking on as his touring buddies from a few months back, the Rolling Stones, performed. Their latest hit record, "(I Can't Get No) Satisfaction" was a song with an opening guitar line and drum pattern that bore a passing resemblance to Roy's "Oh, Pretty Woman." Sullivan graciously invited Roy up onstage for a bow, but, as enthusiastic as the reception was, he would have much rather been plugging his latest release, because Roy's run of hits in America now seemed as good as over.

His next pair of singles during 1965, "Ride Away" and "Crawling Back," did little to stop the rot. The latter may have been a flop commercially, but it was a gutsy effort. "Roy put himself at risk with 'Crawling Back,' for what he thought was the truth," Bill Dees figured. He was referring to how men of their generation were unlikely to admit their need for a partner, let alone consider "crawling back" to a woman. "That is definitely our song, but it's in his heart because he . . . realized [Claudette's] worth more and wanted her back."

Another song from this period, "Breakin' Up is Breakin' My Heart," was, according to Dees, "very real, true to life"—again, clearly, a statement about Roy's situation with Claudette. Commercially, the sweeping "Ride Away" was the most successful of these tracks, although it ground to a halt at number 25 on the *Billboard* Hot 100. Once again, it was Roy's overseas fans that responded most strongly: "Ride Away" and "Goodnight" both made it into the Australian top 10, while "Crawling Back" reached number 5 there and charted for almost four months. Canada too remained a strong market for Roy: "Ride Away" became his third number 1 north of the border in the late summer of 1965. These regions would become increasingly key for Roy as his career in America headed steadily downhill.

By the time of these none-too-subtle statements about his troubled love life, however, Roy had made a significant career change. He'd moved on from Fred Foster and Monument Records, Roy's very own house of hits, where he'd recorded his best-known and most powerful songs. Roy signed a new record deal that seemed to him as though he'd hit the jackpot. But that proved to be far from the truth.

CHAPTER 12

You can keep all your birthday presents. The best one I could have had is Claudette

When Roy was asked why he left Monument for MGM Records at the end of June 1965, he cited his disappointment with the failure of a mid-1965 single called "(Say) You're My Girl" as the catalyst, coming as it did at the end of a series of minor hits and outright flops. According to Roy, "That convinced me." There was also conflict between Wesley Rose and Fred Foster about songs Roy chose to record, especially tracks for which Acuff-Rose didn't control the publishing. But at the heart of Roy's decision were two key factors: money and a burning desire to be a film star. "Ambition had taken over," said Bill Dees, "as he wanted to be in the movies."

Singers moonlighting on the big screen had become commonplace. By the summer of 1965, Elvis Presley had pumped out something like twenty good, bad, and indifferent feature films, while Johnny Cash had starred in the well-regarded 1961 crime drama *Five Minutes to Live*. Carl Perkins had cameoed in a movie called *Hawaiian Boy* and Ricky Nelson acted alongside John Wayne in the big budget Warner Bros. Western *Rio Bravo*. Even Conway Twitty appeared in a few B movies, including *Platinum High School* and *Sex Kittens Go to College*. ("You never saw a student body like this!" teased the film's poster.) Roy, however, had done little more on celluloid than strut around awkwardly on the roof of a London department store in the film clip for "Oh, Pretty Woman." His new deal would give him a chance to see if he could make it in the movies.

MGM Records, Roy's new label, was part of the Metro-Goldwyn-Mayer empire. The agreement was worth $1 million and was good for twenty years, if all of Roy's options were exercised. It also contained an option for Roy to star in films—including, perhaps, his own life story. As one newspaper report noted, Roy was hot property, "the fair-haired boy in record circles, and several labels tussled to sign him." Fred Foster had no intention to lose his star client and had countered with his own $1 million offer to entice Roy to stay with Monument. But, as Foster revealed, Wesley Rose, who was negotiating on Roy's behalf, "was also insisting on prime-time television appearances and a motion picture deal. [And] I didn't have a movie company." Wesley Rose had history with MGM—he'd managed Don Gibson, who recorded for the label, and his father was involved with MGM when he brought Hank Williams to the label in the late 1940s.

Roy may have sometimes felt Fred Foster got too much credit, but he knew how crucial he had been for his career. "He didn't put his foot in his mouth by suggesting I sound like this or that. He just liked what sounded good to him, which is the best producer you could have." But the MGM offer was simply too good to resist. "The money was so big it was scary," said Roy, who cried when he told Fred Foster of his decision. ("I'm talking about honest to goodness tears," said Foster.)

MGM's president, Robert H. O'Brien, announced the news of Roy's signing in the first week of July 1965 (although Roy signed his deal with the head of MGM Records, Mort L. Nasatir). "It represents a talent acquisition of major significance," read the MGM press release, which pointed out that Roy would make music and motion pictures (two, with options for additional films) for the company. Already there was talk of Roy's first movie for MGM, a musical, according to the press release, "in which he will write as well as sing the title song." Shooting was scheduled to begin in October. (At the same time, a rumor appeared in the press that a film called *The Fastest Guitar in the West* would be Elvis's next movie for MGM.) Robert H. O'Brien would turn out to be the first of many MGM presidents during Roy's tenure with the company.

Roy would soon discover that there was one key difference between Monument and MGM—with his former label, he was the star, the main attraction, whereas at MGM, he was merely another big name on the roster. Roy was now *product*, whose contract stipulated that he generate at least three singles and three albums per year, which was a hefty output. One of many artists recording for MGM was Conway Twitty, whom Roy had warned off signing with Sun Records. Sheb Wooley too had scored big for MGM with his novelty song "Purple People Eater" and "That's My Pa," a song that was as country as a hay bale. Also having success with the label was British group Herman's Hermits, as well as Sam the Sham and the Pharaohs, whose "Wooly Bully" was in the *Billboard* Top 5 and was fast becoming the bestselling song of the year. Roy was no longer top dog, even though he was currently being promoted as "the world's number 1 vocalist" and demanded upwards of $10,000 every time he stepped onto a stage.

"Ride Away" had been Roy's first single for MGM, released in August 1965. "The Roy Orbison sound is getting a little worn out and tired," admitted one reviewer. "I wonder how long he can go on being successful with the same old formula?" As it turned out, at least in America, Roy would never better the chart ranking of "Ride Away"—number 25—while he was alive. He could now only look on as younger acts—the Beatles, the Rolling Stones, Bob Dylan, Marvin Gaye, the Supremes—took over the charts that he once ruled.

By the time of "Ride Away," Roy had already recorded his first long player for the label, *There Is Only One Roy Orbison*, which appeared in August '65. Wesley Rose, Roy's manager, music publisher, and namesake for his third child, produced the album with Jim Vienneau, an MGM staffer who'd produced Conway Twitty's "It's Only Make Believe." They would be Roy's producers for this and other early MGM recordings. Among the LP's dozen tracks was Roy's take on "Claudette." Clearly, Roy's first love was very much on his mind, as they went about rebuilding their relationship.

Bill Dees, who was still working with Roy and contributed five tracks to the album, was startled by the heavy demands that MGM had put on their new signing—Roy's contract stipulated that he record about forty songs a year for the label. "Roy would come in off the road on Friday and say that we needed six songs by the following Thursday." It wasn't a great omen for what lay ahead.

Still, reviews for Roy's first MGM LP were positive: "The distinctive Orbison style comes off in first-rate fashion," noted one critic. "[It's] destined for a chart-buster." But *There Is Only One Roy Orbison* wasn't a big hit, only reaching number 25 in the USA and selling around

200,000 copies, much less than MGM anticipated. It would be the last album of original material from Roy to chart in America for more than twenty years. *There Is Only One Roy Orbison* hit number 34 in the UK and number 12 in Australia. The album's progress Stateside was stymied by the looming release of *The Very Best of Roy Orbison*, a collection of Roy's Monument recordings curated by Fred Foster. It was a replay of the situation when Roy left Sun and Sam Phillips packaged together his old material for release. Roy was, in essence, once again competing with himself.

In fact, one of Roy's newer chart rivals was the highly photogenic Bobby Goldsboro, who'd been his guitarist for hundreds of shows. Goldsboro's recent singles—"See the Funny Little Clown," "Little Things," and "It's Too Late"—had fared better in the charts than much of Roy's recent work. He'd also appeared as a solo act on *Hullabaloo*, *Shindig!*, and various other TV programs, all with Roy's blessing, as Goldsboro made clear. "He told me not to hesitate—to do it and get started on my own career." When Goldsboro played a show at the Columbus (Georgia) Municipal Auditorium at the end of August, the headline in the *Columbus Ledger* captured Roy's dilemma in bold black newsprint. It read: BOBBY GOLDSBORO TO SING IN COLUMBUS WITH—in a much smaller font—ROY ORBISON.

The early months of 1966 were as lively as ever for Roy, but he struggled to regain his chart prominence in the US. He had a new album on the market, his second for MGM, *The Orbison Way*, the feature being a cinematic ballad written by Bill Dees entitled "This Is My Land." The LP wasn't a hit in America, where it peaked at 128, despite a prediction from *Cashbox* magazine that "Roy Orbison can expect enthusiastic reaction to this package." In the UK, however, it charted for ten weeks and reached number 11.

Roy returned for his next tour of the UK in late March 1966. It was an extensive run of more than fifty dates, playing theaters, cinemas, and halls. Roy would remain in the country until May 1, when he'd appear at the *NME* Awards show at the Wembley Empire Pool, sharing the bill with Herman's Hermits, Dusty Springfield, chart-topping Australian folk quartet the Seekers, and Stevie Winwood. Winwood, the teenage singer and keyboardist for the Spencer Davis Group, had recently turned critic and reviewed Roy's single, "Breakin' Up is Breakin' My Heart" for *Melody Maker*. "It's Roy Orbison," figured Winwood, "he always comes up with something good. I don't like all he does, but I admire him." (The single made it to number 22, his nineteenth charting hit in the UK.)

During a rare free day, Roy attended a motorcycle racing event at Hawkstone Park, near Birmingham on March 27. Fully aware that he was an avid rider—Roy had said that "riding a motorcycle gives you the feeling that fast cars, fast boats, water skiing, and horseback riding don't quite give you"—the organizers invited Roy to enjoy a "lap of honor" on a 250cc bike. But, as thousands of people looked on, he fell and injured himself. "We hit a sandpit on the course," Roy explained. "I came off altogether." Despite this, Roy remounted and completed a second lap with English motocross star Dave Bickers. Roy tried to convince his minders that it was merely a sprain, but he'd fractured his ankle. Fortunately, he was insured, to the sum of £250,000.

Roy played his next show at the Granada Cinema in London while seated, his foot in a cast, and continued to play that way for the rest of the tour. When he arrived at the Blossoms Hotel prior to a show in Chester, Roy was carried through the front door and into the lobby, hardly the best look for a visiting American star. It was proving to be a difficult tour, because Roy's support acts also had their problems. Scottish singer Lulu had been sidelined with a sore throat, while expat American duo the Walker Brothers, currently red-hot on the strength of their broody ballads "The Sun Ain't Gonna Shine Any More" and "Make It Easy On Yourself," were involved in a car crash on their way to a show in Bristol. (The evening's running order was altered, reported the *Evening Post*, because the still-shaken Walkers "insisted on washing their hair before going onstage.") It reached a point where Roy was forced to play one show without any supporting acts.

On stage, Roy may have been sitting down, but his magic hadn't faded. When he performed "Crying," reported the *Cheshire Observer*, "one would have heard a pin drop." Backed by an eight-piece ensemble, Roy delivered a set that contained nothing but hits—"Oh, Pretty Woman," "Running Scared," "Only the Lonely," "Dream Baby (How Long Must I Dream)," and "In Dreams" all featured—and he "had the audience magnetized . . . Roy is a great artist and the audience gave him the attention he deserved." (HOBBLING ROY ORBISON FAULTLESS AS EVER was a headline from later in the tour.)

Roy also turned on the charm away from the stage. Between shows he talked shop with John Orgill, a reporter from the *Evening Telegraph*, who wrote that "he looked completely calm, and his hair was, as ever, immaculate." Roy worked his way through a packet of French cigarettes as he spoke fondly of his beloved cars—he currently owned a Corvette, an E-Type Jaguar, a Volkswagen, a Ford, and a Mercedes—and his upcoming star turn in a movie now titled *The Fastest Guitar Alive*. As Orgill reported, "He was quite willing to talk about his wife Claudette, whom he recently remarried"—in late December 1965—"and hoped that she might be able to join him later in the tour."

When Claudette received news of his accident, she flew to the UK and took in every show from the rear of the venues that Roy filled night after night. Roy turned thirty on April 23, and they celebrated at an exclusive Soho restaurant. Roy quietly turned to one of his guests, writer Michael Housego, and said, "You can keep all your birthday presents. The best one I could have had is Claudette." When asked about Roy's accident, Claudette revealed that she too enjoyed riding motorcycles. In fact, it was her favorite pastime. "Why should it be more dangerous for a girl than a boy?" she asked. "I just don't see it."

Claudette confided to journalist Chris Hutchins that she feared Roy was working too hard; this tour alone included almost forty one-nighters. But that didn't stop Roy hosting a seemingly endless procession of reporters in his various hotel suites as he traversed the country. Toward the end of the tour, Roy spoke candidly with yet another writer: "I don't think I'm a really sad person. It's just that when I sit down to write a song, bad times tend to spring to mind much more easily than the good times."

And what lay ahead for Roy Orbison was the saddest of all possible times.

On Monday, June 6, Roy and Claudette were riding home from Bristol, Tennessee, where over the weekend they'd been enjoying the Spring Nationals drag races. Roy was on his Harley; Claudette was riding a

Honda. It was the beginning of what they intended to be a holiday after his lengthy UK tour.

By the early evening of June 6, they'd reached the town of Gallatin, about thirty miles outside of Nashville. Roy was riding slightly ahead when he glanced behind him and couldn't spot Claudette. As he later recalled, "I looked back and she wasn't there." He did, however, see an ambulance racing to the intersection of South Water Street and Coles Ferry Road, its siren wailing. Roy followed the ambulance and was horrified by what he saw.

Claudette had been struck by a truck, driven by thirty-year-old Kenneth Herald, who told police that he hadn't seen Claudette's bike when he entered the main street of Gallatin—running a stop sign—at Highway 109 South and Coles Ferry Road. She was thrown into the air and ended up beneath the truck. "She was blue," said an onlooker, one of the first people on the scene. "I thought she was already dead."

Roy rode in the ambulance with Claudette, but two hours later, at 9 p.m., she died from her injuries in Sumner County Memorial Hospital. She was twenty-four. Claudette was survived by her sons, Roy Dewayne, who was eight, Anthony—known to all as Tony—who was soon to turn four, and baby Wesley, who'd only just turned one. She was the fifth person to die in a motorcycle crash in Tennessee within four days.

When Roy broke the news to his children, Tony asked him, "Did Momma go to heaven on a Honda?"

Claudette's death was front-page news. ROY ORBISON'S WIFE DIES IN CRASH, reported *The Nashville Tennessean* the following day. TRAGEDY AS THEY GO HOME BY MOTORCYCLE. PRETTY WOMAN IS KILLED, was the headline in the UK's *Daily Record*. Claudette was rightfully eulogized as "the inspiration behind many of her husband's successful songs." Kenneth Herald was charged with involuntary manslaughter and was released on a $750 bond, but Roy decided not to prosecute. He felt that Herald had suffered enough. Claudette's body, meanwhile, lay in rest at the Phillips-Robinson Chapel in Hendersonville.

Roy was grief-stricken, devastated. Fred Foster, upon hearing the terrible news, drove to Hendersonville, where he found Roy sitting in silence, staring at the floor, completely dumbstruck. Roy's parents, who'd moved into a nearby property in Hendersonville to help out, were also in the room—Orbie Lee was holding Wesley. When Roy realized that Foster was there, he jumped up from his chair "and kind of leaped on me," said Foster. "He was beating his fists on me and crying. It was awful."

Orbie Lee pulled Foster aside. "Thank God he's crying at last," he told him.

Claudette Frady Orbison was laid to rest at the Woodlawn Memorial Park in Nashville; the Reverend Courtney Wilson presided over the service. Among her pallbearers were her brother Bill, as well as Fred Foster, Chet Atkins, and Bill Dees. Persistent rain made a miserable day all that much sadder.

Roy had never experienced tragedy on this level and had no idea how to deal with his pain. "I was devastated," he said. "My whole life just crashed around me."

In later years, Wesley would ask Roy, "What was my mother like?"

"She was beautiful," Roy would reply. "Very sweet. You remind me a lot of her, so it's a little hard to talk about."

CHAPTER 13

It's no good pretending—I need another wife and a mother for my three children

In the wake of Claudette's death, "naturally everything was at a standstill," said Roy's manager and friend Wesley Rose. "He's one of the strongest people I know, but it was hard to ask him to go into the studio or get him involved in writing." Yet somehow, Roy found the strength to travel to Los Angeles for an appearance on the teen dance program *The Lloyd Thaxton Show*, which aired on KCOP on June 16, just ten days after Claudette's death. It was a rare public appearance from Roy during his period of mourning.

But Roy knew that work was good therapy, and he had a feature film to make, having banked, quite literally, on movies as his next big career move. And in late October 1966, news broke that Roy was to appear in *The Fastest Guitar Alive*, ending the rumor that it was to be Elvis Presley's next starring role. (Elvis sent Roy a congratulatory telegram when he heard about the role.) "I'm going out to California in a month to start it," Roy said. "It's about the Civil War, and I play a happy-go-lucky guitar-playing soldier." How Roy would be able to carry that off, considering the emotional turmoil he was going through, was anyone's guess.

When asked about his role, Roy replied, "I'm starring," adding that he was also writing nine songs for the film. "This is a progression I'd like to make," Roy said about his big-screen future. He'd set up his own production company, in association with MGM, which he named Kelton. *Billboard* quickly picked up on the story. "Soon: Orbison the Film Star," they announced, revealing that "Orbison will have a romantic lead" story, portraying Johnny Banner, a singing cowboy-*cum*-Confederate spy. Roy had already put in four studio sessions to record music for the film. "It was work that saved my sanity," he admitted. "Some of the work was therapeutic, but I did it because I was obligated."

The film's producer was Sam Katzman, known within the industry as "the king of the quickies," a master of delivering B-grade movies rapidly and on budget. A New Yorker who'd relocated to the West Coast during the Golden Age of Hollywood, Katzman, now in his sixties, had produced dozens of low-budget features, starring everyone from a very young John Wayne (1933's *His Private Secretary*) to Bela Lugosi (1936's *Shadow of Chinatown*). More recently, Katzman had produced the 1956 hit *Rock Around the Clock*, starring Bill Haley and His Comets, which grossed a staggering $4 million (on a $300,000 budget). He'd also produced two Elvis Presley features, *Harum Scarum* and *Kissin' Cousins*.

Katzman needed a director and placed a call to Michael "Mickey" Moore, who'd been assistant director on dozens of films, including *The Ten Commandments*, *Gunfight at the O.K. Corral*, and several Elvis Presley movies. By his own admission, Moore had no idea who Roy Orbison was, but agreed to meet with him in Nashville prior to filming. As Moore recalled, "He showed up all in black and wearing dark glasses. Not being at all familiar with him, I wasn't quite sure what to think." When Roy removed his glasses, Moore was concerned: "His eyes had a strained appearance and [he] didn't focus well. I knew we'd have to shoot him very carefully." It was agreed that Roy would wear contact lenses on set, rather than his usual glasses. But this was a problem, according to Bill Dees, who cowrote the songs for the soundtrack based on plot points that Roy described to him. "Roy found it uncomfortable [on set] to be wearing contacts instead of glasses." Without his dark shades, Roy was almost unrecognizable on-screen.

Despite his concerns, director Moore had no problems on set with Roy, whose costars included Sammy Jackson, who'd appeared in the TV shows *Maverick* and *77 Sunset Strip*, and Maggie Pierce, a former nurse who'd recently starred in NBC's fantasy comedy *My Mother the Car*. "It was a fun picture to do, a very nice cast to work with, and a good atmosphere," said Moore. "Knowing it was Roy's first movie"—and fully aware of his terrible recent loss—"all the people were especially helpful to him." A rumor circulated that Roy broke his leg when some scenery fell on him, but, according to Moore, "it just didn't happen." When the shoot wrapped in late 1966, Moore kept a memento: a prop guitar with a gun, made especially for Roy's character in the film.

With a release scheduled for mid-July 1967, Roy badly needed *The Fastest Guitar Alive* to connect with an audience, because his recent records hadn't succeeded in America. "Twinkle Toes" had barely scraped into the top 40, while "Too Soon to Know," released in July 1966, had flatlined at number 68 in the *Billboard* Hot 100.

Roy was beginning to question if his decision to follow the money and sign with MGM had been especially wise. "It didn't take me long to learn that money wasn't happiness," he said. Roy wasn't entirely satisfied with his early recordings for the label, and he'd play just a handful of shows in America during 1966 (and would play very few during the final years of the 1960s). Amid new music from the likes of the Monkees, the Temptations, the Byrds, and the all-conquering Beatles and Rolling Stones, along with the burgeoning psychedelic scene, Roy seemed like a relic from a past age, a dinosaur. He just didn't fit. "The hippie thing," Roy admitted, "was not my kind of thing."

Yet there was a lifeline for Roy—the enthusiasm for his music in the UK and Australia remained strong. One of his best mid-1960s cuts, "Communication Breakdown," which stalled at number 60 on the *Billboard* Hot 100, was a top 10 hit in Australia during early 1967. Roy still had an audience and that would dictate his movements for many years to come. It would also help put some distance between Roy and the memory of Claudette, his beautiful "woman child," the first great loss of his life.

Roy was back in Australia in late January 1967, touring with the Yardbirds, and for the second time, the Walker Brothers. Roy was photographed on arrival at Sydney Airport, shades solidly in place, being greeted warmly by nineteen-year-old Gay Robbins, who worked for the tour's promoter, Harry M. Miller. Roy was all smiles, but his good nature was tested when he was repeatedly quizzed by the press about Claudette's accident. It reached the point where *Sydney Morning Herald* columnist Mike Walsh published what he referred to as the "Golden Yawn Award," which he dedicated "to all those booring [sic]

interviewers who persistently questioned Roy Orbison over his wife's tragic death." Enough was enough.

Roy's first performances were staged in the Sydney Stadium, an aging barn in the city's eastern suburbs, where the Beatles had created pandemonium three years earlier. The sixty-year-old venue was a firetrap; its worst feature was a revolving stage, which sometimes seized up and belched smoke mid-performance. (Ringo Starr had been forced to physically move his drum kit between songs when the motor seized up.) But on Roy's opening night, which was attended by about 8,000 fans, there was a different kind of problem. "Twelve girls collapsed and one was taken to hospital during a hysterical pop musical performance," read the story the following day. "The heat and hysterical screaming affected many of the audience." As for the show itself, "Roy was the star of the night," reported *The Sydney Morning Herald*.

An unexpected controversy arose during Roy's third visit to Australia. A regional branch of the Returned and Services League (RSL) protested to local radio station 2PK, who'd been playing Roy's "There Won't Be Many Coming Home," a teaser of the soundtrack from the yet-to-be-released *The Fastest Guitar Alive*. They argued that the song was in "bad taste," given that many servicemen from the region had been killed in Vietnam. The station manager, Frank Spicer, agreed to "examine the record" to see if there were grounds for complaint. It took a terse observation from a Sydney reporter to shut the issue down: "All that controversy about Roy Orbison's new record . . . being a sick record because it refers to Vietnam is rather pointless. Roy sang it in a film he has just made about the American Civil War." Roy and Bill Dees did write a song specifically about Vietnam, entitled "The Defector," but it wasn't released until after he died.

Roy made it clear that it wasn't some kind of Vietnam commentary in disguise; he'd leave that to rebels like Kris Kristofferson, whose "Viet Nam Blues" was a recent top 20 hit for Dave Dudley. When an English critic, Wayne Stierle, suggested that "There Won't Be Many Coming Home" wasn't released in the US because it was somehow anti-Vietnam, Roy put him straight. "He sure has got his wars muddied up. The song was about the Civil War. It was written for the film."

Roy kept a low profile during the Australian tour, although he became friends with Yardbirds guitarist Jimmy Page—the pair bonded over Fender equipment, even though Roy favored Gretsch guitars. "He was brilliant," said Roy. "He was miles ahead of everybody."

Just weeks later, Roy was in the UK, headlining a six-week, thirty-two-city package tour that also featured the Small Faces and another young Brit guitarist, Jeff Beck, who, like Jimmy Page, had done time in the Yardbirds. (Opening night wasn't Beck's best: He had equipment trouble and stormed offstage, muttering "I knew it was a waste of time," before jumping in his car and driving home.) Roy had a new single in the stores, "So Good," but it felt half-cooked, a song in search of a hook—it was a far cry from the newly released two-sided masterpiece from the Beatles, "Strawberry Fields Forever" and "Penny Lane." The two very contrasting releases were reviewed together in the *Western Daily Press*, whose critic was being generous when he wrote, simply: "Roy Orbison's 'So Good' isn't as good." "It sounds like a group practising in a pub," was the assessment of another critic. It was only in Australia that "So Good" cracked the top 30—in the US, it stalled at number 132. Roy's American career was in a tailspin.

Between shows in England, Roy interviewed local applicants for the job of nanny for his three boys, who would return to the States with him and live at Hendersonville. Roy was envisaging a long-term position. According to one report, he was "meeting and talking to English girls anxious to work and travel with him for the next ten or fifteen years." This would enable him to bring his sons along with him when he toured—or made movies. "I miss the children," Roy confessed. "They are quite nice people."

"I decided on an English nanny," Roy explained, "because American nannies are difficult to find . . . I don't mind if she is a homely girl, or a glamorous one, so long as she makes a good nanny." And being an Orbison fan wasn't mandatory: "It does not matter if she has never even heard of me," Roy clarified. About 600 hopefuls applied for the job, and Roy allowed a photographer to snap away while he was deep in discussion with contenders.

Roy eventually hired thirty-year-old Dorothy Cook from Gateshead, having realized that a married woman "was less likely to leave quickly." Roy also hired her husband Bob to be his chauffeur. He'd be responsible for Roy's collection of sixteen cars, which now included a mint condition 1926 Studebaker with only 20,000 miles on the clock and a shiny new white Excalibur SSK.

In between interviewing potential nannies and playing for the faithful, Roy visited the BSA motorcycle factory in Birmingham, shopping for a new bike. He admitted that he was "still mad" about motorbikes. Claudette's tragic death hadn't dampened his need for speed. And Roy hoped to remarry and the sooner the better, as he admitted to *Daily Mirror* writer Don Short. "Since my wife Claudette died," said Roy, "I've been the loneliest person in the world. It's no good pretending—I need another wife and a mother for my three children. I've gone into deep depression [but] when I'm sure I've met the right girl I'll marry again." Roy had been seeing a twenty-three-year-old flight attendant named Francine Herack, who was said to resemble Claudette. "They are quite alike in a lot of ways," Roy agreed. "[But] there will be no rush decisions." They had a post-tour holiday planned in the Caribbean.

Roy was asked about the ongoing appeal to British audiences of American acts such as himself and fellow tourist Gene Pitney, who was also going through a very dry patch Stateside (he hadn't reached the top 40 since early 1966). Roy figured that it all came down to humility. "I think the reason both Gene and myself have lasted in Britain is because we are both unassuming," replied Roy. "I have always tried to be friendly." Roy was toying with the idea of buying a home in London's St. John's Wood, perhaps basing himself in the UK for at least six months each year.

Roy's UK popularity was sometimes confirmed in unusual ways. One evening, while dining in a restaurant, he was hounded by autograph hunters, even though award-winning film star Laurence Harvey was seated at the next table. Both flattered and a little bemused, Roy greeted his fans and commenced signing autographs.

Roy's next move was not a strictly commercial decision. He'd always had a strong connection with singer-songwriter Don Gibson, both as a fan, dating all the way back to the Wink Westerners and via Wesley Rose, who had managed Gibson. Roy had earmarked his song "Crying" for Gibson before deciding to record it himself. He'd also shared several bills with the thirty-nine-year-old native of Shelby, North Carolina, a key player in the "Nashville Sound." Famously, Gibson, working with Chet Atkins, had cut his two best-known songs, "I Can't Stop Loving You" and "Oh, Lonesome Me," during one afternoon session in 1957, which helped get him out of the East Tennessee trailer park where he was living at the time. Gibson, like Roy, had his music published by Acuff-Rose, but unlike Roy, he was still in touch with the charts, having recorded a string of eight US country hits since 1964.

Roy had begun working on an album of a dozen Gibson originals in June 1966, just before Claudette's death, but didn't finish the record until filming had wrapped on *The Fastest Guitar Alive*. It was clear that Roy connected with the powerful sense of pathos that was prevalent in Gibson's music. His take on such tracks as "Oh, Such a Stranger," "Too Soon to Know," and "Sweet Dreams," songs awash with strings and heartache, were as potent as anything he'd recorded in recent years.

Roy Orbison Sings Don Gibson was treated with due reverence on its release in the late winter of 1967, but it was never going to be a hit record. It didn't even chart, although reviews were generous. "The combination of Roy's mellow, mature and emotional tones, and the wonderful country-blues of Don Gibson comes across well," noted *Record Mirror*. "You all know what Roy is like singing sad songs, well, Don Gibson does tend to write some pretty heartbroken material."

In what seemed like a backup plan, MGM had issued a best-of, *The Classic Roy Orbison*, just a few months before his Don Gibson tribute. And as if that wasn't enough, Fred Foster continued plundering the Monument archives and released *More of Roy Orbison's Greatest Hits*. ("First class Orbison," declared an Australian reviewer.) Three long-players from Roy were in the market, without a single new Orbison song among them.

Roy's *Don Gibson* LP did rate a mention in the "Pop Special Merit" reviews section of the March 11 issue of *Billboard*. "It's indeed a tribute to [Roy's] talent that he can take some country standards and give them a twist that puts a fresh glow to listening." *Cashbox* also reviewed it favorably: "This album shows off his singing ability to good advantage. Those who enjoy the artistry of both Orbison and Gibson should find this set a winner."

But *Solid Goldsboro*, the new LP from Roy's former guitar picker, featured more prominently in *Cashbox*'s "Pop Picks" column. It was clearly a sign of the times. And quite unintentionally, Bobby Goldsboro played a part in the fracturing of the relationship between Roy and Bill Dees. Dees had written a song called "Little Girl, Walk On," which Goldsboro and his partner Bob Montgomery offered to produce. "Chances are," Dees admitted, "I could have had a hit." But Dees told them that he'd have to check with Roy first, explaining that he was "responsible for my income."

Goldsboro and Montgomery weren't thrilled. "Is he your mother? Do you have to check in and out?"

Dees told them that he believed it was the right thing to do and he called Roy, expecting his blessing. After all, Roy had given Goldsboro the okay to pursue a solo career, so how could this be different? But Roy wasn't happy.

"He sounded hurt," said Dees. "In fact, he hung up on me."

When Dees finally got Roy back on the line, it was clear that he was stung by what he saw as an act of betrayal. But eventually Roy gave him the go-ahead and left Dees with an assurance: "We'll do a big session when my next check comes in." Although they'd work together again, that next big songwriting session never eventuated (and Dees's song was not recorded).

Dees admitted that in the wake of this clash, he and Roy "got real petty with each other." Their days as a writing duo were numbered.

Roy's feature film debut, *The Fastest Guitar Alive*, shot during the most difficult time of his life, was released in September 1967. "Roy Orbison sings and shoots," stated ads for the movie, while a poster proclaimed that Roy was "A Singing, Shooting, Son of a Gun!" A subsequent print ad declared: "His guitar makes staccato music like bullets." The hype was laid on very thick.

Roy, in his role as Confederate spy Johnny Banner, appeared in the movie's opening scene, riding a stagecoach, strumming his guitar while traveling with a medicine show selling Dr. Ludwig Long's Magic Elixir. They were en route to San Francisco. Trailing behind the stagecoach was a wagon holding six young women—the Chestnut sisters—who were busy hanging their laundry on a line strung between the two wagons.

Roy's first line, on sighting a tribe of Indians closing in on his wagon train— "They sure don't look like they're selling blankets"—made it clear what kind of movie he'd signed on for. During a chase scene early in the movie, Roy fired his modified "guitar gun," which looked more like a prop from a Z-grade spy flick, at the fast-approaching natives.

"Hey, Steve, they quit," Roy said to Sammy Jackson, playing his partner Steve Menlo, while looking over his shoulder.

"That's good," he replied, "because you never hit anyone with that contraption yet."

"Maybe not," Roy replied, "but it sure scared them to death."

Roy's acting was as wooden as the stagecoach he rode in on.

"In the movie," wrote the critic for the *Tampa Tribune* with admirable precision, "Orbison's guitar converts into a rifle and he emerges a hero." Few other critics even bothered reviewing the film or commenting on Roy's secret weapon. Even Roy wasn't sure what kind of film it was. "I didn't know what it was all about until it was all over," he admitted. And even then, it was hard to tell: Was it a comedy, a Western, or a farce?

Although it was mainly played for laughs, most of the scenes featuring Native Americans—or actors pretending to be Native Americans—were so corny and culturally sketchy that the film was lucky to pass muster in 1967, let alone today. (ABC's *F Troop* did it much better and a whole lot funnier.) Roy was woefully miscast as a musical Lothario, or a sort of Confederate mariachi in the scene where he was performing "Pistolero" dressed in a bolero jacket and matching black hat. To his credit, Roy looked more comfortable on camera when he was singing and cradling a guitar—ideally without its secret gun—especially during the scene when he performed the lovely, elegiac "River." Likewise, "Whirlwind," a minor Orbison classic. But when he was dependent purely on the generic script of Robert E. Kent—another B-movie veteran—Roy looked lost. As for Roy's make-out scene with one of the Chestnut sisters, it allowed for some smutty innuendo thanks to his customized (and highly phallic) six-string. It was perhaps the most uncomfortable scene in a film not short of awkwardness.

"I thought it was a terrible movie," said Fred Foster, who felt that the project was so bad that it embarrassed Roy. Much later, when asked about the movie, Roy explained that it was "intended to be a serious film but [that's] not how it worked out." It went into production not too long after the Jane Fonda-Lee Marvin hit *Cat Ballou*, and Roy suspected there was an attempt on the filmmaker's part to capture some of the same comic spirit. They failed.

Still, there was the accompanying Orbison-Dees soundtrack, of which "There Won't Be Many Coming Home," which didn't appear in the film, was the highlight (and became a minor hit in both the UK and Australia). Quentin Tarantino liked it enough to feature it on the soundtrack of his 2015 Western *The Hateful Eight*.

Despite the hype, *The Fastest Guitar Alive* was the type of B-movie seemingly made for drive-ins, where it sometimes screened with reruns of Elvis's *Viva Las Vegas*, *Spinout*, or *Double Trouble*. Although it continued screening well into 1968, it would be the only feature film Roy made for MGM, despite promises of further roles. Roy blamed in-house "financial trouble," but the hard truth was that he lacked the on-screen charisma and sex appeal of Presley.

When it came to acting, Roy Orbison was one hell of a singer.

CHAPTER 14

I was in shock. I was so confused

The demands of his million-dollar MGM deal meant that Roy all but lived in the studio when not touring overseas. But, as Bill Dees witnessed, Roy wasn't in the ideal mindset for making music; he was still adjusting to life without Claudette. "He felt he should keep on working, but he was vulnerable and delicate. [Yet] he didn't like to let anyone down." Dees insisted that it was the two of them who did the bulk of the work in the studio while Roy was with MGM, particularly when the hits stopped flowing. The credited producers, according to Dees, were usually "out drinking coffee." And oddly, Roy's next album, *Cry Softly Lonely One*, was released in October 1967, while *The Fastest Guitar Alive* (and its accompanying soundtrack) was still screening. There didn't seem to be any kind of marketing plan or strategy for Roy's music.

Cry Softly's best cuts, such as "Communication Breakdown" and "She," were cowrites with Dees, who believed the latter—"a great song"—could have been a hit for someone like Barbra Streisand with a simple switch of pronouns to "he." As far as Dees was concerned, the subject matter was obvious. "Roy didn't say it was about Claudette, but he didn't have to." The mournful ballad "Memories" was another track that could only have been inspired by Roy's awful loss.

The LP had a stronger country flavor than previous offerings from Roy, heard most explicitly in the big ballad "Time to Cry." Though unintentional, this slight shift of direction could have been opportune, given the current success of Glen Campbell, whose hit album, *By the Time I Get to Phoenix*, was released at the same time. (A big Roy Orbison fan, Campbell cut the Orbison-Dees classic "It's Over" for his next studio album, *Hey, Little One.*) But Roy's record was not a hit. And in strictly commercial terms, *Cry Softly Lonely One* was only significant because the title track, when released as a single, reached number 52 on the *Billboard* Hot 100, which would be Roy's highest chart placing in America for two decades. His hot streak at home was well and truly over.

Roy sounded uncharacteristically jaded when he spoke with a reporter about yet another failed release. He gave the impression that he needed a break from the studio. "I prefer to wait until I make [another] record which satisfies me personally and which also happens to be commercial," Roy said.

Roy didn't play a single show in America during 1968, although a string of nine dates across the border, at the Club Embassy in Toronto, earned him both strong notices—"You can't hardly get that kind of uncluttered singing anymore," noted the *Toronto Star*—and a handy $90,000 payday. When Roy attended a ceremony for the 1968 Grammys, held in Nashville in March, he was a shadowy figure, standing off to the side of a group photograph with two-time nominee Joe Tex, who'd scored big with his million-seller "Skinny Legs and All." Roy was yet to claim his first Grammy.

Nonetheless, Roy had retained his die-hard fan base outside of North America. A stretch of singles through 1967 and 1968—"So Good," "She," "Walk On," and "Heartache"—all did reasonable business in Australia and the UK, and it came as no great surprise that Roy focused even more strongly on those markets. "Roy can still pack 'em in at theatres and clubs all over Britain. His following is loyal—and immense," stated the *NME*.

Roy returned to England in mid-July 1968, this time playing larger clubs—as he'd predicted the year before—such as the Talk of the Town in London, and the 1,750-capacity Batley Variety Club in West Yorkshire, where he had a weeklong residency. Roy's set list remained stacked with his greatest hits: "Only the Lonely," "Crying," "Dream Baby (How Long Must I Dream)," "In Dreams," "Oh, Pretty Woman," and many others among them. Roy's onstage style was also unchanged and despite his lack of razzle-dazzle, the shows were an unqualified success. As the *NME* reported, "All Roy Orbison really does is stand there, with hair looking like black PVC and as action-packed as our dining room table. But with Orbison, who needs action?" Roy's voice could still leave an audience spellbound.

After a show at the Batley Variety Club on July 24, Roy was talked into going to a local discotheque, which was out of character—he usually headed straight back to his hotel. While in the club, Roy noticed a striking young woman seated nearby and had one of his group approach her and ask if she'd like to meet him. The woman was an eighteen-year-old German medical student who was living in London and visiting a friend in Leeds. Her name was Barbara Anne Marie Wellhoner Jakobs, and she was the daughter of a wealthy German industrialist.

"I ignored them," Barbara said of this first encounter, but Roy's friend was persistent, and she eventually agreed. When they spoke, Roy asked if she knew who he was. Had she heard his music? "No, I haven't," Barbara admitted. Roy was taken aback, but they continued chatting.

"That's a terrible-looking jacket you have on," she said, running her eyes over Roy's borrowed Levi's jacket.

"Come to the show tomorrow night," Roy countered, "and I'll show you my finest suit."

Barbara agreed. Soon enough, she would be playing a very large role in Roy's life.

Towards the end of his six-city, thirty-date tour, Roy played a week of shows at the Birmingham Theatre. "It was tremendous," reported the *Birmingham Post*, "enthusiastic to the point of frenzy." After the last show, Roy sat down with Terry Widlake from his touring band and proudly showed him photos of his three sons, which he kept in his wallet.

"He gazed with love and pride at the pictures and confessed how he was looking forward to seeing them in a couple of days' time," Widlake remembered.

Roy also showed Widlake photos of his trophy home by the lake in Hendersonville, which he declared was "virtually fireproof." Unbelievably, at almost the exact time he uttered those words, Roy's home, and his life, was going up in flames.

The news report on September 14 couldn't have been bleaker. It read: "Two small sons of singer Roy Orbison were missing and presumed dead Saturday night after fire destroyed the country music star's lakeside home." Fire had broken out at around 6:30 p.m. and Roy's parents, Nadine and Orbie Lee, who were minding the children along with Roy's secretary, Betty Young, almost had the three children out of the house when, according to Gallatin Fire Chief George Thompson, "an explosion erupted in the basement" and shook the burning residence. "One of the youngsters got out," said the fire chief, "but we believe the other two were trapped inside." Roy's parents and Ms. Young escaped without injury and lay sprawled on the front lawn with three-year-old Wesley, gasping for breath. However, eleven-year-old Roy Dewayne and six-year-old Anthony were trapped inside and died in the fire. Tommy Butner, the assistant chief of the Hendersonville fire department, was overcome by smoke and was given emergency treatment at the scene.

A neighbor named Billy Brown was one of the first people to arrive on the scene. He raced to the front door, "but I could not open it because of the smoke and the flames." Brown said that he could hear the children inside the house, crying for help, but was unable to save them. "It was pitiful," he said. "I couldn't get the door down." Another neighbor, Rex Goosetree, climbed up and looked in the den window, "but I couldn't see anything. The room was full of smoke." And yet another neighbor, Frank Mir, said that "it was mostly smoke at first. A few minutes later, flames were busting out everywhere."

Hundreds of people had gathered outside the property as the blaze erupted and a small group managed to salvage some of Roy's cars. But the house was destroyed; when the fire was extinguished, only the chimney remained. Little was salvaged, apart from the cigarette lighter that had been a gift to Roy from the Rolling Stones, and a portrait of Claudette, which hung above the fireplace and somehow survived the inferno. Claudette, allegedly, had sworn an oath when she and Roy reconciled—if they were ever separated again, she was taking the children with her. Now this had played out in the most tragic of circumstances. (The boys' bodies were recovered on the evening after the fire, near the indoor swimming pool.)

Roy was in Birmingham when he received the dreadful news via his road manager, Bobby Blackburn. The remaining dates of Roy's British tour were hastily canceled. He was sedated and put on the next flight back to the United States, returning to Nashville via New York.

Roy's life had come undone for the second time in barely twenty-four months. "I was in shock," he said. "I was so confused." The details of Roy's latest tragedy were splashed across newspapers all around the world. The front page of *The Nashville Tennessean* read: 2 ORBISON SONS DIE IN FIRE; underneath was a photo of Roy Dewayne's body being removed from the rubble. The UK's *Daily Mirror* ran a photograph of a smiling Roy and Claudette from 1964, who were playfully swinging Roy Dewayne by his arms—they were the perfect modern family. The heartbreaking caption read: "The singer . . . in happier days." In an unfortunate coincidence, Roy's latest release in America was a single called "Heartache."

Captain Bill Derring of the Gallatin fire department told the press that the fire was an unfortunate accident. "From what we've been able to piece together," he said the day after the inferno, "the two children who were killed were playing with an aerosol can in the basement of the house." And while this was given as the official cause, Roy's mother Nadine later told Terry Widlake a very different story. She said that there had been a problem with the central air-conditioning system that hadn't yet been repaired, and that may have started the fire. According to Nadine, any suggestion that the boys were playing with matches or cigarette lighters was false. "Nadine told me how she held onto young Wesley as tightly as she could," said Widlake, "and appealed to God to open the door. They spilled out into the fresh air only to discover that Anthony and Roy were not with them. The two boys had fled back [inside] the house in an attempt to escape the smoke. The rest is history."

A grim-faced Roy was photographed changing flights at JFK, assisted by a TWA passenger relations agent. This time, his dark glasses were absolutely necessary. He was devastated, grief-stricken. First, he'd lost Claudette, now two of his boys. It made no sense at all.

His sons were laid to rest on September 16. The service was presided over by Brother Ira North and among the pallbearers were Roy's brother Sammy and Claudette's father Chester, as well as Acuff-Rose's Wesley Rose, Don Gant, and Robert McClusky. The boys were buried at Woodlawn Memorial Park in Nashville, where Claudette was also at rest.

Roy's neighbor, Johnny Cash, was on the road with June Carter

Cash at the time of the fire, but upon hearing the news, he canceled his remaining dates and chartered a flight back to Hendersonville. As they unpacked their bags, the Cashes could see the ruins of what had once been Roy's home. In an awful coincidence, Cash's longtime guitarist, Luther Perkins, had died in a Hendersonville house fire only a month earlier.

John and June were among the mourners at the funeral, but, as Cash wrote, "I couldn't even approach Roy . . . for the first time in my life I was at a total loss for words, gestures, anything." Cash too had suffered his fair share of grief. His younger brother Jack had died after almost being cut in two by a table saw, when Johnny was twelve years old. He understood loss. About a week later, Cash got Roy on the phone and said, simply, that he loved him. Roy told him that he'd be all right, but, as Cash later wrote, "I couldn't imagine how he could be."

After the service, Roy moved in with his parents, who lived nearby, and they placed a NO VISITORS sign at the entry to the house, as Roy mourned. Orbie Lee and Nadine would care for Wesley. Cash occasionally saw Orbie Lee and asked how Roy was doing. He was told that he was shut away in his bedroom and wasn't speaking with, or seeing, anyone. One day, Cash decided it was time to act and he told Orbie Lee that it was important, he needed to see Roy. "And there he was," observed Cash, "so pale that he could have been dead himself." Roy was sitting on his bed, dark glasses in place, watching a TV set with the sound muted. Cash wasn't even sure that Roy knew he was there. Again, Cash told Roy that he loved him. He also said that he had no idea how he would handle such a loss. "I don't know how to handle it, either," Roy said. Then he fell silent again and Cash left.

Over time, Roy decided to begin building a new home on an adjacent lot and offered Cash the block of land where his house had once stood. They came to an understanding. "I told him," wrote Cash, "that I'd never build on it or sell it to anyone else." As good as his word, Cash planted a vineyard and an orchard on the site. "I think he was glad that strangers wouldn't live where his children died," Cash figured. (Cash would eventually sign the land over to Roy's son Wesley.)

In early October, Roy made a rare public appearance at Hillbilly Day, a charity fundraiser, in Madison, Tennessee. He sat at the wheel of a 1929 Bentley, alongside Democratic vice-presidential candidate (and future secretary of state) Edmund Muskie. In the rear seat was Tennessee congressman Richard Fulton. As for Roy's film *The Fastest Guitar Alive*, it was still screening at a few suburban drive-ins, now teamed with Elvis Presley's *Speedway*. Meanwhile, an announcement was made that Roy would return to playing live, having agreed to play two shows in Canada during February 1969. "I went ahead and did what I normally did," Roy said of this dark phase of his life, "and then let love and time and things like that take care of everything."

A few months after the fire, Roy called Nashville session guitarist Harold Bradley, who'd played on several of his biggest hits, and asked if he'd like to see him. Roy was now staying in a hotel and, as Bradley recounted, it was clear he'd been there for some time, judging by the mess. "He didn't have a home," said Bradley. "Inside it was absolutely dark, food wrappers scattered all over the room." Roy didn't want to discuss his feelings or what he was going through. "He wanted to talk about getting some guitars. I think that was kind of a way of regaining his sanity," Bradley recalled. "What is nice, is that life didn't end in that hotel room."

On January 21, 1969, a little over four months since the death of his sons, Roy returned to the studio. He'd already completed an album, *Roy Orbison's Many Moods*, back in May 1968, although its release was put on hold until Roy was able to promote the record. But Roy now wanted to record another batch of new songs. He had Canadian dates to play in February, followed by yet another UK tour starting in April, including an even lengthier two-week stretch at the Batley Variety Club, so he needed to work around these commitments to finish this new album.

Yet again, Roy had no live dates booked closer to home. "As much as I would enjoy touring and performing in America, there's just not enough time," he explained. "By the time I do a two- or three-month stretch of shows abroad, the only thing I want to do is come home and relax." What Roy wasn't saying was that demand from the UK and Australia was far stronger than the USA, where he was viewed as some sort of relic from the past. What interest he did get from American promoters was to appear on oldies shows, alongside ageing acts like Bill Haley and Little Richard. "Where do I fit in this picture?" Roy would ask these promoters. "I didn't have a hit until the spring of 1960." Roy refused to buy into the idea that he was some kind of veteran—he felt that he didn't belong with these artists. "They quit recording, more or less, even before I had a hit record," said Roy, who had a current record deal and was still making new music.

Roy was now working in the era of the concept album, which had been in vogue since such trailblazing records as the Beatles' *Sgt. Pepper's Lonely Hearts Club Band* and the Beach Boys' *Pet Sounds*. Contemporary artists weren't just growing their hair and getting high—they were now striving to record albums that worked as one complete piece, rather than the old method of patching together LPs from singles and whatever else remained on the studio floor. And while Roy was still very much a product of that latter era, there was a clear connection between the stronger songs that he recorded during the early months of 1969. The overriding mood was as unmistakable as the inspiration: These were songs about real loss and sadness, heard most powerfully in standouts "Sweet Memories" and "Leaving Makes the Rain Come Down." Roy had rarely been in better voice; his vocal on "One of the Lonely Ones," a song drenched in strings and melancholy, was one of his best. It felt as though Roy was trying to sing away all the demons that had plagued him since that fateful phone call in September 1968.

Bill Dees cowrote five of the album's dozen tracks, while "Little Girl (In the Big City)" was a stand-alone Dees composition, his last major contribution to a Roy Orbison album for many years. Satisfied with what he'd achieved so far, Roy headed to Canada in early February.

Roy's relationship with Barbara, the German medical student that he'd met in Leeds around the time of the fire, had become a full-fledged romance, and they were now living together in Roy's new home, an 11,000-square-foot chalet with a home recording studio, six bathrooms, and three kitchens. "If you have six bathrooms, you obviously need about three kitchens," Roy managed to joke with a writer.

While Roy was in Canada playing shows in Victoria and Saskatoon, there was a visitor to his new home in Hendersonville. Barbara answered the door and was stunned to see that Bob Dylan had come calling. He'd been recording his *Nashville Skyline* LP at Columbia Studio

A and decided to visit Roy, whom he greatly admired. As Dylan would write in his memoir *Chronicles, Volume One*, it was "Running Scared" that had made him a Roy Orbison convert. "He sounded like he was singing from an Olympian mountain top and he meant business . . . There wasn't anything else on the radio like him." Dylan, a close friend of Johnny Cash, now looked nothing like the Tambourine Man of the mid-Sixties: He was sensibly dressed, his once wild hair was cut short, and a little stubble lined his face. But, still, it was very clearly Bob Dylan. Barbara told him that unfortunately, Roy was on the road.

While disappointed to have missed meeting Dylan, Roy was thrilled when he got the news. "That was a compliment," he said. "Anytime anyone takes the time to come to your home and knock on the door, it's marvelous." Roy was sure that he and Dylan would make music together one day.

Just weeks before Roy set out for England, what was perhaps the most intriguing song he ever cut was released. Produced by Acuff-Rose's Don Gant, who'd been a pallbearer at the funeral of Roy Dewayne and Anthony, Roy's new single was "My Friend," but its flip side was the outlier. It was called "Southbound Jericho Parkway," which Roy had recorded on January 30, at the end of a lively month where he'd cut a dozen new songs during four recording sessions. While Roy felt no affinity with what he called "the hippie thing," "Southbound" had the same feel and scope of Jimmy Webb's 1968 epic "MacArthur Park." "Southbound" was written by Bobby Bond (real name Robert William Reinhardt), a twenty-five-year-old who'd started playing in bands in Michigan when he was a teenager, before moving to Nashville in the mid-1960s. Bond wrote songs for Acuff-Rose, which led to "Southbound Jericho Parkway" being recorded by Roy.

"I thought the story itself was really good," said Roy of this seven-minute-long meditation about life and death, which was broken down into distinct sections, à la Webb's "MacArthur Park." If nothing else, it was worth it just to hear Roy sing such unlikely lyrics as "the psychedelic sign read: Peace." Though the release wasn't a hit, just scraping into the top 40 in the UK, "Southbound Jericho Parkway" became a touchstone for Orbison devotees.

Roy had a big surprise for the always supportive English media when he arrived in April 1969 and introduced his "attractive wife" Barbara. "I don't think the news has broken in America yet," Roy told reporters at Heathrow. A few days earlier, on March 25, they'd been married at Madison, Tennessee. The minister who presided over their ceremony, Ira North, had laid Roy's sons to rest. (They'd visited Barbara's family in Germany en route to the UK.) "Roy arrives—with his surprise wife," announced the *Evening Standard*. He was still front-page news in England.

When the Orbisons posed for photographers in London, Barbara was radiant, while Roy looked dapper in a dark suit and checked tie. The newlyweds had reason to smile: This current tour would be one of the most lucrative yet for Roy. According to a report in the *Daily Mirror*, he stood to earn some £100,000 from a run of dates that would keep him in the country until the end of May. Roy assured the press that he was now on the mend, despite his recent terrible losses. "[I'm] very much full of life," he said. "The last few years have left me a little older and a little wiser. I'm full of good feelings. I never felt better."

While speaking with *Melody Maker*, Roy hinted at a second movie, a more "contemporary" project than *The Fastest Guitar Alive*—most recently screened in Papua New Guinea, of all places—which he hoped to begin during the fall. "I feel that films are just an extension of my singing career, a natural progression," Roy said. While he wasn't crazy about "all the hanging around" that came with moviemaking, Roy enjoyed the teamwork, "the fun you have with the people on the set."

But there'd be no second film for Roy at MGM. Nor would his latest set of songs, which he completed upon his return to the USA, see the light of day during his lifetime. (The tapes were thought lost until they were unearthed and released by his family in 2015, as *One of the Lonely Ones*.) At the time, Roy blamed "contract disputes" for the shelving of the material he'd recorded in early 1969, but his son Alex, speaking long after his father's death, had a different take. "I think maybe his management was a little afraid of going in that deep," he told *Goldmine* magazine. Alex referred specifically to the title song, "where he so specifically spells out being sick and tired and uninspired and not wanting to be where he was heading, which was to be one of those glum, lonely people."

Instead, MGM released *Roy Orbison's Many Moods*, a more conservative, middle-of-the-road option, a very different record to the highly personal *One of the Lonely Ones*. Despite the usual praise from *Cashbox*—"The latest Orbison outing is a compelling package that showcases the unique talent in a variety of moods . . . sales sure to follow"—it came nowhere near a chart.

CHAPTER 15

I have no wish to be a pedant, but I would just like to get the record straight

During Roy's latest UK tour, he'd met an English songwriter named Sammy King, a former salesman who'd worked in a touring band called the Voltairs and currently led the Sammy King Duo. King offered Roy a song that had been inspired by a visit to what the British called a "penny arcade," an amusement center filled with coin-operated gaming machines. "I was enjoying the final moments of an unbelievable sunset," King told the *Yorkshire Evening Post*. "Within a matter of moments, I had the first two lines of the song." Hoping to appeal to a broader audience, King opted not to refer to British currency—sixpence didn't sing so well—so he used the term "dime" in his lyric. It worked perfectly.

Roy recorded "Penny Arcade" in mid-July 1969, along with a second King song, "After Tonight," and it was released in Australia in late September. Roy hadn't had a top 40 hit in Australia since March 1968's "Born to Be Loved by You," and almost immediately, "Penny Arcade" found its audience—Australians, after all, loved to gamble. "American pop idol and millionaire, Roy Orbison, seems to be on top of the blues after having suffered three years of heartbreak," reported *The Age*. "'Penny Arcade' seems to reflect a happier frame of mind." And the song *was* upbeat, almost chirpy, very different to Roy's best-known hits. On its first week in the Australian charts, "Penny Arcade" reached number 39, and then it began to climb. Competition was fierce: Roy's buddy Johnny Cash was riding high with the tragicomic "A Boy Named Sue," while the Beatles' "Something," Neil Diamond's "Sweet Caroline," and Elvis Presley's "Suspicious Minds"—all great songs—were clinging tightly to the business end of the top 10. Yet by the first week of November, "Penny Arcade" had breached the top 20. A week later, it had hit number 7.

Come November 29, Roy had his first Australian number 1 since 1963's "Blue Bayou"—and "Penny Arcade" was still in the top 5 at the end of the year, selling more than 100,000 copies in the process. It would chart for twenty-four weeks, eclipsing "Working for the Man," Roy's previous best, by two weeks. Yet Roy didn't know that he'd topped the Australian chart until he and Barbara reached Sydney in mid-January 1970, where he was booked for a residency at the upscale Chevron Hotel. "It was terrific," Roy said after getting the news, "a massive hit. It sold more copies than any other record has ever sold there."

Just like the British press, the Australian media were fascinated by Barbara—they mistakenly referred to her as a model, which was understandable: She was a beautiful woman. Her protective feelings toward Roy were obvious when he headed to Melbourne for a show at Festival Hall. That afternoon, during a meet-and-greet with press and DJs, Roy the perennial crowd-pleaser was doing his best to speak with as many people as possible, all demanding their five minutes, when she called out: "Don't tear him apart!"

Johnny Cash was dressed in white tie and tails when he spoke with the audience on the set of his ABC show in April 1970. "Tonight, I'd like you to meet a very good friend of mine," Cash announced, his voice the usual mix of sand and gravel. "This young man lives next door to me." Cash went on to describe how the plot of land that lay between their properties—where Roy's former dream home had once stood—"is a nice garden and an orchard, and in the spring, we share the fruits thereof. Make welcome my good neighbor, Roy Orbison."

Roy was making his third appearance on Cash's popular variety show, promoting a new song called "So Young," which he'd recorded for an MGM film directed by Italian Michelangelo Antonioni called *Zabriskie Point*. Putting a whole new spin on the man in black, all the way down to the acoustic guitar that he strummed, Roy performed one of the best songs he'd cut in recent times, which he'd recorded with a new producer, Mike Curb, a twenty-five-year-old overachiever, who composed film scores, established a record label, and now ran MGM Records. Curb was a huge Orbison fan, who got along well with Roy. "So Young" had all the drama of his Monument hits, and Roy pushed his voice as far as it could stretch—which was pretty damned far. At thirty-four, despite thousands of gigs and twenty-plus years on the road, Roy's pipes were as supple as ever.

After Roy's song, Cash joined him on the set and reminisced about their early days in the 1950s, pointing out how Roy had since become a superstar. "Despite the fact," Roy interjected, "that you told me to change my name and lower my voice." This brought a grin to the craggy face of Cash—the camaraderie between the two singers was unmistakable. "I like your name and I like your voice," Cash clarified, still smiling, before exiting stage left. Roy then performed a rapid-fire medley of "Only the Lonely" and "Oh, Pretty Woman," leaving the audience in raptures.

Perhaps the warm feelings on the set had something to do with Roy having learned that Barbara was pregnant with their first child—she was due in October. Together they were rebuilding Roy's life, of which Johnny Cash was also a very big part. Roy's parents Nadine and Orbie Lee, who cared for Roy's son Wesley, now lived on the same Hendersonville street as Roy and Barbara.

"So Young" was intended to be heard over the closing credits of Antonioni's film, but there'd been a complication. The film was completed when Roy and Mike Curb came up with the track, which was a last-minute addition. "They wanted a song written for the movie," Roy explained to Australian journalist Glenn A. Baker, "so it could be an Academy Award proposition." (A report in *Billboard* said that it was an attempt on MGM's part to "bring back Orbison as a major record act in the US," and an Oscar would have helped that immensely.)

Roy was traveling with Barbara, his parents, and Wesley when he was told by those who'd seen *Zabriskie Point* that "So Young" didn't appear on the soundtrack. "I can't believe it," said Roy, who called the producers. They told him that they hadn't been able to squeeze the song onto the first few prints of the film. "It didn't make any sense to me," said Roy. It was only then that "So Young" was added to a film that was widely panned. "Their voices are empty," critic Roger Ebert said of *Zabriskie Point*'s protagonists, "they have no resonance as human beings." Any hope of an Oscar for Roy was gone.

Roy's appearances in America were rarer than Orbison songs on the hit parade, so when he agreed to perform on August 29 at Centennial Park as part of the Nashville Music Festival, it was an event—a big free event, with a crowd of about 75,000 anticipated. MGM had just released *Hank Williams: The Roy Orbison Way*, so he had new product to promote. The show was sponsored by local radio station WMAK. Aside from Roy, the daylong outdoor concert featured Ronnie Milsap, Jimmy Buffett, Bobby Bloom, and a variety of rock bands. These included an unsigned act named Steel Mill, who'd been spotted playing in Richmond by some college students with connections to the festival's organizing committee. Among the members of Steel Mill were guitarist Steven Van Zandt and a twenty-year-old front man named Bruce Springsteen, who'd been an Orbison devotee ever since he first heard "It's Over." Steel Mill hadn't played in front of a crowd anywhere near this size.

Their trek to Nashville was arduous; the band spent fifteen hours in the back of a U-Haul truck. But, as Springsteen made clear when he inducted Roy into the Rock & Roll Hall of Fame in 1987, the memory of the headliner's performance was indelible. "He came out in dark glasses, a dark suit, and he played some dark music," said Springsteen. He couldn't get over how still Roy stood onstage: "It seemed like if you went up to him and tried to touch him, your hand would go through him. It seemed like he'd fallen from another planet." Roy introduced himself to Springsteen after the show, and they got along well. "His honesty and openness struck me," said Roy. They'd meet again.

A few weeks after this one-off show, Roy and Barbara welcomed their first child into the world, on October 18, also in Nashville. Johnny Cash was in the waiting room at the hospital, offering support to his "good neighbor."

"Well, what is it?" Cash asked Roy when he emerged from the delivery room.

"It's a baby," said Roy, clearly overcome with joy, and more than a little bewildered.

Roy and Barbara named their newborn Roy Kelton Orbison.

They introduced him to the wider world with a release that read, in part: "Announcing . . . A New Star in his first personal appearance at Hendersonville, Tennessee . . . a sweet and innocent, 7 pound 10 ounce dream baby."

Roy Jr. traveled with his parents and his half brother, when Roy made yet another pilgrimage to the UK soon after the birth. In the wake of the Hendersonville fire, Roy had made a commitment to this family: Whenever possible, they'd be by his side, no matter where the road took him. Barbara too had made a commitment, giving up her studies to travel with Roy and dedicate herself to his career. "Taking my family with me on trips makes it a working holiday," Roy told a reporter, but there was more to it than that: In no way he did he want to risk a repeat of the horrors of September 1968.

Steel Mill's Bruce Springsteen wasn't the only young rocker paying homage to Roy Orbison. There was no hotter American rock band in 1970 than Creedence Clearwater Revival, who were fronted by John Fogerty, a twenty-five-year-old Californian with a wardrobe full of flannel shirts and a rock and roll heart. (His first band, the Blue Velvets, played nothing but covers of early rockers like Little Richard and Fats Domino.) In a remarkable stretch that began in September 1968 with "Susie Q," Creedence had recorded eleven charting singles, seven of them top 10 *Billboard* hits.

When Fogerty was a kid learning the basics of the guitar, the first single he purchased was Roy's recording of "Ooby Dooby." He prized it so highly that Creedence recorded the track and included it on their fifth studio album, *Cosmo's Factory*, a number 1 hit in six countries, including the US, the UK, and Australia, on release in July 1970. Creedence didn't mess with the formula: Their version was every bit as raw and fresh as Roy's 1956 hit single. "I really dug the guitar breaks," wrote Roy Carr in the *NME* upon hearing "Ooby Dooby," "which brought back much nostalgia. Very basic yet very exciting."

Roy might have shuddered at the mention of the word "nostalgia"—he'd recently told a reporter "I feel contemporary"—but he too was impressed by the Creedence cover. It was a handy reminder that while he may have gone AWOL commercially, he hadn't been cast aside by the current generation. "That makes me feel good," he said upon hearing it. "It may sound corny, but that's one of the better things you get from being in the business." After years of neglecting "Ooby Dooby," Roy understood that it had historical value and meant a lot to his fans and began playing it again during his live shows. Coincidentally, around the same time, Elvis Presley dusted off his Sun Records hit, "That's All Right, Mama," for the first time in many years. "We didn't acknowledge [their significance] until it became popular to do so," Roy explained. "Being part of history was very important."

The admiration of true believers like Fogerty and Springsteen showed that Roy hadn't been forgotten, but it didn't help his commercial fortunes, especially in America. Roy had recorded several songs while under contract to MGM that never saw the light of day, beginning with 1967's "Blue Teardrops (Are Falling)" and continuing, more recently, with "Kelly's Warriors," which he cut in February 1970. (More unreleased recordings followed in 1971 and 1972.) Instead, Roy was represented in the marketplace by a series of best-ofs and greatest hits collection, released by both MGM and Monument—and Sun, who pieced together *Roy Orbison: The Original Sound* in 1971—or oddities such as 1970's *The Big O*, which he recorded with English group the Art Movement at the Batley Variety Club, while on tour. It included unlikely covers of the Beach Boys ("Help Me, Rhonda"), classic Motown ("Money"), and the old folk song "Scarlet Ribbons (For Her Hair)" and featured Roy's recent Australian number 1, "Penny Arcade." The album was only released in the UK, where it reached number 27. It was the final record of Roy's to chart in England during his lifetime.

Roy had often been the victim of misconceptions—there were rumors that he was blind and that he was a hermit, rock's very own Howard Hughes. There was even a misunderstanding, backed up by the *San Francisco Examiner*, that "oldie goldie Orbison went into retirement in recent years, following a period of personal tragedies." A lengthy think piece published by the *NME* in October 1971, written by Wayne Stierle, didn't help matters. It was worryingly titled "Orbison a Victim of '45 Decline." Essentially, Roy's problem, Stierle argued, stemmed from being a great singles artist in what was now an increasingly album-oriented age. "A big part of the Orbison magic," he wrote, "was Monument Records. They gave Roy the sound of a huge crashing orchestra." Cowriter Joe Melson was also a big boon for Roy. "Suddenly a fairly good rockabilly artist," Stierle wrote, "became the leader in a big rock beat ballad sound. Monument knew exactly how to handle Roy, and his moves were nothing short of brilliant."

Roy responded by letter to Stierle's comments, and his response was published in the October 16 *NME*. And Roy wasn't happy. He dismissed much of Stierle's article as "complete bull," strong words for a mild-mannered man. "I have no wish to be a pedant," Roy wrote, "but I would just like to get the record straight." His first beef was regarding television, which Stierle believed that Roy hadn't fully utilized during his peak. "I did major network shows in the States. I did *The* [Ed] *Sullivan Show*. I topped the bill at the *Sunday Night at the* [London] *Palladium* five or six times," Roy wrote. "I did major television programs everywhere I appeared—including Australia."

Roy also made it clear that it was he, not his producer, who was responsible for the strings that featured on his Monument hits. "I had to plead with Fred Foster for strings," he wrote. "Nobody else had used them, except for Buddy Holly on the last record before he died." (Roy was probably referring to "True Love Ways," which Holly recorded a few months before he died in a plane crash in February 1959.) Stierle had complimented Bob Moore's contributions to the Monument records, but Roy also disputed that. "What is all this nonsense he writes about the Bob Moore orchestrations?" Roy asked. "Bob Moore only played bass . . . Joe and I wrote the songs. We arranged [the songs], gave the arrangements on tape to Anita Kerr, and she took them down." Roy also disputed that Monument was selective and chose his releases carefully. "No, they weren't," wrote Roy. "They got what I gave them."

Roy had almost always been genial and forthcoming when dealing with the media and his written outburst was out of character. Perhaps the frustration of having dropped off the charts and being seen as some kind of museum piece, was taking its toll. Roy firmly believed that his time would come around once more—he just had to stay hopeful and be patient. "I didn't hear a whole lot I could relate to," Roy said of this era in music, "so I kind of stood there like a tree where the winds blow and the seasons change and you're still there and you bloom again."

But Roy couldn't have imagined how long it would be before he bloomed again.

Roy could take some solace, however, in his earning potential as a live act. In May 1972, he set out on what would be his biggest-ever world tour, playing hundreds of shows in numerous countries. Industry insiders believed it was the largest world tour ever undertaken by a Nashville-based artist. "We'll perform somewhere every day," Roy said before departing, "except, of course, when we have to take a day off to travel." Roy's itinerary was so extensive that some of the same US media outlets that thought he had retired were suddenly paying attention. "Orbison is as popular via records and in person in foreign lands as he is in the USA, maybe more," noted Red O'Donnell in Kentucky's *State Journal* newspaper.

Roy's UK tour would include an opening show at the Royal Albert Hall in mid-May, a two-week residency at the Golden Garter in Manchester, a week at the Talk of the Midlands in Leicester—and then he'd pretty much stay on the road for the next five months, which he'd round out with yet another run of dates in Australia (where Melbourne radio station 3UZ intended to play nothing but Orbison songs for an entire day). The road would also take Roy and his ten-piece band to much of Europe and southeast Asia, where they'd play in Japan, South Korea, Hong Kong, and Taiwan. There seemed little left of the world for Roy to conquer, although he did have a wish list. "I'd like to play Russia and Red China someday," he admitted. (He'd come close when he played a show in Bulgaria during 1982.) Roy's father Orbie Lee would be part of his entourage, in the role of tour manager. Many years earlier, Roy's brother Sammy had gone out on the road with him. Touring was very much an Orbison family affair.

Roy's desire to play live hadn't abated. "I guess you could say that I enjoy singing while others may do it for different reasons—money or fame," Roy told a reporter in Melbourne, Australia. "Even if I wasn't making money, I'd still want to do it."

Roy would earn around $1 million from the tour, and it was estimated he'd entertain something like 500,000 fans. The money would prove handy, as Roy hadn't lost his obsession with cars. In a recent two-day period, he'd traded no less than three brand-new vehicles. He'd bought a Dodge Charger, but backed it into a utility pole, so he returned it to the dealer and swapped it for a Pontiac Grand Prix. But when that car began blowing smoke, he drove back to the dealer and exchanged the Grand Prix for a Porsche. "I didn't back it into a utility pole and it didn't blow smoke," Roy said of the Porsche. "So, I kept it." His collection currently stood at around forty vehicles, although Roy wasn't quite sure of the exact amount. "The cars I own now are all special for some reason or other," he made clear. Roy's pick of the bunch was a 1957 Thunderbird.

On October 3, a TV film crew captured Roy's opening night at Melbourne's Festival Hall, a 1,700-capacity venue on the western side of the city, where the Beatles had played in 1964. The lights dimmed and Roy walked to center stage, as a huge neon sign flashed out his name, and his seven-piece touring band and a full orchestra readied themselves. He looked as sharp as ever—his cream-colored stage outfit was in stark contrast to his dark glasses and jet-black hair, which Roy was wearing a little longer. And Roy got straight to business, launching into "Only the Lonely" while a few latecomers were still finding their seats.

For the next hour, Roy held the Festival Hall audience spellbound as he performed "Crying," "Running Scared," "Blue Bayou," and many more of his solid-gold hits—crowd favorites, every one. He merely had to sing the opening line of "Dream Baby (How Long Must I Dream)" and the crowd began clapping along so loudly that they threatened to drown out the musicians onstage. They did the same, maybe even louder, during "Penny Arcade," while "Oh, Pretty Woman" went over so well that Roy opted to return to the stage and play it again as an encore. These die-hard Aussie fans simply loved the Big O, even when he threw out a curveball like Simon & Garfunkel's "Bridge Over Troubled Water." While undeniably a great song, it wasn't really necessary, given the depth of Roy's catalog. Still, the applause that greeted its big finale was deafening. Roy also covered "Sweet Caroline," a song from Neil Diamond, whom Roy had met on a prior Australian visit and joined onstage. Together they played "Oh, Pretty Woman"—well, *almost* together. After a few bars, Diamond realized he was "excess baggage"—his words—and opted to step back, thereby allowing "the master [to] do one of his masterpieces alone."

Between-songs patter had never been Roy's style, and he said very little during this and the many other shows on his 1972 tour, other than smiling and murmuring the occasional "thank-you." ("His stage act is nonexistent," sniffed one hard-to-please critic. "He hadn't even said what a wonderful audience we were," grumbled another. "Not a word to us.") But Roy's songs and his polished performance connected so powerfully with his fans that all he really needed to do was breathe deeply and sing his heart out, stopping occasionally to wipe the sweat from his forehead. "People come to hear the hits, so I sing them," Roy figured. It made perfect sense.

During a sit-down with a Sydney reporter a few days after his Melbourne show, Roy let it slip that all was not well on the MGM front. "I've been at cross-purposes with my record company," Roy admitted, "and that stopped any recording." Yet he intended to write new material once his lengthy road trip was over and he'd recovered. "It's the longest tour I've ever done, and it's starting to take its toll," Roy said as he prepared to board yet another flight.

A week later, after a final show at the City Hall in Hobart and a two-night stand at the Sheraton Ballroom in Waikiki, Roy returned to Hendersonville, a lot wearier but a whole lot richer. "It was strenuous," Roy said, "but it was profitable. I really doubt if I'll ever consider doing it again. [But] the crowds were almost unbelievable."

It was time for Roy to take stock and plot his future.

CHAPTER 16

People started sort of rediscovering me

Roy spent much of the early 1970s in the shadows, running down the clock on his MGM deal, a contract that he'd been battling to extricate himself from for several years. "I tried to get out of that thing from 1970," he admitted. "But all that time I would go to Australia and I'd have a hit record." He'd seen a procession of presidents join and then leave the company in the wake of Robert H. O'Brien, who was in charge when Roy began recording for the label. It was clear that MGM Records was in a state of flux (and would be sold to PolyGram in 1972). When asked why he'd signed with them in the first place, Roy had an admission to make: "I was just too immature to know any better." He'd been seduced by the big money on offer, and the chance of a career in movies.

Roy had recorded some quality material during his eight years with MGM Records—"Ride Away" rated among his best songs and deserved to be a bigger hit. He'd also stretched his wings with "Southbound Jericho Parkway" and scored an international hit with "Penny Arcade." All in, Roy recorded eight studio albums—including *The Fastest Guitar Alive* soundtrack—and released more than twenty singles for the label. He was nothing if not productive, as his contract demanded. But it certainly didn't compare with his time at Monument, which he described as "five years of super success and a couple of years of nice success." Being an MGM Records artist was not the high point of his career. "They were good songs but not done all that well. They didn't do anybody any good for a while," said Roy. The only movie he made for the company, *The Fastest Guitar Alive*, was now relegated to screening on early morning TV in outposts like Greenville, South Carolina or Pottstown, Pennsylvania.

It was especially frustrating for Roy that an album of genuine substance, *One of the Lonely Ones*, was sitting on the shelf unreleased, while his three final LPs for the company—*Roy Orbison Sings* and *Memphis*, both released in 1972, and 1973's covers-heavy *Milestones*—had a steady supply of strong performances and songs, such as "Harlem Woman," where Roy really sang his heart out, and "Why a Woman Cries," but barely registered a murmur with the public. *Billboard* did, however, acknowledge that *Memphis* was "one of the best efforts that Roy Orbison has come up with in years," yet it just didn't sell. Roy didn't help his cause by focusing more on the UK and Australia than North America during the early years of the 1970s. As far as his home audience was concerned, Roy may have well been a ghost.

Roy's wife Barbara would state a little later that Roy's commercial drought and his withdrawal from the US music scene had an upside: It gave him time to focus on family. "The music in the Seventies had gone somewhere Roy really didn't really want to go," she said. "The Seventies he really enjoyed because I think he got to catch his breath."

Roy was approached, however, in late 1972 by the producers of a coming-of-age film titled *American Graffiti* who wanted to use "Oh, Pretty Woman" on the soundtrack. Roy rejected their offer, not because of the terms, but because he saw no music from Elvis Presley or the Beatles on the proposed track list. "If you're talking about the Sixties, you have to mention the Beatles," Roy figured, so he passed. But it did turn out to be a star-studded soundtrack and a triple-platinum smash, featuring music from Bill Haley and His Comets, Del Shannon, Buddy Holly, Chuck Berry, the Big Bopper, and many other stars of what was now being referred to as "the golden age of rock and roll." It was much more 1950s than 1960s, truth be told, so Roy's decision-making was askew.

Roy saw *American Graffiti* when it was released in August 1973 and gave credit to the film for kick-starting a nostalgia boom, grabbing the attention of music fans who "thought that whole era was a milestone of some sort." Roy may not have appeared on the soundtrack and probably still had issues with the word "nostalgia," but he gradually detected more interest in his work. "People started sort of rediscovering me."

Roy even agreed—perhaps reluctantly—to appear on *Dick Clark Presents the Rock and Roll Years*, alongside the Byrds, Tommy Roe, Gene Vincent, and Paul Anka, and he also hosted an episode of *The Midnight*

Special, which aired in February 1974. "Welcome to the solid gold show, with great songs from the Fifties and the Sixties," Roy, a vision in a powder-blue jumpsuit, announced a little stiffly to the gathering inside NBC's Burbank studio and a TV audience in the millions. (*The Midnight Special* aired directly after *The Tonight Show Starring Johnny Carson.*) Also on the bill was Del Shannon—he and Roy joked about how their live-wire fellow guest, Jackie Wilson, "was never gonna have an energy crisis"—as well as Bobby Vee, with whom Roy had once helped judge a Miss Teenage America quest. On air, Roy also related the story about how Duane Eddy, yet another guest, had pulled out of the Beatles' UK tour of 1963, "so I had to fill in for him. I think they could get me cheaper." Scripted patter didn't sit so comfortably with Roy, however. He looked much more at ease on set when singing and strumming "Dream Baby (How Long Must I Dream)," "Only the Lonely," and "Running Scared," which had the studio audience up and cheering.

Glen Campbell also helped Roy's cause when his cover of "Dream Baby (How Long Must I Dream)" had become a chart hit in the UK and North America in 1971. The song may have been written by Cindy Walker, but it was synonymous with Roy and his peerless voice. And more hit covers of Roy's work would follow in the future.

In 1974, Roy was finally able to switch labels, signing a one-record deal with Mercury Records. The label was headed by Jerry Kennedy, a friend of Roy's who'd played on "Oh, Pretty Woman" and "Mean Woman Blues." Roy's new labelmates were a very mixed bag. Among them were country act the Statler Brothers (not siblings, weirdly enough); Rod Stewart, a bottle-blond Brit with a raspy voice and an eye for supermodels; and Canadian rockers Bachman-Turner Overdrive. Roy, along with another new signing, country singer Jeannie C. Riley—of "Harper Valley PTA" renown—posed for the camera alongside Mercury president Irwin Steinberg for a photographer from *Cashbox*. "Mercury flashes," the magazine announced, heralding Roy's latest move.

In May, Roy was invited to perform at a high school in Potomac, as part of an event called "Where Were You in '62?" The turnout, according to a member of the Woodbridge Jaycees, who arranged the event, was "less than meager." There were rows of empty seats, stark evidence that Roy's drawing power remained weak. Roy had been forced to strip his touring band back to a basic four-piece, which included two Nashville twentysomethings, Joel Warren on piano and drummer Monty Mendenhall, as well as Terry Widlake and Alan Painter, who'd been playing with Roy for several years.

After the Potomac show, Roy bristled ever so slightly when asked what he'd been doing since 1962. "I've sold seventeen million records," he reminded writer Cyndi Young, while sipping a Coke and wiping his brow. Roy once again mentioned how he'd been "trying to get out of some contracts" but confirmed that yes, he'd just signed with Mercury.

A few months earlier, while on his latest successful Australian tour, Roy had been asked whether he was "slipping." He was, after all, nearing forty—a veteran in pop music terms—and his last two singles to make the charts in Australia, 1970's "So Young" and 1972's "Memphis, Tennessee," had only reached number 82 and 84 before quickly fading away. "Penny Arcade" they definitely were not. "Well," Roy explained, and not for the first time, "the only reason I haven't had a hit record lately is because I haven't recorded anything at all." That was about to change.

Roy finally emerged with a new song, "Sweet Mama Blue," in August 1974, a cowrite with Joe Melson, with whom Roy crafted his early hits for Monument. It was a curiously old-fashioned cut that nodded in the direction of the sleek, polished Nashville Sound that had been in vogue a decade or more earlier. Roy's voice was as strong as ever, but he sounded as though he was caught in a creative time warp. The song was "lacking the crispness and confidence of earlier Orbison material," in the view of *Crawdaddy* magazine. It certainly sounded nothing like the big-sellers of the moment, such songs as Eric Clapton's "I Shot the Sheriff," Roberta Flack's sultry "Feel Like Makin' Love" or "Takin' Care of Business," a hit for Roy's new labelmates Bachman-Turner Overdrive.

Roy traveled to Chicago to promote his new song and try and rebuild a relationship with the American media. Before being granted an audience with Roy, journalists had been given a grim warning by his new PR person. "Keep it clean," they were advised, "they tell me he's very religious. And don't mention the accidents. They really destroyed him." Yet Roy, wearing green-tinted glasses, a pack of Salems in his breast pocket, showed no obvious signs of distress when he greeted reporters, as Greg Mitchell wrote in *Crawdaddy*. "The voice is unbelievably soft, the manner unmistakably modest, the face unforgettably unique," Mitchell observed. "There is only one Roy Orbison."

Roy dined with select members of the press and Mercury execs at an upscale eatery on the ninety-first floor of Chicago's John Hancock Building, and a murmur began as soon as he took his seat. "That's Roy Orbison," announced a diner from a nearby table—clearly, not everyone had forgotten him. Roy smiled and resumed reading the menu, which was in French. "I'm generally satisfied with cheeseburgers," he laughed.

When chat at the table turned to contemporary music, Roy made it clear that right now, "nobody fractures me." His tastes, he confessed, currently ran to the middle of the road, such artists as Australian songbird Olivia Newton-John and Barbara Fairchild, a country-gospel artist who'd scored a country number 1 with the six-Kleenex weepie "Teddy Bear Song." A little earlier in the year, Roy had taken his family to see his old labelmate and friend, Elvis Presley, perform in Murfreesboro, Tennessee, and was disappointed. "It was terrible," Roy said afterwards. But he did retain fond memories of the man known as "the King." Roy regaled the Chicago gathering with a story about their first meeting, at a show in Memphis in the 1950s, when Elvis told him—"in the nicest form," Roy stressed—that "he would never work the same show I worked. Which was marvelous, whether he meant it or not."

Roy disliked the word "comeback" almost as much as he disliked the idea of being some kind of nostalgia act, but that seemed to be how this press blitz was interpreted. "It's not an attempt by me to make a comeback," he told a British reporter. "I hate to use the word. I'm making more money now that I did before." It must have been especially trying for Roy, given his ongoing success overseas as a touring act, to somehow have to validate himself all over again. His friend Del Shannon had the same problem, having just signed to the Island label and collaborated with Jeff Lynne of the Electric Light Orchestra. When asked if it was his attempt at a comeback, Shannon replied: "I've never been away."

As it turned out, Roy's "Sweet Mama Blue" wasn't a hit—it didn't even chart in Australia, where his music almost always connected. His manager Wesley Rose conceded that the failure of "Sweet Mama Blue" forced him to shut down a proposed US tour. "We thought we could ride the single," said Rose, who blamed "the people upstairs" at

Mercury for having "juggled the agenda" with Roy's first release for the label. But Rose hadn't abandoned Roy in any way—he remained a true believer. "I still look for Roy to be the world's biggest artist again," Rose insisted. "We're not jaded. We're very happy where we are."

Roy backed this up: "I don't have a burning desire to recreate what I've already done," he said. "[But] I think the best songs are yet to come—and the best performances. I can say that without any reservation."

Reviews of Roy's debut album for Mercury, *I'm Still in Love with You,* were as rare as radio play for his new material. Yet San Francisco–based *Rolling Stone*, which under the stewardship of publisher Jann Wenner had established itself as America's leading music magazine, did cover the LP—and perhaps Roy would have preferred that they didn't. For the first time in his career, Roy's voice came under critical scrutiny. "Once a prodigious instrument," Jim Miller wrote in the December 18, 1975 issue, "it now sounds shopworn, wobbly, a shadow of its former self." Another problem, according to Miller, was the work of producer Jerry Kennedy, who "takes a stab at duplicating the bolero buildup that producer Fred Foster used to such telling effect during Roy's Monument days. But the music lacks punch."

Bruce Springsteen, the rock and roll dreamer who'd opened for Roy in Nashville back in 1970, had name-checked Roy in "Thunder Road," a standout of his recent breakthrough album, *Born to Run*. And this was something that didn't escape reviewer Miller's attention. He felt that Roy might have benefited from the New Jersey singer-songwriter "invoking his name and influence," but that was not to be—*I'm Still in Love with You* was a flop, whereas *Born to Run* sold seven million copies. Springsteen featured on the covers of *Time* and *Newsweek* and became a superstar, a household name. As for Roy, he was currently referred to as "Nashville's mystery man," whom many people thought was either blind or retired, possibly both. Maybe even dead.

Springsteen, to his credit, never shied away from talking up one of his idols. He revealed that during 1974, prior to recording *Born to Run*, he'd devoted a lot of his listening time to *All-Time Greatest Hits Of Roy Orbison*, a Monument collection from the early 1970s. As Springsteen explained, he would lay on his bed, the lights very low, with Roy's best-known songs "fillin' my room . . . Roy's ballads were always best when you were alone and in the dark. They were scary, his voice was unearthly." Springsteen's fans would roar when he sang the line in "Thunder Road" about Roy "singin' for the lonely," even though many were too young to remember the golden voiced singer that Bruce was celebrating.

Roy, meanwhile, in 1975, had to resort to booking high school auditorium shows at places like Appleton West in Wisconsin, an event advertised as "A Concert for Lovers" (and a steal at $4 cover charge), where he was to share the bill with Joleen Benoit, a singer and former Miss Minnesota. The specifics of Roy's success—"Over 30 Million Records Sold"—which was printed on the handbill, felt more like a memory-jogger than a sales pitch. But this and a handful of other shows in the area didn't go ahead. Prior to a concert at Green Bay, Roy demanded full payment of his fee, rather than the usual process of receiving 50 percent in advance and the rest on show day. The manager of the auditorium, Michael Gebauer, argued with Roy and called him a "has-been." That was enough for Roy, according to Gebauer. "The man packed his bags and walked out the door."

Yet Roy remained a very bankable act elsewhere and undertook yet another successful string of dates in Australia during early 1975, his ninth tour of the country, which included four sold-out nights at the recently opened Sydney Opera House. "Roy Orbison is doing huge business," reported *The Sydney Morning Herald*. It was a dilemma—a well-paid one, admittedly—that Roy shared with such peers as Gene Pitney, Neil Sedaka, and Del Shannon, who were all reliable draws internationally, but virtually unemployable at home. In an intriguing coincidence, Don McLean, a fan of Roy's and someone who'd play a part in his future career revival, had performed at the Sydney Opera House the week before Roy.

While in Australia, Roy also took part in a meet-and-greet with prisoners at Pentridge, a maximum-security prison on the outskirts of Melbourne, where he'd played the year before. Roy was presented with a white toy koala bear and two portraits, one in oil, the other pencil, painted by inmates. "They're fantastic," gushed Roy as he posed for a photo with nineteen-year-old prisoner John Farrell, who'd discovered Roy's music on the prison's in-house radio station. Before leaving for a sold-out show at Festival Hall, Roy said that he felt a "sympatico" and "kindred spirit" with the jail's inmates. Roy's neighbor Johnny Cash, who'd recorded hit live records behind the prison walls of Folsom and San Quentin, must have been impressed.

Roy's association with Mercury Records was brief. It didn't last beyond the poorly received album and three failed singles, one of which, "Hung Up On You," was dismissed as "another throwback to the days of rock 'n' roll past" by the usually supportive British press. Dismissing his association with Mercury as a failure, Roy chose to head back to the past and re-sign with Monument, which now had a distribution deal with Columbia Records and had Kris Kristofferson, Dolly Parton, and Larry Gatlin on their artist roster. Despite making some less-than-flattering comments about Fred Foster since leaving the label for MGM, Roy was convinced that they could work together again—and maybe even re-create the magic of the early 1960s. "Fred and I are honest enough with each other that if we believed our time was past, we wouldn't have gotten back together," Roy explained.

A photo of Roy signing his new contract appeared in *Cashbox*, while Foster predicted a big, bright future when he spoke with a reporter from *Music City News* in February 1976. "Working with Roy Orbison was always a vibrant and unique experience," he said. "We're anticipating making many hit records." Roy's new deal with Monument was described as a "long-term exclusive recording pact," and he and Foster had already been in the studio, cutting a new track called "Belinda." It was written by Dennis Linde, who'd hit the jackpot in 1972 when Elvis's version of his song "Burning Love," which he'd knocked off in twenty minutes, hit number 2 on the Hot 100.

"We're getting close again to what is reality for me," Roy said somewhat cryptically when asked about rejoining Monument. He currently had yet another collection, *The Best of Roy Orbison*, riding very high in the UK album chart, while Jim Capaldi, the cofounder of English band Traffic, had recorded an up-tempo version of Roy's 1961 B-side, "Love Hurts" that, according to *Rolling Stone*'s Dave Marsh, "he sings almost as well as the original." It reached the top 10 in the UK and Australia. ("I loved the song," said Capaldi. "He was one of my all-time favorites.") A

Roy Orbison impression was now part of the repertoire of British TV comic Freddie Starr, who had his own show on BBC2. (Starr also "did" Gene Pitney and Elvis Presley.) Canadian singer-comic David Proud, meanwhile, did his own "Orbison act" on the Vegas circuit. It seemed that echoes—even facsimiles—of Roy were everywhere.

Roy had a new album planned for release later in 1976, to coincide, hopefully, with his first major US tour of the decade. But before that could happen, Roy went offshore again, revisiting the Sydney Opera House in March, for what was promoted as a "10th Anniversary" show. (It had been eleven years since he first visited the country, but who was counting?) Roy liked Australia so much he'd been considering building a rural hideaway for himself and celebrity buddies when they visited the country. Roy was shown a plot of land that was so vast the real estate agent described it as "bigger than Belgium." "I don't think I want to buy a whole country," replied Roy.

Then Roy flew to the UK, where his performance at the International Pop Proms in April just about brought the house down. Roy stepped onto the stage at the Granada Television studio, dressed in trademark black from head to toe, his sideburns now stretching to his cheekbones, a touch more flesh around his chin, and launched into "Only the Lonely," backed by a full orchestra. Though a little tentative at first—an orchestra could be intimidating, even for a singer as good as Roy—he soon found his groove, delivering a powerful "It's Over," the studio audience bobbing their heads in time with the emotionally charged music. Come "Oh, Pretty Woman" and he had the crowd completely under his spell, as they clapped along loudly and sang Roy's lyric almost as loudly as the man himself. Many were on their feet when Roy took a bow after his three songs, yelling for more—he looked genuinely thrilled when he returned for a final bow. Roy may have played thousands of shows to millions of fans, but this response was hard to top.

CHAPTER 17

You'll never see something like Roy Orbison disco music

Released in November 1976, Roy's first album under his new Monument deal ran for barely twenty-six minutes—it could hardly be called a long player. The record had its moments, such as Roy's take on Tony Joe White's "(I'm A) Southern Man," and "Something They Can't Take Away," which was written by Monument artist Kris Kristofferson, but it was hardly the chart-topping return that had been hoped for by Roy and Fred Foster. Roy later blamed a lack of studio time for its failure, stating, "I only had a few days to do the album." But the truth was that there was no genuine standout among the ten tracks that featured on the optimistically titled *Regeneration*.

Still, Roy was in fine form when he reached Detroit in late November for a rare US show at the Allen Park Civic Arena, where he was promoted as "the Lonely Man of Rock." Tellingly, Roy didn't perform any new material when he and his band, now expanded to a six-piece, stepped out for this and another gig in November '76 at Wisconsin's Sheboygan Armory. Instead, they stuck with a set of hits that stretched all the way back to "Ooby Dooby" (or "Hoobie Goobie," as reported by the proofreader-shy *Sheboygan Press*). "Give them the hits" was Roy's MO, and he did just that.

When asked why he wasn't playing shows in the big music cities—New York, Chicago, or LA—Roy explained that it harked back to his time growing up in Wink, a town that was rarely, if ever, visited by big stars. "I always said to myself that if I ever get successful, I'm going to play the smaller areas. We've been doing that." There was more to it, of course, because it was unlikely that Roy could fill venues in those larger cities, at least not right now. For the time being, despite his failed new album, Roy seemed to be reveling in smaller gigs like the Armory, so much so that he invited a twelve-year-old local named Jimmy Yurk, who he'd met at sound check, to work the lights. After the show, as the local paper reported, "Orbison had his whole band autograph two record albums and slipped his helper a $5 bill."

Roy crossed the border for some work later in November, and as a writer from the *Hamilton* (Ontario) *Spectator* noted, there'd been a shift in his audience—and not just with twelve-year-olds operating his lights. "A large portion of the crowd," observed critic Lyle Slack, "was in its late teens, early 20s. These are people who would have been between 5 and 10 years old when Orbison was at his peak. Yet they know the songs and they come."

"This isn't a revival for me," Roy said. "But I think there is a new interest in older performers like me. I still feel as young as ever." One thing he would never do, Roy made clear, was conform to current trends. "That's why you'll never see something like Roy Orbison disco music," he stated firmly. Then Roy slipped away into the night, heading off to the next gig.

In late May 1977, Roy played a one-off club show in San Francisco, at the Old Waldorf. After the concert, several members of the Eagles—who were experiencing massive success with their *Hotel California* album—came backstage to meet the man with the golden voice. Roy had been a huge influence on the band's music and in particular their 1972 hit "Take it Easy." Jackson Browne, who cowrote the song with Glenn Frey, revealed that the lyric in "Take It Easy" about a woman "slowing down to take a look at me" was their update on one of Roy's most famous lines, the unexpected about-face that closed "Oh, Pretty Woman." "Glenn's culminating line was perfect," said Browne. "He grabbed that line like Roy Orbison did on 'Oh, Pretty Woman.' [Frey] was a big Orbison fan."

When the Eagles met Roy at the Old Waldorf, they had a question for him: "When are you coming to LA?" Roy's mission was still to play shows in smaller cities and towns, avoiding the "music cities" like Los Angeles, but he agreed to a show at the Santa Monica Civic Auditorium on August 18. Advertised as "An Evening with the Legendary Roy

Orbison," it was a huge success, as Roy ran down the hits: "Only the Lonely," "Running Scared" (which went over so well he played it twice), "Blue Angel," and many more—they were "triumphant, emotional workouts," in the words of Richard Cromelin from the *Los Angeles Times*. "Orbison's performance essentially boiled down to two ingredients," he wrote, "an absolutely majestic voice and some great songs."

A few days later, Roy performed for 1,500 fans at Portland's Civic Auditorium and the response was equally enthusiastic. "Roy Orbison," reported *The Oregonian*, "is alive and well and performing in a puce-colored jumpsuit with white fringes and silver chains dangling from it . . . [and he] still brings tears to the eyes with 'Only the Lonely,' 'It's Over,' and 'Crying.'" Roy was thrilled by the response—there was momentum building, he could sense it. "That showed me that there was some sort of popularity there."

As well-received as these shows were, it was a bittersweet return to the spotlight. His friend, Elvis Presley, the man who said he'd never share a stage with Roy—for the best possible reasons—had died just days before his LA concert, on August 16. Presley was only forty-two. "Once you get on that road of abusing substances," Roy said of Presley's demise, "your judgment gets clouded." Roy felt his loss deeply.

"We were very close because we were the two from Sun who went more pop than country," said Roy. "We would send messages. We were very kindred souls, Elvis and I." Roy had caught up with Elvis in early December 1975. Presley had flown Roy to Graceland on his plane, the *Lisa Marie*, and later welcomed him from the stage at the Las Vegas Hilton, describing Roy to the audience as "one of the finest singers of all time." Yet perhaps Elvis's most telling tribute was that he didn't successfully cover any of Roy's songs. Roy had spoken with Presley around Christmas 1976 and Elvis said that he'd been trying to record "Running Scared" and "Crying," but "they just didn't jell." How could he improve on what Roy had achieved?

Roy was invited by Presley's family to pay respects to his former friendly rival at the Liberty Bowl football game in Memphis on December 19. After singing snippets of "Don't Be Cruel" and "Hound Dog," as part of the halftime tribute to the King, Roy began to make his way to the press box, but grew dizzy while scaling the stadium's steps.

"I feel quite strange," he told Barbara, who was waiting for him. "It is a long way," Roy pointed out, but clearly something wasn't right.

A few days later, Roy was in Hawaii and complained that he still wasn't feeling 100 percent, and checked into intensive care, where he was given the all-clear. But Roy was never a vision of perfect health—he was a lifelong smoker, fond of the occasional cheeseburger and Coke, and often appeared ghostly pale. When he and Barbara returned to Nashville, they met with his doctors, who advised him to "go home and watch the Super Bowl." Three days later, however, Roy still felt unwell and consulted a specialist at St. Thomas Hospital. Roy was given a worrying diagnosis: He had three clogged arteries dangerously close to his heart and required surgery. He was told that the operation would require the removal and transplant of three sections of healthy blood vessels from his lower leg.

Roy was very direct with his medical team. "Let's just get it on," he instructed them. A date of January 18, 1978 was set for surgery. Somehow, despite his prognosis, Roy hadn't lost his sense of humor—as he was wheeled into the theater, he turned to his surgeon with a last-minute request. "Make sure it's a clean, pretty incision. I perform with my shirts open pretty far down." Afterwards, Roy admitted that his doctor "thought I was bonkers." But Roy had dodged what may have been a fatal coronary.

While Roy recuperated at home in Hendersonville, his critical rebirth continued. By the late 1970s, there was no more bankable female singer on the planet than Linda Ronstadt. Born in Tucson, Arizona in 1946, and dubbed the "queen of country-rock," the powerfully voiced Ronstadt was a song interpreter rather than a writer, who gravitated toward the very best material—her cover of Buddy Holly's "It's So Easy" had been a number 5 hit earlier in 1977, while her take on the Everly Brothers' "When Will I Be Loved" climbed to number 2 during 1975. She dominated the reader-voted 1977 *Rolling Stone* People's Poll, claiming the Female Vocalist Award (over Stevie Nicks) and finishing runner-up to Fleetwood Mac in the Artist of the Year. Ronstadt even ranked number 3 in the poll for the Best Country Artist, just behind

Dolly Parton and Waylon Jennings. She was the only female act of her era capable of filling stadiums.

Ronstadt had once discussed Roy's voice with producer Fred Foster. Ronstadt asked Foster candidly what tricks they'd used in the studio: Surely no one could sing that high, she figured. Foster laughed. "He's hitting those notes," he assured Ronstadt. She was impressed.

Ronstadt was managed by expat Brit Peter Asher, one half of the 1960s pop duo Peter and Gordon, and it was Asher, along with songwriter JD Souther and Eagle Glenn Frey, who helped Ronstadt choose material. While "Blue Bayou" might only have been a B-side for Roy (and cowriter Joe Melson) in 1963, when it was suggested to Ronstadt, she knew it was a hit in waiting. In the winter of 1977, she recorded "Blue Bayou" in a relaxed, sensual style, for what would be her sixth studio album, *Simple Dreams*, with another Eagle, Don Henley, providing backing vocals. It was chosen as the lead single, quite the vote of confidence.

"I feel really good about 'Blue Bayou' being the single," Ronstadt told *Sounds* magazine. "All you have to do is recycle it. Really."

Ronstadt's instincts proved to be spot-on. "Blue Bayou" reached a peak of number 3 on the *Billboard* Hot 100 by Christmas Eve 1977, held out only by Debby Boone ("You Light Up My Life") and the Bee Gees "How Deep Is Your Love." It also reached second spot on *Billboard*'s country chart, number 3 on the easy listening chart, and number 3 in Australia, where Roy's original had been a chart-topper. Ronstadt's "Blue Bayou" sold more than one million copies in America alone, her first platinum record, and was nominated for two Grammys, including Record of the Year. Ronstadt liked it so much that she later recorded a Spanish-language version, "Lago Azul (Blue Bayou)." She even performed "Blue Bayou" on TV's huge rating *The Muppet Show*.

Roy was thrilled—and not just by the songwriting royalties. "It sort of makes me feel contemporary," he said. When asked if it was his favorite cover, he replied: "For sure"—and he positively beamed when he posed for a photo backstage with Ronstadt at New York's Lone Star Cafe. Roy sensed that a genuine rediscovery of his work was underway in America—this was backed up by a cover of Roy's "Oh, Pretty Woman" by rock and roll newcomer Johnny Cougar on his debut LP, *Chestnut Street Incident*. Cougar wasn't the only under-thirty performing

Roy's material—manic comic John Belushi had been pulling off a typically way-over-the-top rendition of "Oh, Pretty Woman" on *Saturday Night Live*.

Roy was made aware of Belushi's tribute by another SNL cast member named Laraine Newman and decided to call the program's producer. For a moment, there was a fear in the production office that he was going to threaten legal action—but that wasn't the case, which Roy made clear. "I love it," Roy told them. "It's terrific." Hugely relieved, the show's producers invited Roy onto the program to sing his hit with Belushi, but he let them know that he was on the mend from heart surgery. Perhaps some other time.

Post-surgery, Roy felt like a new man—he genuinely believed that his senses were sharper than they'd ever been. "I seem to think better now," Roy told *Rolling Stone*'s Scott Isler. "They increased the oxygen to the brain." He even felt that his voice, that golden instrument, was now somehow stronger. With Barbara hugging him from behind, Roy posed for renowned photographer Ken Regan, his surgery scar on full display. He certainly *looked* like a new man.

In July 1979, Roy appeared on the British TV show *Be My Guest*, singing "Crying" while strumming a white Fender and accompanied by a studio orchestra. Cutting a stylish figure in his fringed white jumpsuit, Roy's voice was in great shape. Roy seemed a little bemused as he spoke between songs with host Paul Daniels, who'd cheekily slipped him fifteen British pounds for his performance. "Are you sure you can afford this?" Roy deadpanned before leading the house band into a rock-solid "Oh, Pretty Woman." Roy managed to generate some genuine excitement among the middle-aged crowd, who clapped along enthusiastically while he played. British audiences couldn't get enough of Roy Orbison.

It was during this tour that Roy met Michelle Booth, a British woman who'd been attacked and thrown from a train, which left her in a coma. When told he was her favorite singer, Roy sent Michelle a tape, which she played constantly during her recovery. Roy recorded a message for her on the cassette: "Dear Michelle," he said, "this is Roy

Orbison. I'd very much like to wish you all the very best for the future health, wealth, and happiness. Okay?"

When she had recovered and returned home, Roy paid her a visit, arriving in a chauffeur-driven Daimler. They had tea, posed for some photos, and then Roy escorted Michelle to London, where she looked on as he recorded a radio session.

"I was dumbfounded," Michelle said. "It was so life-changing"—perhaps even lifesaving. Roy described his role in her recovery as "the biggest thrill."

In late 1978, Roy's period of record label bingo continued when he signed with Asylum Records, the home of the Eagles, Joni Mitchell, Linda Ronstadt—and Roy's old Sun labelmate, Jerry Lee Lewis. Roy's brief reunion with Fred Foster and Monument had been just that—brief. He requested a release and Fred Foster granted Roy's wish. "I was looking for [record] companies that were big and little at the same time, if that makes any sense," Roy said when asked why he'd signed with Asylum. He duly set to work on a new album, yet another stab at a commercial rebirth.

Just two years earlier, Roy had stated that "you'll never see something like Roy Orbison disco music." But perhaps 1979's funked-up remake of "Oh, Pretty Woman" by Frenchman Dick Rivers had changed his mind, because Roy's next recording misstep, an LP called *Laminar Flow*, veered dangerously close to the dance floor at times. When *People* magazine reviewed Roy's new single, "Easy Way Out," their critic was surprised, noting that it "sounds suspiciously like disco." "I couldn't tell you what disco is or isn't," Roy said. "We just found a groove and rocked right on." ("Easy Way Out" stalled at 109 on the *Billboard* chart.)

Roy had met one of his two new producers, Terry Woodford, while in LA: "He told me how great he was," Roy recalled with a laugh. "I said, 'Well, I'll come see you [play].'" Roy traveled to Wishbone Studios at Muscle Shoals in Alabama, where he met Woodford's partner Clayton Ivey and quickly learned that "he was a genius on keyboards." Roy began working with them in January 1979 and had the tracks completed by the middle of February. "My concept for an album," Roy said, "is to do everything from a beat ballad all the way up to a real rocker."

In May, upon the release of the LP, Roy sat down with the *LA Times*'s Kristine McKenna at the Beverly Wilshire. Dressed all in black—of course—and sporting a diamond ID bracelet, Roy, as McKenna noted with some surprise, "exuded a shy innocence that belies the seasoned showbiz pro he's proven himself to be." Between sips of coffee, Roy validated much of his past decade. "I haven't been suffering any sort of artistic block," he maintained. "I've been recording steadily for the past ten years, but nothing was released because I didn't feel comfortable with the label I was with."

This wasn't strictly true: *Laminar Flow* was his sixth studio album in seven years, although Roy referred to his earlier 1970s LPs as "semi-released," because they'd suffered from a lack of both exposure and interest. Nothing had registered with American radio programmers, or inspired Roy's longtime fans to seek out anything other than his many greatest hits collections, so his "semi-released" comment wasn't that far off the mark.

McKenna asked about "the Orbison mystique," most recently perpetuated by Bruce Springsteen's "Thunder Road," but the tag seemed to make Roy uneasy. "The 'Orbison Legend' became very worrisome to me for a while," he said, before steering the conversation elsewhere. "I never want to be the kind of person who says, 'Today's music is terrible.' It's not terrible, it's magnificent," Roy insisted. Even punk rock had its appeal. "If there's something innovative about it, I'm all for it."

But the same couldn't be said about *Laminar Flow*, named for an aviation term, a nod to Roy's model aircraft hobby. Roy had always been treated with respect by *Rolling Stone*—"Orbison delivered songs that broke the standard songwriting formula," David McGee wrote of his Monument classics, "and came on instead like mini-operas"—but that didn't prevent *Laminar Flow* from copping a brutal pasting in their August 23 issue.

"What riles me isn't so much that the LP is an embarrassing travesty ill-suited to one of rock's minor masters, but that such a debacle was totally unnecessary," barked critic Dave Marsh. He blamed the producers, Clayton Ivey and Terry Woodford, for creating "what may be the most soulless album ever recorded in Muscle Shoals. *Laminar Flow* is a whimper, not a bang." A reviewer from *Musician* magazine was equally appalled. "On *Laminar Flow*, Orbison's unique voice was pickled in soft-funk and disco (!) arrangements that sound more dated now than his older hits ever will." Or, as Peter Trollope half-joked in his column in the *Liverpool Echo*, "the thought of bumping into Roy Orbison full of Travolta flash on a disco floor is rather grotesque, but that's where he seems to be heading for." William Carlton, writing for the *Daily News* in New York, provided a rare positive review: "This collection of 11 tunes is an effortless and beautiful blend of screamers and ballads."

Not everything on *Laminar Flow* was drenched in synths and strings and slick grooves. One saving grace of the album was Roy's gently moving tribute to Elvis entitled "Hound Dog Man." At first, Roy was concerned that it would be mistaken for some kind of cash-in, but eventually agreed to cut the track when he felt that a reasonable amount of time had passed since Elvis's death. "It was long enough after all the exploitation," Roy explained. "Also, I've got credentials to sing it." Roy's decision was made easier when he was told that it had been written while Presley was still alive. "Hound Dog Man" was unusual for Roy; it was one of the few songs he recorded that he didn't care if it was ever played, or even heard. Roy called it "a private track," a personal exchange between he and Elvis, "just something I wanted to do." In his otherwise damning review in *Rolling Stone*, Dave Marsh singled out "Hound Dog Man," describing it as "probably the most moving Elvis tribute ever written."

Elvis's death had left its mark on Roy and it ran a little deeper than the heartfelt "Hound Dog Man," or his halftime tribute at the Liberty Bowl. But rather than worry about his own longevity, Roy had adopted a more philosophical approach to life. "I get this feeling now that what I want to do is gonna happen," Roy told a *Rolling Stone* reporter. "It's just a plain old down-home feeling. My home life is fantastic . . . I'm very content."

Roy and Barbara were considering a move to the West Coast. They felt sure that their children, including Alexander, who'd been born on May 25, 1975, would enjoy the sunshine and good life in Malibu. (Although Wesley would remain in Hendersonville with Roy's parents.) "I would like to have commercial success," Roy admitted to a reporter, "[but] it never was a super big thing with me."

If they did make the move, Barbara would have to give up a role she'd taken on as cochair of the Nashville Symphony Orchestra. Roy's career and contacts had its benefits, because Barbara solicited donations from Fred Foster and Wesley Rose to help support performances from the Symphony at Nashville's Opry House. "I'm not a musician," Barbara admitted, "but I'm interested in classical music."

After the critical and commercial beating dished out to *Laminar Flow*, Roy was in no hurry to return to the studio. When asked about the record by the *NME*, Roy sounded underwhelmed by the experience, which he described as "about a year and a half making an album, writing a couple of songs, negotiating, doing this, that and the other." Roy admitted that right now he preferred performing to writing. "The rewards are immediate," he said, whereas with songwriting, "You know it's a success when you get the checks." As it turned out, *Laminar Flow* would be the last album of original material that Roy completed during his life. He'd rather be out on the road, playing to the faithful.

When Roy turned forty-three on April 23, 1979, his father Orbie Lee called him.

"How old are you?" Orbie Lee asked.

"Dad, you know how old I am."

"No," he insisted, "tell me how old you are."

"I'm forty-three."

"You're almost as old as I am!" chuckled Orbie Lee, who was now sixty-six.

Orbie Lee, when not tour managing his son, had reveled in middle age, getting his pilot's license at forty-three and buying his first Harley at fifty-one. "He's still rockin'," Roy said, impressed by his father's zest for life. Maybe, Roy figured, he should be doing the same.

CHAPTER 18

There have been times when I felt like a prophet without honor in my own country

Roy saw in the new decade with an unlikely return to the big screen. Many of his peers had dabbled with acting in recent years, in some cases with great success. Willie Nelson acted in such Hollywood-goes-country films as *The Electric Horseman* and *Honeysuckle Rose*; Johnny Cash made a series of TV movies, while Dolly Parton produced a star turn in the box office smash *9 to 5*. Elvis Presley, of course, had made far too many mainstream Hollywood films during his life: some hits, some awful misses. There'd already been a made-for-TV Elvis biopic in 1979, starring Kurt Russell, as well as *Living Legend*, a low-budget film from 1980 that was a thinly veiled study of Elvis's later career. Roy contributed ten songs to the soundtrack, including cuts from *Laminar Flow*, but only about 100 copies of the album were pressed and distributed.

Roy, who could never lay claim to being much of an actor, agreed to a guest appearance in the screwball 1980 flick, *Roadie*, which starred Meat Loaf. Roy sang "The Eyes of Texas" in a roadhouse scene alongside Hank Williams Jr., stopping a wild brawl in the process, before disappearing into the night. It was unlikely to win Roy any awards, but it was a step up from *The Fastest Guitar Alive*. Roy's scene was shot at the Soap Creek Saloon in Austin, Texas. "It was fun," he assured Australian writer Glenn A. Baker.

Soon after, Roy was filmed in another roadhouse, this time on the hit TV show *The Dukes of Hazzard*, singing "Oh, Pretty Woman" after being snared in the "celebrity speed trap" set by Hazzard's top cop Boss Hogg. Roy did his best to keep his cool as a barely dressed Daisy Duke watched him intently, smiling and swaying while he played. Song over, Roy rejected an offer for a beer, offering an explanation: "I really need to get out of Hazzard County as soon as I can." He'd never delivered a line of scripted dialogue so convincingly.

As for the cottage industry that was Roy Orbison covers, it continued apace when Don McLean cut a version of "Crying." Roy was a little surprised; he felt that if anyone could cover that track successfully, it'd be a woman—perhaps it would be right for Linda Ronstadt, who'd done such a great job with "Blue Bayou." "It just seems logical to me," Roy figured. "A man's falsetto ending in a song that calls for full voice would be bad."

McLean, who'd met Roy at Johnny Cash's house after the 1972 Grammys, had recorded the song in 1979—and his motivation was very clear: "I recorded 'Crying' because I had a nervous breakdown in the Seventies, and I knew what it felt like to have that kind of emotional turmoil," he said. McLean understood the feeling of the song, but didn't try to replicate what Roy had already achieved. That way was madness. "Nobody can touch Roy's original record, of course. But I felt I could do something different with it, that would add to it."

Released as a single, McLean's "Crying" hit a US high of number 5 in March 1981. It was his second biggest hit after "American Pie," a 1972 number 1. It also reached number 1 in the UK, staying at the top of the singles chart for six weeks and selling a whopping 750,000 copies. "I heard Roy Orbison likes it," McLean said, which was hard to dispute—the royalties alone were huge.

Roy believed that successful covers such as McLean's "validated" his work, "in that some of them have become standards. As a songwriter, that's the best thing you can hope for."

Now fully recovered from his open-heart surgery, Roy returned to the road, but opted to focus mainly on North America. The tide was changing at home, Roy could feel it. "For years I didn't pay much attention to any place in the United States," Roy told a journalist from *The Tennessean*. "There have been times when I felt like a prophet without honor in my own country." But things were now different for Roy. "I started touring in America almost exclusively and realized that you could tour America forever, almost," he said.

Critics and audiences certainly seemed to have no issue with Roy's return to American stages. "Roy Orbison's hour came very close to perfection," reported *Trouser Press* magazine when he played the Town Hall in New York in early 1981. And it hardly mattered, as their writer noted, that Roy took the stage "looking like a vanilla popsicle in a black wrapper," because "the Big O stood motionless but for gentle guitar strumming and easily hypnotized the crowd."

Yet behind the scenes, Roy had business troubles. He was once again between labels, having recorded just the one album for Asylum. "Considering his still-awesome talent," noted *Trouser Press*'s writer, "that's criminal." But Roy had bigger problems: In early 1981, he instigated an audit of Acuff-Rose Publications and Acuff-Rose Artists Corp., which resulted in he and Barbara eventually filing a $50 million mismanagement suit in Davidson County, Tennessee against Wesley Rose and thirteen Acuff-Rose companies. The suit demanded $25 million compensation for lost songwriting royalties and a further $25 million in punitive damages. The Orbisons were also seeking to void Roy's publishing, management, and booking contracts with Rose and regain copyright to his songs. Their case went all the way back to 1958 and the publishing rights for "Claudette," which had been on the B-side of the Everly Brothers' hit "All I Have to Do is Dream." Roy had recently switched his concert bookings to the William Morris Agency, ending a two-decade relationship with Acuff-Rose Artists.

The wording of the thirty-six-page legal document was damning. It stated that Rose, Roy's "manager, confidant and trusted advisor," had "availed himself of plaintiff's ignorance for his own personal/financial gain." The Orbisons stated that Rose had misused this trust for personal gain, citing "double commissions" paid to Acuff-Rose from tour grosses and the 1965 publishing contract that Roy had signed when he was dealing with the fallout of his (brief) divorce from Claudette. The document stated that "Rose took advantage of . . . Orbison's mental state and financial condition by instructing him to enter into" that publishing deal. They also cited an instance of Rose overcharging them in an exclusive 1976 booking contract and a 1969 agreement between Rose and Barbara regarding her future interest in copyright renewals that they believed to be misleading. Their complaint alleged that Rose had instructed Roy not to trust any other music publisher, and that there was no need to read his contracts.

After more than twenty years with Acuff-Rose, it was a very messy situation.

Roy may have cut huge hit singles and sold millions of records, but he hadn't won a Grammy. Not one. It made no sense—Johnny Cash had six trophies on his sideboard, while Elvis had claimed seven Grammys during his life, yet Roy had just the single nomination, in the Best Rock and Roll Recording category, for "Oh, Pretty Woman," which was somehow "beaten" by Petula Clark's "Downtown" in 1965. This was about to change.

Fred Foster had introduced Roy to Emmylou Harris, a native of Birmingham, Alabama, who'd brilliantly covered "Love Hurts"—the flip side of Roy's 1961 hit "Running Scared"—as a duet with the late Gram Parsons. Roy visited Harris and her then husband Brian Ahern at their home, and the impression he left was indelible. "It was just one of those picking parties that happen sometimes," Harris told *Rolling Stone*. "I remember commenting that I'd probably never sell that house because Roy Orbison had sung in it."

As well as his brief cameo in the film, Roy had been asked to contribute a song to the *Roadies* soundtrack. He cowrote "That Lovin' You Feelin' Again" with Chris Price, a twenty-eight-year-old Oklahoman who'd played in Roy's band, and recorded it as a duet with Emmylou. An MOR ballad with a gentle hook, it was a handy reminder of Roy's musical roots. "I've never had a country hit," Roy mentioned to *Rolling Stone*, and although it didn't chart beyond number 55 in the Hot 100, "That Lovin' You Feelin' Again" was nominated for the Best Country Performance by a Duo or Group with Vocal at the 23rd Grammys.

At the event, staged at Radio City Music Hall in New York on February 25, 1981, Roy and Emmylou's competition was stiff: Their fellow nominees included the Charlie Daniels Band and Glen Campbell and Tanya Tucker. Nonetheless, "That Lovin' You Feelin' Again" was declared the winner, a first Grammy for Roy and a third trophy for Harris. "I'm in shock," Roy's cowriter Price said afterwards.

Spending time with Emmylou Harris had its moments beyond their shared Grammy. One night, Roy was chatting with Harris and Linda Ronstadt and a wild-haired thirtysomething whom he couldn't quite place. The man pulled Roy aside and said that he'd seen him play in Winnipeg in the early 1960s and his performance had inspired him to become a musician. "You really moved me," he said. He added that they'd spoken briefly on the night, when Roy stepped out of a motor home, trailed by his band the Candymen.

Roy said thank you and then the man left.

"Who was that?" Roy asked.

Emmylou Harris smiled and said, "That's Neil Young."

If turning up by chance in *The Dukes of Hazzard*'s favorite roadhouse wasn't peculiar enough, in the early years of the 1980s, Roy and his song "Oh, Pretty Woman" began appearing in the most unusual places. Roy's son Wesley was now a high school student and one day, he was approached by some classmates who had a question for him. "Did your dad write that Van Halen song?" As Wesley recalled, they seemed shocked when he told them that, yes, "Oh, Pretty Woman," which the hard rock band covered on their recent *Diver Down* LP and sometimes used to close their live sets, was written by his father. Not only that, but the song was almost twenty years old.

Although intended strictly as an album track, Van Halen's version was released as a single—its B-side an even weirder heavy metal take on the Roy Rogers theme "Happy Trails"—and rose all the way to number 12 on the *Billboard* Hot 100 during April 1982, further evidence of the enduring popularity of Roy's music. When asked why they'd chosen Roy's song, extroverted front man David Lee Roth had a typically quotable answer: "Van Halen is the world's most successful bar band in history, and 'Pretty Woman' is probably the most successful bar-band song in history."

In a bizarre mistake, the first pressing of the record made it to stores with the songwriting credit: "Orbison/Melson/Rush," which related to another song Roy had cowritten called "Pretty Woman," recorded in 1962 by Curtis Byrd and the Joe-Rag Singers. As Bill Dees, who *was* the cowriter of "Oh, Pretty Woman," recalled, "Acuff-Rose had to get Joe

Melson and Ray Rush to sign a form relinquishing their rights." Dees only learned about the error when his nephew bought the Van Halen record and pointed out the incorrect credit.

But this wasn't the only unexpected appearance of "Oh, Pretty Woman" in 1982. Roy rerecorded it for a national TV ad for Sasson jeans ("Sasson woman / the kind I'd like to meet"), which featured a cameo from the man himself. Roy uttered his immortal line "mercy" from the back of a car, glancing out the window, as the "Sasson woman" sauntered by. Although it'd be considered borderline stalkerish by twenty-first-century standards, the Sasson ad was tame when stacked up against the video Van Halen shot for "Oh, Pretty Woman," which was one of the first clips to be banned by MTV. Apparently dwarves fondling a captive transvestite didn't play so well, even on the very permissive cable network. "The plot," writer Lisa Robinson pointed out in Newark's *Star-Ledger*, "has absolutely nothing to do with the song."

Just to prove how versatile a song "Oh, Pretty Woman" truly was, it had been adapted by Henry Gwiazda, an assistant professor of music, for a composition he called "Mercy!" It was performed at the Walker Art Center in Minneapolis by the St. Paul Chamber Orchestra. "Sometimes, if I'm successful," Gwiazda said of this commingling of classical and pop styles, "you can't pin down where one ends and the other begins."

Not everyone was completely thrilled by Roy's return to the American live circuit and his return, of sorts, to the charts. In early February 1982, he played two concerts at a venue called Ziegfield's in Tulsa, and while the audience loved what they heard—his first show drew three standing ovations—a local music critic proved harder to please. Writing in *Tulsa World*, Tom Carter took aim at Roy's vocals ("the voice is gone, the power is absent") and his stage presence, which he felt "hints of a Steve Allen satire about the 1960s." (Roy wore an ebony jumpsuit with matching leather belt and plastic ebony love beads, perhaps not his best wardrobe choice.) While Carter fully acknowledged Roy's legacy, describing him as "a William Shakespeare of American rock 'n' roll," he also felt that he was "the Muhammad Ali of music. He just doesn't know when it's time to quit." As flattering as it appeared to compare Roy to the giants of the sporting and literary worlds—a rare double—Carter kept harking back to what he called "that ugly phrase 'has-been.'"

Admittedly, Roy was still stuck in the twilight zone between his legendary past and a present in which he hoped, somehow, to return to commercial relevance. Grammys and fawning audiences and hit covers of his songs were satisfying, as were the financial returns, but he hadn't been anywhere near the lively end of the *Billboard* Hot 100 since March 1966, when "Breakin' Up is Breakin' My Heart" reached number 31. And while he continued to fill big venues in Australia, Roy hadn't had a top 40 hit there in over a decade, since 1970's "Break My Mind," a song also recorded by Linda Ronstadt. It was a similar situation in the UK, where Roy hadn't charted since 1969's "Penny Arcade." Perhaps he was destined for the dreaded nostalgia circuit, playing his old hits to easily pleased audiences, much like the final act of Elvis Presley's career.

Yet this was of no consequence to *The Daily Oklahoman*'s Gene Triplett, who saw Roy in action at a venue named Henson's, his next 1982 show after Tulsa, or the crowd that gave him a standing ovation at the end of his set. "It's been a long time since the last hit single," Triplett wrote of Roy's concert, "but timeless originals like this man can rest on their laurels indefinitely. This was the finest rock 'n' roll performance to hit Oklahoma City in years."

The residents of Austin, Texas felt likewise when Roy filmed a segment for the renowned *Austin City Limits* program in early August 1982. Performing with a full band, featuring three backing vocalists, a black-clad Roy—with the exception of his white shoes—did what he did best, delivering a set of solid gold classics, played impeccably, and sung with heart and soul. And the audience inside Studio 6A on the University of Texas campus were with Roy all the way, bursting into spontaneous applause when he hit his first high note during the evening's opener, "Only the Lonely," and rarely letting up during his sixty-minute set, which included note-perfect renditions of "Leah," "Dream Baby (How Long Must I Dream)," "In Dreams," "Blue Angel," and "Blue Bayou." Roy delivered his songs like knockout punches, one after the other, hit after hit, rarely stopping for a breath.

By now, it was no secret that when onstage Roy would let his songs—and his supple voice—do the talking for him. What did he have to say, really? But every now and then during his *Austin City Limits* set, Roy's poker face would break into a gentle smile as the crowd's applause washed over him. "Thank you, thank you," he whispered after a dynamic "I Got a Woman," which featured one of Roy's trademark growls. The crowd, who were on their feet by the time of "Crying," loved it. Roy's *Austin City Limits* performance was released as a concert video in 1982.

Stellar performances like this were a feature of the early 1980s for Roy, as he balanced time on the road in America, England, and Australia with a quiet life away from the spotlight. "Roy drove the kids to carpools, he was very involved as a father," said Barbara. The Orbisons had decided to move to the coast and now lived a comfortable life in Malibu, in a property Roy described as an "unostentatious house high in the hills overlooking the beach." The driveway, like their former home in Hendersonville, was clogged with Roy's many cars, a Corvette and a Mercedes convertible among them. Roy would drive into town for groceries, go to the bakery, have breakfast, buy guitar strings at the mall, basically do mundane, normal things for perhaps the first prolonged period of his adult life. He once lived next door to Johnny Cash; now his neighbors included such celebrities as Rick Springfield, Ozzy Osbourne, Madonna, and Sean Penn. "I see them around some time," Roy casually mentioned, "and we say hello."

Roy was filmed in LA by a crew from *Lifestyles of the Rich and Famous*, "shopping for flashy fashions on trendy Melrose Avenue," and then at home with Barbara and the children. It seemed that Roy dressed in basic black even when reclining by the family pool. "I'm not really a recluse," Roy made clear. "It's very peaceful [here], it has a very calming effect. Being close to the ocean settles me down a bit." He and Barbara practiced Transcendental Meditation, while Roy had swapped his beloved soda for Evian and was working with a Hollywood personal trainer, Jackson Sousa, having been encouraged by his family to work on his fitness and health. "I'm a better friend and a better husband and a better everything," Roy insisted.

When not playing his own shows, Roy occasionally turned up at gigs. He stood backstage with members of the Oak Ridge Boys, with whom he'd toured, at a Bob Seger concert in Nashville during March 1983, when Seger dedicated his hit "Old Time Rock & Roll" to Roy. A few years further along, Roy and Seger would share the stage at the Grammys, presenting an award to U2.

Roy had also undergone what his former cowriter Bill Dees described as a "religious awakening" in the late 1970s. Roy made no secret of this—when he spoke with rock writer Lisa Robinson and was asked how he'd dealt with his many hardships, Roy replied, simply: "Faith in God." Bill Dees too had moved to Malibu, where he reconnected with Roy. "We were both believers," said Dees.

Roy's faith provided him with the necessary strength when Orbie Lee, his father and sometimes tour manager, died from a heart attack on December 5, 1984 at the age of seventy-one. Almost until the day his father died, Roy would still have to assure people that, yes, Orbie Lee Orbison was his dad's real name. "It's not a nickname," he'd say repeatedly.

Orbie Lee was laid to rest at Woodlawn, the same Nashville cemetery as Claudette and Roy's sons, Roy Dewayne and Anthony, and Roy's older brother Grady Lee, who'd died as a result of a car crash on November 26, 1973, aged just forty. His wreck occurred at Gallatin, close to where Claudette had been killed.

For the first half of the 1980s, Roy released no new music and remained between record labels. But he knew his time would come. "A lot of people are interested in me recording for them," Roy insisted, although he hadn't signed another deal—and wouldn't do so for some time yet.

As it turned out, Roy had other business matters to resolve. His lawsuit with Acuff-Rose, which was filed in August 1982, was eventually settled out of court in 1985, saving both parties a costly court battle (although Roy's legal bills were still considerable). While Roy's touring business was now managed elsewhere, in the summer of 1985, Roy signed a new publishing deal with Acuff-Rose. The arrangement would guarantee Roy $70,000 per annum for five years in exchange for at least ten "marketable" songs a year, as spelled out in the contract. Now all he needed was a record deal.

Roy had been fielding phone calls from Virgin Records for some time, asking him if he was interested in recording new material. Roy was starting to find the idea tempting, despite his disappointments with Asylum, Mercury, and also Monument the second time around. (Monument filed for bankruptcy in March 1983, ending Fred Foster's four decades as a successful independent.)

In fact, Roy was on a considerable upswing. With Barbara at his side—"We're a team," he said, "we're a duet, in a way"—he had recently adopted what *Goldmine* magazine described as "a new aggressive outlook on his career," hiring manager Jim Mervis, who'd learned the trade with Columbia Records, to look after his affairs. "A lovely man, a sweet man, a very generous man," Mervis said of his new client. Roy had also given LA's Triad Artists the role of booking his live work.

And Roy had been busy with one-off projects. He'd contributed a power ballad called "Wild Hearts Run Out of Time," cowritten with Will Jennings, for the soundtrack of the noirish Nic Roeg movie *Insignificance.* (It would later appear on Roy's 1992 posthumous album *King of Hearts.*) There'd also been whispers of a full-length project with hit-making Bee Gee Barry Gibb, with whom Roy—and Larry Gatlin—had just recorded a track called "Indian Summer" at Middle Ear studio in Miami. And Roy had recently rerecorded "Leah" with Bertie Higgins, the voice behind the yacht rock chart-topper "Key Largo."

Roy had even agreed, perhaps ill-advisedly, to a cameo in a short-lived ABC series called *Just Our Luck.* He was cast as the emperor of an alien planet whose anthem was "Oh, Pretty Woman," wearing an unflattering silver suit that made it seem as though he was clad in aluminum foil. "This is the strangest gig I've ever played," Roy dead-panned to camera. He wasn't kidding.

With Monument now out of business, Roy entered a studio in Sherman Oaks, California during January 1986 and rerecorded nineteen of his best-known songs, including "It's Over," "Crying," "Dream Baby (How Long Must I Dream)," "Oh, Pretty Woman," and "Running Scared." The collection of songs was self-released in 1986 as *The Great Roy Orbison*, and then rereleased by Virgin Records a year later as *In Dreams: The Greatest Hits.* Bruce Springsteen contributed liner notes, while T Bone Burnett, a lanky Texan who'd toured with Bob Dylan, helped with production, along with Roy and Michael Utley. "It was an incredible experience," wrote Paul Leim, who played drums on these new recordings.

But Roy's next move would take him even deeper into his storied past.

In the late summer of 1985, producer Chips Moman, who'd worked with Elvis Presley during his late-career resurgence, became the ringleader of a project designed to promote the musical heritage of Memphis. He reached out to Carl Perkins, Johnny Cash, and Jerry Lee Lewis, all alumni of the famous "Million Dollar Quartet," which had grown out of a Perkins recording session at Sun Studio three decades earlier. Moman's project was dubbed *Class of '55: Memphis Rock & Roll Homecoming*. Of course, Moman needed a "new" Elvis and got in touch with Roy. Because he knew the others like family, Roy agreed to participate.

Roy, Cash, Perkins, and Lewis would return to Sun Studio in September 1985 to record an album, which Moman would produce. Strictly speaking, it wasn't the first time the foursome had worked together—they'd performed "This Train" as a quartet on a 1977 TV appearance, *The Johnny Cash Christmas Special*, shot at the Grand Ole Opry House—but it was a momentous occasion nonetheless. *Bandstand* host Dick Clark would document the event for a TV special.

Roy, Perkins, Lewis, and Cash had a lot of shared history: They were all poor country boys when they first met at Sun, but things had changed by 1985 when they got together at the start of the project. Roy arrived in a chauffeur-driven limo, having jetted in from Malibu, where he'd recently settled into a new property on Sierks Way overlooking the Pacific. Johnny Cash reached Memphis on his tour bus, his initials emblazoned down the side. Jerry Lee Lewis, meanwhile, pulled up in what was described as a "flashy red and white sedan," while Carl Perkins was behind the wheel of a new white Mercedes, his golf clubs in the trunk.

A meet-the-press event was staged in Memphis's Peabody Hotel on September 16 at the beginning of a week that Perkins would describe as "very emotion packed." Roy and the others weren't quite sure what to expect, but when they entered the hotel's lobby, it was overflowing with media. Country musician Marty Stuart was in the mix, and as he recalled, "The place exploded. There was five minutes of applause, hollering, and tears."

Once the press conference was done, Roy and the crew got down to business with producer Moman. Roy had brought one particularly strong track to the sessions, "Coming Home," which he'd cowritten with JD Souther and Will Jennings, who'd started writing with Roy in the late summer of 1984. (It too would reappear on the 1992 posthumous release, *King of Hearts*.) Jennings had written "Up Where We Belong," a huge hit for Joe Cocker and Jennifer Warnes, and admired Roy enormously: "I just loved the cat, ya know? He had a royal quality, a princely quality. His spirit was strong." As for Roy's voice, which at least one critic had recently questioned, Jennings believed that it was as strong as ever. It was "as big as Texas," according to Jennings. As if to prove the point, Roy sang "Coming Home" beautifully and it was one of the standouts of an album that *Billboard* noted "effectively blend[ed] standards with worshipful derivatives."

Inside Sun Studio, Roy, Perkins, Cash, and Lewis paid their respects to Elvis during a heartfelt ballad called "We Remember the King." The famous four shared a single microphone as they sang about their old friend and Sun labelmate. While they listened to the playback, Perkins turned to the others and said, "God, I love you all." The four men embraced, tears clouding their eyes. "Elvis is with us in spirit," Roy said afterwards. "I wish he was here with us. Wonderful fella."

CHAPTER 19

I was aghast, truly shocked

As stipulated in his new contract, Roy's second $10,000 payment from Acuff-Rose was due on June 8, 1986, but there was a problem. According to Acuff-Rose, Roy failed to deliver the ten "marketable" songs he'd agreed upon and he was advised that they were withholding the advance. Acuff-Rose's representatives believed that Roy had been copyrighting the songs he did write with Orbisongs, his own music publisher, and they were considering legal action. (Acuff-Rose sued for more than $1 million in 1989, after Roy's death.)

But Roy had other distractions at the time, in particular a controversial new film that featured one of his best songs performed in a totally unexpected manner. The movie was *Blue Velvet*, which was being shot in North Carolina while Roy was involved with the *Class of '55* project. *Blue Velvet* was a genuinely perverse thriller, starring Kyle MacLachlan, Laura Dern, Dean Stockwell, and Dennis Hopper and directed by David Lynch. As anyone who'd seen Lynch's previous films *Eraserhead* and *Elephant Man* would attest, the eccentric director was no stranger to on-screen weirdness, but *Blue Velvet* came on like a cinematic nightmare.

In one pivotal moment—described by Lynch as the "eye of the duck scene"—a primped and preened Dean Stockwell, playing a drug dealer and bordello owner, mimed Roy's "In Dreams." He used a lamp as a microphone and elicited a series of bizarre reactions from Hopper's Frank Booth, who was obsessed with the song. "Let's fuck!" Frank roared. "I'll fuck anything that moves!" Roy's song also played on Frank's car stereo when he drove MacLachlan's Jeffrey to a remote spot and beat him savagely.

When asked about his relationship with Roy's music, Lynch explained that he was in a taxi with MacLachlan, driving through Central Park, when "Crying" came on the radio. The film at this point was still in preproduction. "That could go on *Blue Velvet*," Lynch thought to himself. He bought a copy of one of Roy's greatest hits collections and changed his mind when he listened to "In Dreams." "If ever there is a song that fits in this film," Lynch figured, "this is the song. It grew out of that." At first, Roy rejected the idea—he was very protective of the song—but Lynch called him and said that it was crucial to the movie. Only then did Roy agree to its use.

The film was released in September 1986 and immediately caused a huge stir—the *LA Times*'s Sheila Benson declared it as "the most brilliantly disturbing film ever to have its roots in small-town American life." Roy decided to see what the fuss was about and ducked into a Malibu cinema without being observed. Then the lights went down. "Oh, God," Roy said of the experience. "I was aghast, truly shocked." Many of his songs had appeared in movies before, but none had been used quite like this. This definitely wasn't *The Fastest Guitar Alive*.

Lynch, by his own admission, was a rusted-on fan—"I loved Roy Orbison from the first time I heard his music. I grew up with Roy Orbison"—but he didn't get to meet Roy until after the film was released. During their time together, Lynch learned just how significant the lyrics of "In Dreams" were to Roy, who admitted that he disliked *Blue Velvet* on first viewing. But, as Roy also explained to Lynch, he'd changed his opinion since that afternoon in a Malibu cinema. A friend had suggested that he watch it again, which he did one night on his tour bus. "I really got to appreciate it," said Roy. "*Blue Velvet* really succeeded in making my music contemporary again." According to Barbara, Roy came to understand the film and "he could see that it was just confronting the dark side."

Roy's "In Dreams" was a feature of the film's official soundtrack, which also included music from Julee Cruise ("Mysteries of Love") and frequent Lynch collaborator, composer Angelo Badalamenti. Lynch would work again with Roy, adding his song "Crying" to the soundtrack of his movie *Mulholland Drive*.

Roy and Lynch also spent time together when the opportunity arose for Roy to rerecord "In Dreams" for release as a single, with an accompanying video. Lynch was in the control booth when Roy was cutting his vocal, and he asked the engineer if there was a quiet space he could use. As Lynch reached for the door, Barbara Orbison asked what he was doing. When he told her he was going to meditate, she pulled him up.

"Roy and I do TM," she said. "We're going with you."

Roy had entered the phase of his career where, like so many of his peers, he spent a good chunk of his time graciously receiving awards, many of them long overdue. He'd finally won his first Grammy in 1981, followed by another in 1987, for Best Spoken Word, which he shared with his *Class of '55* alumni, Carl Perkins, Johnny Cash, and Jerry Lee Lewis, specifically for the interviews they undertook as part of the Memphis project. Roy was inducted into the Nashville Songwriters Hall of Fame in 1987, even though, as he admitted, "I've never had a country hit." And in 1987, Roy was in line for another impressive gong.

The Rock & Roll Hall of Fame had been opened in Cleveland, Ohio in 1983. It was the brainchild of Ahmet Ertegun, the founder and chairman of Atlantic Records, with the assistance of such key industry players as Jann Wenner, the publisher of *Rolling Stone*, and Sire Records founder Seymour Stein. Three years later, the Hall of Fame began inducting honorees. The original inductees, the "Class of 1986," featured such innovators as Chuck Berry, Bill Haley, Ray Charles, and the Everly Brothers, and Roy was thrilled when he was told he was among the following year's intake. His fellow inductees included Carl Perkins, his longtime friend, and Ricky Nelson, who'd also contributed to the *Class of '55* Memphis project. The ceremony would be held at the Waldorf-Astoria in New York on January 21, 1987.

Perkins, who was sharing a table on the night with Roy, was inducted by Sun Records founder Sam Phillips. Looking just fine in a tailored suit, his tinted glasses firmly in place, and wearing blue suede shoes (of course), Perkins took the stage and spoke about how big a thrill it was to be honored in this way, "and what a night it is for a sharecropper's son to stand here in this beautiful building." When Perkins returned to the table, Roy leaned over and said, "I'm proud of you, Carl. I wish Elvis had lived to experience this."

Then Roy moved to the wings as Bruce Springsteen stepped up to the dais. The thirty-seven-year-old superstar spoke about his first close encounter with Roy at Nashville during the summer of 1970, when he looked on in awe as Roy played what Springsteen described as "some dark music." Springsteen also described how it felt to be a young man playing Roy's greatest hits, alone in a darkened room, letting songs like "It's Over" seep into his very soul. Springsteen also had a confession to make. Over the years, he'd come to recognize that even though he'd love to be able to create the same musical magic as Roy's best work, that was simply impossible. "Most of all," Springsteen said in closing, "I wanted to sing like Roy Orbison. Now everybody knows that nobody sings like Roy Orbison." The crowd stood as one and applauded long and loud as Springsteen ended Roy's induction with a growl and a "mercy!"

Roy was genuinely thrilled by the speech. "I thought Bruce Springsteen was just going to say, 'Ladies and gentlemen, da da, ya know?'" Roy said afterward. "Anyway, he went into this soliloquy almost . . . I was really touched, really deeply moved. I felt I had been truly recognized." *The Washington Post* clearly agreed, because they ran the full text of Springsteen's speech in their February 1 edition.

After the induction formalities, Roy jammed "Oh, Pretty Woman" with Springsteen, Bo Diddley, B. B. King, and numerous other inductees and musicians on a very crowded stage. It was shambolic, as these all-star jams tended to be, but the mile-wide grin never left Springsteen's face as he traded vocals with Roy. It wouldn't be the last time Roy and Bruce Springsteen shared a stage.

In the wake of Roy's Hall of Fame induction, the support of such boosters as Springsteen, and the attention given to *Blue Velvet*, the Orbisons decided that it was time for a new recording contract. As Barbara later revealed, an exec named Jordan Harris had been calling them repeatedly, and Roy agreed to a deal with Virgin Records America. It helped considerably that Virgin's US head, Jeff Ayeroff, was a huge fan of Roy and his work. After seeing *Blue Velvet*, Ayeroff firmly believed that the film "made Roy's music current again."

"I have re-found my drive and love for the business," Roy announced after signing his contract.

It was agreed that his first Virgin release would be titled *In Dreams: The Greatest Hits*, which compiled all of Roy's recent rerecordings that he made a year earlier, including his new version of "In Dreams," and was scheduled for release in May 1987. (Roy had rerecorded these nineteen songs fearing that Monument would destroy the original recordings if their legal dispute wasn't resolved, leaving his classics lost forever.)

Sarah McMullen was a publicist for Virgin America. "There was a lot of interest in him, but also a lot of misconception," she said when news broke of Roy's new deal. The Virgin strategy was to invite writers to Roy's shows, so they could get a sense of what he could still accomplish live. The move worked, as McMullen revealed: "They came away talking about his voice. They didn't think of him as a Sixties act anymore." When Roy performed at the Burbank Center for the Arts a few days after the Hall of Fame bash, 3,100 fans snapped up tickets for two sold-out shows. "Orbison still rocks and rolls," wrote Dan Taylor in the (Santa Rosa, California) *Press Democrat*, "using his dramatic, immediately identifiable voice the way other rockers use lead guitar . . . fans applauded when Orbison hit a high note, as they might for an opera diva." Onstage, Roy was in a buoyant mood, joking with the audience: "We've had a lot of requests tonight, but I'm going to sing anyway."

Finally, it appeared that Roy was no longer seen as a man past his prime. His next trick was to find the right studio partner. As Roy explained, "I want a producer I can work *with*, not be produced by." Roy had been busy, writing with Rodney Crowell, a Nashville-based singer-songwriter, and Steve Jones, a former Sex Pistol now living in America. They may have seemed like an odd pair, but Roy had no issues whatsoever with Jones's punk past, or the way he rolled up to his house on his Harley, a guitar slung over his shoulder. "A good songwriter is a good songwriter," Roy told the *Arizona Republic*. "It struck me how similar we were. He's a really personable fellow."

Roy had also worked with hard rocker Glenn Danzig on a song called "Life Fades Away," which appeared on the soundtrack to the 1987 movie *Less Than Zero*, and later as a bonus track on the *King of Hearts* LP. "Roy was really cool," said Danzig. In the studio, Roy noticed that Danzig didn't bring a guitar, so he offered him one of his. Danzig was impressed by the instrument and asked Roy what it was worth. "About $3,000," Roy replied, at which point Danzig immediately put the guitar back in its rack. "No, no," Roy insisted. "Guitars are meant for playing."

"Life Fades Away" was produced by bearded studio guru Rick Rubin, who'd work with Johnny Cash on his revered *American Recordings* series of albums. (Danzig too would work with Cash.) Although Roy had sworn off drinking soda, he asked for a Coke while working on "Life Fades Away" and Rubin obliged. As the producer revealed to *Rolling Stone*, "He'd never made a record in his whole life without having a Coke. This wasn't going to be the first one." Rubin, like Danzig, was charmed by Roy's good manners—most singers he worked with swore like sailors when they messed up, but not Roy. "When Roy would make a mistake," Rubin laughed, "he'd go, 'Mercy.' 'Mercy' was his big line."

While still on the lookout for the perfect producer, another prime—prime-time, perhaps—opportunity arose for Roy, a pay-per-view concert video for Cinemax. Barbara and Texan musician T Bone Burnett had pitched the idea to Stephanie Bennett, the wife of Roy's former manager Jim Mervis, who produced the *Cinemax Sessions* series. She agreed to work with Roy on the project.

There was a successful precedent. In October 1985, Carl Perkins had broken new ground when he was the star of a similar production for Cinemax. Titled *Blue Suede Shoes: A Rockabilly Session*, Carl was surrounded on a London soundstage by friends and admirers, including George Harrison, Paul McCartney, Eric Clapton, Roseanne Cash, Dave Edmunds, and members of rockabilly revivalists the Stray Cats. Together they blissfully worked their way through Perkins's many classics. The video was a commercial and critical hit and helped remind the wider world just how big an innovator—and an influence—Perkins was. Roy made a cameo during the preconcert segment of the video, where he spoke about his relationship with Perkins: "He's a wonderful, sincere man. I love him. Always have and always will."

Roy and Barbara hoped to create the same kind of magic with their Cinemax project, titled *Roy Orbison and Friends: A Black and White Night*, which would be filmed at LA nightclub the Cocoanut Grove. Situated inside LA's Ambassador Hotel, the Cocoanut Grove, which opened in 1921, was once known as Hollywood's "first playground of the stars," where movie greats and fellow A-listers could go about their private business away from the glare of the paparazzi. Bing Crosby had been discovered at the venue, while scenes from the 1947 and 1954 versions of *A Star Is Born* were filmed there, and it was sometimes used as the site for the Academy Awards. Frank Sinatra, Nat "King" Cole, Judy Garland, and Barbra Streisand had all graced the Cocoanut Grove's stage.

But by September 30, 1987, when Roy fronted Cinemax's cameras and an audience peppered with A-listers, the venue was past its prime. Roy's concert would prove to be the last major event staged at the Cocoanut Grove; the doors would be closed for good two years later. But none of this mattered to Roy and his sixteen-piece all-star ensemble who, for one night at least, managed to bring the Cocoanut Grove back to life.

However, there had been problems during the final rehearsal for the show. Backup singers were coming in at the wrong times, while the numerous guitarists were still searching for the right licks—it seemed as though everyone was struggling to find their place. Sensing this, Roy spoke to the ensemble during a break. "The main thing for me," he explained, "is that it's a thrill for me that you guys are here. I'm grateful that you came by to help out." Roy's wise words did the trick—when the cameras began rolling, the musicians had found their groove.

The show opened with "Only the Lonely," the cameras of producer Stephanie Bennett and director Tony Mitchell zooming in and around Roy, making it abundantly clear that he was the main event. Lighting designer Lee Rose gave the set—and Roy—a strikingly retro feel, a natural fit for the black-and-white film that was used to shoot the concert. In a black fringed jacket, his favorite Maltese cross around his neck, and having shed a few pounds, Roy looked great. The cameras loved him.

Bonnie Raitt, k.d. lang, and Jennifer Warnes, who were among the six backing vocalists, all watched Roy intently during "Only the Lonely," smiles lighting up their faces. Seated stage left, strumming guitars, were Elvis Costello and Bruce Springsteen—dressed almost identically as on the cover of his album *Tunnel of Love*—who were also clearly enjoying the moment. Tom Waits sat in on organ, looking very much like Schroeder from the *Peanuts* cartoon strip, a study in concentration, his hair a wild mess. This was a love-in, a gathering of the Roy Orbison Appreciation Society. "We were like disciples in a way," observed k.d. lang, who'd record a wonderful "Crying" single with Roy for the film *Hiding Out*. "I can just remember feeling like somebody who was really there working for the man."

"Dream Baby (How Long Must I Dream)" was early in Roy's set, and already the audience, who were seated close to the stage, supper-club style, were totally engaged, clapping along as Springsteen shared a mic with Roy during the chorus. As the song neared its end, Roy slowed everything down, then looked at Springsteen, who, after a pause, uttered a growl and brought the band back in to finish with a bang. It was a great moment, completely natural and spontaneous. "Ooby Dooby," meanwhile, featured Springsteen and James Burton, one of four former Presley sidemen playing with Roy on the night, trading guitar licks, Roy looking on like a proud parent. When the time came for a loose and funky "Go! Go! Go! (Down the Line)," Roy was now in the front line, swapping licks with Burton and Springsteen.

"Uptown" was another feature—the first and only live recording of the song—as Elvis Costello, stage left, blew some harmonica, while Springsteen again shared vocals with the Big O. He was the only musician to break protocol on the night and venture into Roy's zone center stage, but it was done with absolute respect. For Springsteen, this had to be more fun than living up to such tags as "the future of rock and roll" and the "new Dylan." He was having a blast—or, as one reviewer put it, he looked "positively enthralled beside his boyhood idol." (At one point, off camera, Springsteen turned to Roy and whispered, "Should I be nervous?" "No," Roy assured him, "you let me handle that.")

T Bone Burnett, who'd recently been in the studio with Roy, stepped up to the microphone after "Blue Bayou." He informed the crowd that they were about to play a new song "that Orbison just recorded," called "The Comedians." "It was written by Declan MacManus," Burnett chuckled, referring to Costello by his birth name. The track was an overly wordy slow burner, a brave attempt to replicate Roy's Monument-era sound, accurately described by *Musician* magazine as "Elvis Costello's turn at a Roy Orbison song." (It was, however, included on Roy's 1989 posthumous album *Mystery Girl*.)

Although appreciated by the crowd, it was the standards that really lit up the room, such as a stellar "In Dreams," a song enjoying a brilliant second coming thanks to *Blue Velvet* and David Lynch, who was looking on from the audience (as was Billy Idol, Kris Kristofferson, Patrick Swayze, and various other celebrities). By the time of "Crying," Roy had the crowd and his supporting musicians transfixed, his voice as supple and emotionally powerful as ever. He blew a wild blues harp during "Candy Man," driving the band hard—even though Roy, possibly the coolest man to ever strap on a black Gibson guitar, barely broke a sweat. During a sublime "It's Over," if someone dared drop a pin, you could have heard it as Roy's voice, and the song itself, built to a mighty climax. The natural closer was "Oh, Pretty Woman," Roy delivering his "mercy" punch line with a wry grin, the crowd roaring their approval.

The next morning, just before 8 a.m., a 5.9-magnitude earthquake rattled the Cocoanut Grove and the surrounding Whittier section of LA. In the ballroom where Roy had performed, several chandeliers collapsed, smashing into the containers that stored the 35mm film footage of the concert. In what must have been some kind of blessing from the musical gods, nothing was damaged, although it took twenty-four hours before the tapes could be found amid the rubble.

Roy Orbison and Friends: A Black and White Night was first broadcast on January 3, 1988 and critical response was positive. Extremely positive. "Roy Orbison shines in Cinemax concert show," declared the *Honolulu Star-Advertiser*. "Orbison's singing is as beautiful and unsettling as ever." *The Tennessean*'s Thomas Goldsmith was also impressed: "A crowd of stars surround Roy Orbison," he wrote, "but he stands head and shoulders above them all." The *San Francisco Chronicle* went one step further—by their estimation, *A Black and White Night* was "one of TV's finest concerts ever."

The *Black and White Night* video was a big hit when released commercially by Virgin. It sold 50,000 copies in the USA and did similar business in the UK, but in Australia, where the love for Roy had never faded, it shifted a whopping 165,000 units. "It's a classic," stated Melbourne newspaper *The Age*, "featuring Orbison leading a stellar ensemble."

"I'm a bit overwhelmed," Roy said of *A Black and White Night*. "I'm very grateful that all these wonderful people came by to help me out." Roy made his feelings very clear to the *LA Times*'s Robert Hilburn when he said: "This has to be one of the greatest moments in my life."

CHAPTER 20

If I'm just remembered, that'll be okay by me

A Black and White Night was a great celebration of Roy and his music, but if he was to stage a full-scale comeback, he needed new music in the market—even a hit, if that was possible. But exactly how was he to achieve that at a time when the charts—and the all-important MTV—were dominated by the likes of George Michael and INXS and Whitney Houston, acts with whom Roy had nothing in common? Perhaps the best thing Roy could do was to stick with the style and the sound that had served him so well during his golden run in the 1960s. For that he needed an empathetic producer, someone with both an understanding of Roy's work and an ability to make modern-sounding records.

As it turned out, Roy employed several producers for his new record, which, as T Bone Burnett mentioned during *A Black and White Night*, was already underway. In March 1988—while Roy was guest of honor at New York's Hard Rock Cafe before appearing at the Grammys—news of the project broke in the press. One writer joked that perhaps it should be called "My Little Fan Club," due to the involvement of Springsteen, Elvis Costello, Bono from U2, and the Eagles' Glenn Frey. Roy and his new record company hoped the album would be released by the summer of 1988.

Speaking of fan clubs, in early April 1988, Roy played a show at Celebrity Theater in Anaheim. In the audience were Jeff Lynne, Tom Petty, and George Harrison, three of his biggest admirers, who were in the process of teaming up with Roy in what would be dubbed "the ultimate supergroup" by *Rolling Stone*—the Traveling Wilburys.

It all began in the most inauspicious way. Harrison needed to record a B-side for the European release of "This is Love," a single from his successful 1987 record, *Cloud Nine*, which he'd coproduced with Lynne. Harrison, who was in LA overseeing the film *Checking Out*, a production of his HandMade Films company, intended to write, record, and produce a song during his one free day. He organized dinner with Lynne—who'd been recording with Roy in LA and invited him along—and laid out his plan. Over dinner, Harrison asked Lynne if he'd like to help. But there was one problem: How could they find an engineer and a studio overnight?

Roy had been taking this in and said, "I'd like to come along and watch."

Harrison agreed in a heartbeat. He and Roy had become good friends during the ensuing twenty-five years since Roy's first tour of the UK, when he stood outside a theater and asked, "What's a Beatle?" In particular, they bonded over Brit comics Monty Python, whose various members Harrison had worked with across several movie projects for HandMade Films, including *Life of Brian*. "Roy knew every word to every Monty Python song and the dialogue in all the movies and the TV series," Harrison told a writer from *Rolling Stone*. "He had a great sense of humor."

During dinner, Harrison remembered that Bob Dylan had a studio in the garage of his LA home. Like Roy, Dylan lived in Malibu. A couple of years back, Roy had been a guest of Dylan's at the Whitney Museum in New York, when Dylan's *Biograph* box set had been released. When they were photographed together, Dylan cracked a rare smile. They were good friends, fellow travelers.

Harrison called Dylan, who confirmed that his studio was free. On his way home after dinner, Harrison dropped in on Tom Petty, who had one of his guitars. A few months back, Petty had cowritten a song with Roy and Lynne that they called "You Got It," destined for Roy's solo record. (The trio also cowrote "California Blue.") Harrison asked Petty whether he was busy and spelled out his plans for the following day.

"I was wondering what I was going to do tomorrow," said Petty, who was in the midst of a solo project with multitasker Jeff Lynne. “I’ll come.”

Later that night, as Harrison began writing a song for the session, he had a revelation: “If Roy Orbison’s going to come, it’s silly to have him just sitting there. He’s a better singer than anybody.” He duly wrote a small vocal part for Roy.

Before they set to work, Dylan hosted a barbecue for his guests. As they ate, Harrison played the others a sketch of the song he intended to record and challenged them to contribute lyrics. When Dylan asked him what it was called, Harrison spotted the “Handle with Care” warning on a box in the garage, and a song title was born. It was at this point that everyone, Dylan included, agreed to sing on the record. When Roy stepped up the mic, according to Tom Petty, “We all just couldn’t believe it. No one could ever make a sound like that.”

Harrison took the finished song—a catchy, hooky acoustic-pop ditty, featuring a flawless vocal from Roy—to a meeting with Mo Ostin and Lenny Waronker, industry kingmakers from his label, Warner Bros. They could hardly believe what Harrison had in his hands. But as great as it was, they also knew this: “Handle with Care” was too good a song to bury away on an extended play European release. It also wasn’t a *Cloud Nine* track, so it served no purpose in promoting Harrison’s new record. Harrison kept the tape and figured, “If we did that song in one day, if we had another nine days we could make an album.” Maybe it wasn’t a one-off. Lynne and Petty agreed, as did Bob Dylan.

Harrison, Petty, and Lynne laid out their plan for the Wilburys album after Roy had finished his Anaheim gig.

“We want you to be in our band,” they asked Roy.

“Sure,” Roy replied after a beat, “sounds like a lot of fun.”

“All the way home,” Petty recalled, “we were going, ‘Roy Orbison’s in our band!’ I don’t think we ever got over it.”

As informal as the Wilburys project was, there was some haste involved: It was spring and on June 7, Dylan was set to begin what became known as his Never Ending Tour. He’d stay on the road until late October, so they needed to complete the album quickly. Roy had a string of dates booked across the country, so his time too was in short supply. He also had to complete the comeback album he'd been working on with Lynne, as well as Mike Campbell from the Heartbreakers—whose garage studio they used—and T Bone Burnett, under the guidance of Barbara Orbison, who'd been closely involved with the LP.

Dave Stewart from Eurythmics had a studio in Encino and he agreed that the supergroup could use it to record their first record. They started work in May. The atmosphere was very relaxed and natural, even with a film camera capturing the action for a making-of documentary. Guitar parts were recorded in Stewart's kitchen and people wandered in and out as the famous five went about their business.

In-demand drummer Jim Keltner, rechristened Buster Sidebury, sat in on the sessions, and when he first stopped by Stewart's home, the Wilburys were seated together on the front porch, having a fine old time. Right away, Keltner sensed something: "They were obviously all there because of Roy." Roy was sporting a slim black ponytail, a nod to America's founding fathers, whom he greatly admired. But it left a different impression on Keltner: "He looked like some youthful martial arts guy." And Roy seemed in good shape; clearly, he was sticking with his health regime and had shed some weight. "He was looking really trim," Keltner noticed. "Everything was fantastic."

Roy enjoyed working in what he felt was an ego-free zone. "Everyone pitched in. Once in a while, you'd look around and see George Harrison and Bob Dylan and all those guys just sitting there, like normal musicians, and then you'd be taken aback by it, struck by how famous they were. But most of the time, you didn't think about it." Workdays began around midday, first with communal coffee. Then someone would play a riff, suggestions would be offered, and a song would grow from that. Most days finished around midnight, which was when things got really interesting, according to Lynne: "Roy would tell us fabulous stories about Sun Records or hanging out with Elvis." At one point, when Roy had finished a vocal, Petty told him, "Roy, you must be the best singer in the world." Roy thought this through, nodded his head, said, "Yeah," and then got back to work.

Tom Petty wasn't alone in his unbridled admiration of Roy. The Orbisons stayed with the Harrisons during the making of the record, and as Barbara recalled, every morning George would walk downstairs and say out loud, "I can't believe Roy Orbison's in my kitchen."

Jeff Lynne, who coproduced the album with Harrison, understood that Roy's voice was so good that it was best "not to get in the way," which sometimes became a challenge during what was a group project. But as Lynne firmly believed, the Wilburys contained the best singer in the world—Roy—and the best lyricist in Dylan. How could they fail? It was a dream team.

A song called "Not Alone Any More" was one of Roy's big moments on the finished record—"he hurts as good as he ever has," Dylan observed—as was his vocal contribution to "Last Night," a sing-along so breezy that it should have been served with a cocktail. Many of the dozen songs recorded were funny and quirky, slightly out of character for Dylan, who sounded like a man reborn, especially during the whimsical "Tweeter and the Monkey Man." Roy downplayed rumors that the song might have been a gentle swipe at Bruce Springsteen. "Bruce is a great mate of mine," he pointed out. Roy felt the same about Dylan. "Bob was just a prince. I still think of him as the greatest poet of our age."

When asked about the project, Tom Petty said, "It was just a bunch of friends that happened to be good at making music," which was reflected in the finished LP. If anyone was the leader of the pack, it was Harrison—this was his baby, the first time since the Beatles that he'd actually wanted to be part of a band. "George would kind of audition us, which could be really intimidating," said Petty. This was especially the case when Harrison asked Roy to sing a part and then asked for someone else to have a crack at the vocal. Roy was a very hard act to follow. "Damn," Petty thought to himself, "that's really intimidating."

As far as Roy was concerned, it was a blast from top to bottom: "It was my greatest time." It took just nine days to record the songs for the Wilburys LP.

The easygoing nature of the recording extended into the naming of the band and its members. The "Traveling Wilburys" moniker—originally the Trembling Wilburys—had been a running joke between Harrison and Lynne for some time, so that was quickly agreed upon, but the five founding fathers decided they needed their own Wilbury names. Roy chose Lefty, a nod to boyhood hero Lefty Frizzell. Dylan became Lucky

Wilbury, while Harrison was now Nelson Wilbury. Jeff Lynne was Otis and Petty renamed himself Charlie T. Jr. In the spirit of brotherhood, writing credits were simply given to the Traveling Wilburys, rather than individual members.

Clearly enjoying the lark of renaming themselves, the Wilburys decided to invent their own backstory. According to band legend, all five had different mothers, but shared the same father. When asked about their old man, Roy deadpanned: "Some people said Daddy was a cad and a bounder. I remember him as a Baptist minister." Although not credited directly, the album's tongue-in-cheek liner notes were written by Python's Michael Palin, who was mentioned in the various thank-yous.

The finished record's credits came with a peculiar twist: The members all used their Wilbury names. Perhaps their respective record companies decided not to complain or didn't even notice, but rather than having a credit that read, "Roy Orbison appears courtesy of Virgin Records," it read "Lefty Wilbury," and so on, for the entire band. It was "an attempt to prolong our anonymity as much as possible," chuckled George Harrison, who, across the years, had grown immensely weary of music business hassles.

Despite the different labels involved—CBS, Virgin, MCA, and Warners, all majors—releasing the Wilburys record proved to be easier than the famous five imagined. No one had advised their respective record company people; instead, they agreed to make the album in secret and then deal with the politics. "In the end," said Roy, "we just presented it to them."

One exec did call Roy and told him that, frankly, he had no intention of letting politics interfere. "I'm not going to stand in the way of history."

The album would be released on their own Wilbury Records label, through Warner Bros., and wouldn't be mentioned in the press until August 1988. The five Wilburys had done a great job in maintaining their privacy.

With the record finished in time for both Dylan and Roy's summer tours, Harrison and Lynne flew back to the UK with the finished tapes, which they'd mix at George's home studio in Friar Park, his eccentric English mansion. Roy also joined them for a short time, in between live dates. They hoped to have *The Traveling Wilburys Vol. 1* ready for release before the end of the year.

"My wife says it's a man's album," Roy said to *The Boston Globe*'s Steve Morse in late August when he became the first Wilbury to go on the record. "She says it's a bunch of men getting together and talking about women. I guess she's right."

As proud as he was of the Wilburys project, Roy couldn't have predicted how well the album would be received. *Rolling Stone*'s David Wild gave *The Traveling Wilburys Vol. 1* a four-star review on the day of its release in late October. As Wild observed, there'd been plenty of all-star projects like this, but they typically failed to live up to expectations. Not the Wilburys. "This is the best record of its kind ever made, a low-key masterpiece," stated Wild. He believed that the Wilburys were "one of the few rock supergroups actually deserving to be called either super or a group."

Wild also noted how the finished record recalled "the inspired mix-and-match musical fellowship found in the best moments of the Rock & Roll Hall of Fame jam sessions." He singled out Roy and his work on "End of the Line," which he saw as proof that "Orbison has lost none of his tremendous vocal prowess." Wild's praise was backed up in the UK, where *Mojo* gave the album a five-star rating; *Q* considered it worthy of four stars. Even hard-to-impress *Village Voice* critic Robert Christgau gave the record a solid A- rating.

"*The Traveling Wilburys Volume 1* is one superstar project that doesn't disappoint," declared *The Cincinnati Post*. "The album sounds like it was a lot of fun to make, and the mood is definitely contagious." The *Toronto Star*'s Craig MacInnis was a rare dissenting voice. "Would Harrison, Dylan, et al be capable of something so cheap and coy? So self-aggrandizing?" he asked in his review of the album. "No, I'm sure it's all a ruse." He jokingly suggested it was the work of "some clone band working the Ramada Inn circuit."

The Wilburys shot a video for "Handle with Care" in early October, at an abandoned warehouse not far from LA's Union Square. It was directed by Brit David Leland, who'd helmed HandMade's *Checking Out*, the film that brought Harrison to LA at the beginning of the Wilburys project. On the way to the shoot, in the car, Roy had entertained the others with word-perfect recitations of Monty Python sketches—he knew all the lyrics to their X-rated ditty "Sit on my face and tell me that you love me." "We'd be giggling like schoolgirls," recalled Jeff Lynne. The "Handle with Care" film clip was as straightforward as the Wilburys' music, showing a bunch of buddies gathered around a microphone, enjoying themselves immensely. When Harrison sang about "the sweet smell of success," a huge smile lit up Roy's face. He understood how that felt. They *all* did.

"Handle with Care" was a moderate hit in America, reaching number 45 in *Billboard*'s Hot 100, although it climbed all the way to number 3 in Australia. But the album was a keeper. On the week of its release, it charted at number 57, then gradually scaled the *Billboard* chart, where it would remain for a remarkable fifty-three weeks, peaking at number 3. In Australia, it reached number 1 and stuck around for fifty weeks, selling close to 500,000 copies. Over time, *The Traveling Wilburys Vol. 1* sold more than three million copies in America alone and another 600,000 in Canada. Roy was finally back in the charts and in a very big way.

There was so much going on in Roy's world—suddenly, he was in huge demand. He'd met with actor Martin Sheen, another Malibu resident, who hoped to play Roy in a biopic. Roy was hoping to record again with Dylan and maybe even work with Bruce Springsteen. Roy was also considering writing his memoirs. There was talk of a Wilburys movie, perhaps a tour.

Buoyed by the success of the Wilburys project, Roy had gotten back to work on his own solo LP, which he'd been recording in stops and starts since July 1987. Rock and roll luminaries were lining up at the studio door to work with him. Three members of the Heartbreakers—Benmont Tench, Mike Campbell, and Howie Epstein—played on the record, as did legendary Stax session guitarist Steve Cropper and former Elvis bassist Jerry Scheff, who'd helped Roy out during *A Black and White Night*. It was also something of a family affair, because Barbara, and their son Roy Jr., appeared on the album, adding background vocals to a track called "In the Real World." ("I think it sounds like me,"

Roy said approvingly of his son's vocal.) Wesley Orbison cowrote the song "The Only One," which Roy coproduced with Mike Campbell.

Bono and the Edge from U2 wrote "She's a Mystery to Me" for the album, which Roy recorded with Bono at Rumbo Recorders in LA. "I felt completely out of my depth writing a song for him," the Irish singer admitted. The idea for the track came to Bono in a dream after he'd fallen asleep listening to Roy's voice on the *Blue Velvet* soundtrack, which he'd been given as a gift. Despite his obsession with Americana, the singer wasn't that familiar with Roy's work, but Bono played "In Dreams" repeatedly and was spellbound. "It breaks all the rules of pop music. I didn't realize he was such an innovator."

When Bono played the sketch of "She's a Mystery to Me" to his bandmates in U2 prior to a show, he asked: "Does this sound like a Roy Orbison song?" They assured him that, yes, it sounded very much like a Roy Orbison song. In a spooky coincidence, Roy and Barbara turned up backstage at that night's concert and introduced themselves to the band. Roy praised their performance and then asked, point-blank: "You wouldn't have a song, would you?" "Yes," Bono said, he certainly did have a song. He couldn't believe how the stars had aligned.

When they recorded the vocal for "She's a Mystery to Me," Bono got the sense that Roy was merely reading the lyric, because he could barely hear him. But he had a completely different reaction when he listened to the playback in the control booth. "There was this voice, which was the loudest whisper I've ever heard," Bono told a *Rolling Stone* reporter. Jim Keltner played on the song and he couldn't miss the reverence in which Bono held Roy. "It was like Bono was with the president," he said. "He just worshipped Roy." Keltner too was knocked out by Roy's vocal on "She's a Mystery to Me": "It was just totally effortless for him."

Roy also got the chance to work again with his former cowriter Bill Dees, who'd reached out when he learned they were both living in Malibu. Once in the studio, Dees played Roy a song called "The Way Is Love," which spoke about his religious awakening. When Dees finished, Roy excused himself, returning about fifteen minutes later. It was clear that he had been crying. Roy cut a rough version of the track, which he recorded on cassette and put aside. On Roy's finished album, which was wrapped in November 1988, he recorded a Dees-Orbison song called "Windsurfer."

When he'd finished work on the record, Roy spoke with the *LA Times*. "Hopefully, everybody will want to listen to the album," he said simply. "To have an artist you like, to be able to say 'I heard him when I was eight and he still sounds the same' is a wonderful thing. It's like a good car will always be a good car." Roy sensed that divine intervention had played a part in his career renaissance. "We had our plan, and God must have had his plan, too, because a lot of things just happened."

In a conversation with UK journalist Jon Wilde, Roy touched on the weighty issue of mortality and insisted that he didn't fear death. "I just know that I'm not ready to die just now and, yeah, maybe I'll know when it's really time," said Roy. Another matter that he dismissed was the idea of retirement—why would he give up now when his career was on an upswing? "I feel that the creative energy is always there, connected, always alive, always humming." When asked by Wilde how he'd like to be remembered, Roy replied, simply: "If I'm just remembered, that'll be okay by me."

A reporter from NBC's *Today* asked Roy about the renewed interest in his work. He admitted that he couldn't really explain how it came about, "but I can tell you how it feels—Roy, you write a good song, you can sing a good song, and we still love it," he said. "That's what it feels like." Roy laughed off the notion that he was some kind of "living legend." "I used to think that legend was a synonym for old."

With his solo record done and the Wilburys record climbing charts all over the world, Roy spoke to Tom Petty on the phone. They'd grown close during the preceding few months, having bonded over cars when they were first introduced by Jeff Lynne. Petty drove a Corvette and within minutes of meeting Roy, they had the hood popped. ("I thought to myself, *Wow, here I am, checking the oil with Roy Orbison*.") Roy had just been told that the Wilburys album was well on the way to selling its first million. "Isn't it great?" Roy said down the line. "Isn't it great!"

"He was just so thrilled," said Petty.

In late October, Roy met with *Rolling Stone* writer Steve Pond during a gig at the Arizona State Fair in Phoenix to begin work on a cover story that would celebrate his recent success. That night Roy played at the Veterans Memorial Coliseum, whispering to his bassist before he took the stage, "Cover for me on any notes I don't hit." As Pond would note, that was unnecessary. "Everybody in the room knew he'd hit every note of every song, and he did." Backstage, Roy spoke about the health pitfalls of "the life of rock and roll," but insisted that he was feeling good right now, thanks to regular sessions with a trainer. "Everything's terrific," Roy said. "Couldn't be better."

A few days later, Roy flew to Belgium, where he was given an award at a ceremony in Antwerp. Barbara, who was traveling with Roy, stayed behind after the event to visit family in Germany. Roy then traveled to London for some promotion, where he spoke with rock writer Nick Kent. Roy was understandably proud of the Wilburys, boasting how the record was "number 9 with a bullet." While he talked about future recordings—"I mean, it's not like this is the only album I'll ever make. I've got time"—Roy was also in a reflective state of mind. He spoke about his late father Orbie Lee, giving him credit for his well-preserved voice. "It never deepened from the ages thirty to fifty," Roy explained. Roy reminisced about the early days with Sam Phillips and how his success "came by luck rather than inspiration." He also flashed back to seeing Elvis, "this punk kid," at the Big D Jamboree in Dallas back in the 1950s and how he'd tried to keep up with him during his "Ooby Dooby" era. Back then, Roy said, he was "an extrovert, sensation-seeking. I moved around more than Elvis or anyone."

Now, with the twentieth anniversary of his marriage to Barbara approaching in March, Roy was in a great headspace. All his tragedies were in the past, "a long time ago." Roy had risen above the type of loss and heartache that would have ruined a weaker man. "I have spent most of my life in a state of genuine contentment," he assured Nick Kent.

Back in the States, on December 4, Roy played a show at the Front Row Theater in Highland Heights, Ohio. After the concert, he said goodbye to his band, adding: "I'll see you in January." He then returned to his old home of Hendersonville to visit his mother and his son Wesley, who was now twenty-three, with plans to then travel to Europe to film a video for the Wilburys' "End of the Line." Roy also had more live dates booked.

In a recent interview, Roy had been asked why he was working so much right now. His reply summed up his philosophy: "I have found out in life that it's not the goal," Roy said. "It's the journey. It's not about the outcome, it's about the daily appliance to life."

What Roy didn't say, but clearly felt, was this: It was great to be back in the spotlight.

On December 6, Roy was visiting the Nashville home of country singer Jean Shepard and her husband, Benny Birchfield, his friend and tour bus driver. Roy had been flying model airplanes with Birchfield during the day at Sanders Ferry Park and stayed for dinner. Afterward, he visited his mother Nadine, his brother Sammy, and son Wesley at Hendersonville. Barbara, meanwhile, was still in Europe with her family.

While Roy was enjoying some rare downtime, in the meantime in Los Angeles Virgin Records' promotion department kicked into high gear, sending out preview copies of Roy's new album to select writers and other media. The record, *Mystery Girl*, was scheduled for release in the new year. In a retro touch that Roy would have admired, advance copies of the album were issued strictly on cassette.

While with his family at Hendersonville, Roy began to experience sharp chest pains. He went to the bathroom and when he didn't return for thirty minutes, Wesley investigated and found his father slumped on the floor. At about 11 p.m., Sammy Orbison called Benny Birchfield, asking if he could come over, quickly. "Roy's not breathing." The paramedics arrived and performed CPR on Roy for "probably thirty minutes at the house," said Jean Shepard, who'd been advised of his condition. Roy was rushed to the hospital by ambulance, where he was worked on for another half hour, but was pronounced dead at 11:54 p.m. Roy Kelton Orbison was fifty-two years old.

In a bizarre coincidence, the registrar on Roy's death certificate, Naomi Jones, had also been the registrar on Claudette's certificate in 1966.

The terrible news spread quickly and tributes flew thick and fast. "He was a great guy," wrote Johnny Cash. "I will miss him so much." "He was the best rock ballad singer that's ever been in the business," said Sam Phillips, who added: "He wouldn't hurt a pissant if it was biting him." Fred Foster said that Roy was "the greatest talent I've ever worked with." If there was any possible consolation to take from Roy's death, Foster figured, it was that he had a top 10 record when he died. (On December 3, *The Traveling Wilburys Vol. 1* reached number 9 on the *Billboard* 200.) "He was the nicest man I've ever met in showbusiness," stated Chris Isaak, one of many contemporary singers who'd taken their cues from Roy. "I mean, I *really* liked this guy." Canadian k.d. lang, who'd been part of Roy's *A Black and White Night* and had recorded with him, felt his loss deeply. "He was like a Buddha," she said. "He was very quiet and very peaceful and very solid."

Tom Petty spoke on behalf of all the Wilburys when he said, "It was just so painful when Roy died." It was George Harrison who called Petty with the terrible news. "He'll be okay," Harrison reassured Petty. "He's still around." At tragic times like these, Harrison's Krishna consciousness came in very handy.

In his obituary, *The New York Times*'s Jon Pareles described Roy as "one of rock's most gifted singers. His best work expressed a longing, a feeling of isolation." On the West Coast, the *LA Times*'s Robert Hilburn fondly remembered Roy's artistry, but also "his gentleness and warmth." Roy's Australian fans were devastated by the news. "Roy Orbison, whose distinctive, three-octave voice made him a legend, has died of a heart attack," solemnly reported *The Age* newspaper. Within hours of the news breaking, not a single Roy Orbison—or Traveling Wilburys—CD, vinyl album, or cassette could be found in any Sydney music store. His latest best-of, *In Dreams*, rapidly reentered the Australian top 40, while *The Traveling Wilburys Vol. 1* was at number 2. As sad as the news was, one store owner had to laugh about the number of customers who struggled with the Wilburys name—he'd had requests for "the Traveling Woodberries," "the Wandering Tilburys," even "Roy Orbison and the Traveling Ashburys."

Jean Shepard arranged a public memorial for Roy, which was staged in Gallatin, Tennessee on December 11 and attended by his son Wesley, Roy's brother Sammy, as well as members of Roy's touring band and many other musicians. Roy's body was taken to the Phillips-Robinson Funeral Home in Nashville and then flown back to the West Coast for burial at the Westwood Memorial Park, in an unmarked grave, under the shade of two trees.

Will Jennings, Roy's most recent songwriting partner, was one of the pallbearers. "It was a terrible day, raining torrentially," Jennings recalled. "It was just so sad. The weather was ungodly."

A private celebration of Roy's life was held for family and a select few friends, followed by a larger gathering at the Wiltern Theater on December 13, which was attended by Tom Petty, Jeff Lynne, Graham Nash, Kris Kristofferson, Tom Waits, and T Bone Burnett. The Stray Cats performed, as did Bonnie Raitt and JD Souther. Will Jennings recited Lord Byron's "So We'll Go No More a Roving" in Roy's honor. "People loved Roy," he said. "He was a decent man and he bore his talent well."

A little while after the funeral, Barbara was asked whether there were any similarities between Roy's death and that of Elvis Presley in 1977. She was absolutely sure that there were none. "Elvis's was a death in darkness," she explained, "and Roy was very much involved in daily living. Roy was so fortunate not only that other artists loved him and that he could feel the love."

Roy's sudden and tragic demise was hardly the end of his career. Anything but. His *Mystery Girl* album was released at the end of January 1989, accompanied by both Steve Pond's *Rolling Stone* cover story and a lengthy Virgin Records press release, which served as a preview of Roy's final work and a reminder of his amazing career. "The legacy of Roy Orbison is one that holds a special place in popular music," it read. "Sadly, with Orbison's untimely death at aged 52 on December 6, 1988 of a heart attack, the world lost one of its finest musical talents."

Led by the very Orbison-like single "You Got It," which came on like an updated "Oh, Pretty Woman," *Mystery Girl* was an immediate hit—and most critics found a lot to like about the album, irrespective of the sad circumstances. As *Sounds* magazine noted, it was a "pleasing reminder" of Roy's talent "that turned out to be a goodbye." *Musician* magazine agreed: "The various producers here all revere the singer for what he's always done best, and provided sympathetic settings in the Orbison 'tradition.' The result is an anomaly: a new old Roy Orbison album." Writing in the *Orlando Sentinel*, Thom Duffy was a convert, describing the album as "a triumphant reaffirmation of his talent."

McClatchy News Service's David Barton couldn't quite understand why Roy had been a stranger to the charts, judging by the high standard of *Mystery Girl*. "The mystery," he wrote, "is why Orbison went unnoticed so long."

By early March, *Mystery Girl* was number 8 (with a bullet) in the *Billboard* chart, becoming Roy's first studio album to breach the American top 10. It also became the bestselling LP of his lengthy catalog. According to Virgin's Jeff Ayeroff, sales for the album had exceeded one million copies a few weeks after release. "You Got It," meanwhile, had hit number 25, making it Roy's highest US charting single since 1965's "Ride Away." "You Got It" would eventually climb all the way to number 9.

At the same time, the Wilburys LP was sitting at number 4, which meant that Roy had two top 10 albums posthumously, a rare double. Elsewhere in the charts, two collections of Roy's past work, *In Dreams*, his 1987 rerecording of his best-known songs, and a Rhino Records collection, *For the Lonely*, were at numbers 130 and 140 in the *Billboard* 200.

Roy may have been gone, but his music was everywhere. ORBISON FINDS POSTHUMOUS SUCCESS, announced *Billboard*. "Roy Orbison's fans are honoring the late vocalist's memory in record stores."

In Roy's hometown of Wink, mayor Maxie Watts's phone had been ringing nonstop since Roy's death. Spurred on by the many callers who were devastated by the loss of the town's favorite son, Watts decided to establish the Roy Orbison Memorial Fund, with the end goal being a monument in Roy's honor in the town square.

As for the Wilburys, the video that Roy had intended to shoot in the UK with his famous friends was for "End of the Line," the second single to be lifted from their hit album. In the finished clip, shot just four days after Roy's death, the Wilburys were filmed inside a train carriage—shades of the Beatles' *A Hard Day's Night*—yet again going about their business with a minimum of fuss. But when it came time for Roy's vocal solo, the camera cut to a black Gibson guitar that rested on a rocking chair, then to a photograph of Roy. The song, a tuneful, twangy consideration of life and death, had taken on a much greater poignancy with his passing.

"We missed him and wished he was there," said Tom Petty, who believed that Roy was perhaps the only person he knew who was "prepared to leave" if fate dealt him that blow. "He'd lived a lot," said Petty, "and he was a very wise man."

Just before he died, Roy had been asked how he'd like to be remembered. He chewed it over for a moment before replying. "One day when they are mentioning people who had an impact, if they just mention me among the rest of the guys and gals, it would be great."

Even when it came to writing his own eulogy, Roy Orbison kept it simple. And perfect.

Epilogue

What Happened Next

1989:
February 22: Roy won a posthumous Grammy, Best Country Vocal Collaboration, with k.d. lang, for "Crying."

April 8: Roy became the first musician since Elvis to have two posthumous albums in the US top 5 with *Mystery Girl* and *The Traveling Wilburys Vol. 1.*

April 23: A Roy Orbison Day tribute concert was staged in Vernon, Texas.

June 10: Acuff-Rose Music sued Roy's estate for more than $1 million in damages. They alleged that Roy failed to fulfill a 1985 contract to write at least ten "marketable" songs for the company each year.

October: An album version of *A Black and White Night* was released.

Roy was inducted into the Songwriters Hall of Fame.

The Roy Orbison Museum was opened in Wink, Texas.

1990:
February 21: The Traveling Wilburys won the Grammy for Best Pop Vocal Performance, Male.

February 24: Barbara organized a tribute to Roy at the Universal Amphitheatre in Los Angeles, which raised $1 million to aid the Roy Orbison Homeless Fund and was later screened by Showtime. Bob Dylan, the Byrds, John Fogerty, Chris Isaak, B.B. King, the Stray Cats, and k.d. lang were among the performers.

November: *Traveling Wilburys Vol. 3* was released, but the band opted not to replace Roy. They also chose not to call their second album *Vol. 2.*

1991:

February 20: Roy won another posthumous Grammy—Best Pop Vocal Performance, Male, for "Oh, Pretty Woman," from *A Black and White Night Live.*

1992:

May 13: Roy's mother Nadine died, aged seventy-eight.

October: Roy's *King of Hearts* LP, including unreleased tracks from the *Mystery Girl* sessions, was released on Virgin. It reached number 25 in Australia and number 23 in the UK and spawned the single "I Drove All Night." Roy's "Crying" duet with k.d. lang was also included and rereleased as a single, this time charting in the UK at number 13.

1994:

2 Live Crew was sued by Acuff-Rose Music for "Pretty Woman," a parody of "Oh, Pretty Women," but the Supreme Court ruled they did not violate copyright law.

November: The Orbisons' home in Malibu was destroyed by fire. Fortunately, no one was hurt.

1996:

The Very Best of Roy Orbison was released through Barbara's company, Roy Orbison Enterprises.

1997:

Combo Concert: 1965 Holland was released.

1998:

January 19: Carl Perkins died, aged sixty-five.

February 25: Roy was given a posthumous Grammy Lifetime Achievement Award.

July 8: The Roy Orbison estate sued Sony Music, charging that the company owed more than $12 million from overseas royalties. Barbara Orbison now ran ten Nashville-based music business companies.

2001:
November 29: Roy's fellow Wilbury, George Harrison, died at the age of fifty-eight.

2003:
May 15: June Carter Cash died, aged seventy-three.

July 30: Sam Phillips, who signed Roy to Sun Records, died aged eighty.

September 12: Johnny Cash died, aged seventy-one.

2007:
April: The Hendersonville home of Roy's neighbor, Johnny Cash, now owned by Barry Gibb, burned to the ground.

2008:
November: Roy was ranked number 37 on *Rolling Stone*'s "Greatest Artists of All Time" list.

Barbara and Roy Jr. coproduced a four-CD box set, *The Soul of Rock and Roll*, which included twelve previously unreleased tracks.

2009:
The Last Concert LP was released, recorded at Highland Heights in Akron, Ohio, two days before Roy died in 1988.

2010:
January: Roy was immortalized on the Hollywood Walk of Fame; Barbara accepted the award in his honor.

September 8: Roy's younger brother Sammy died, aged sixty-four.

2011:
December 6: Barbara Orbison died from pancreatic cancer, aged sixty-one, on the twenty-third anniversary of Roy's death. After services in Nashville and Los Angeles, she was buried next to Roy at Westwood Memorial Park. At the time of her death, Barbara was the CEO of Orbison Records, Orbison Productions, and Still Working Music. She also supported Orbison House, a residence for Los Angeles's homeless. Her sons Alex and Roy Kelton Jr. took over the reins of Roy Orbison Enterprises Company.

2012:
October 24: Bill Dees, Roy's cowriter on such hits as "Oh, Pretty Woman" and "It's Over," died, aged seventy-three.

2014:
May: A demo of Roy singing "The Way Is Love" was added to the twenty-fifth anniversary edition of *Mystery Girl*.

2015:
December: *One of the Lonely Ones* LP released by Universal (the album was recorded in 1969).

2017:
October 2: Tom Petty, another of Roy's fellow Wilburys, died at the age of sixty-six.

2019:
February 20: Monument Records Fred Foster died, aged eighty-seven.

2022:
October 28: Jerry Lee Lewis died, aged eighty-seven.

Bibliography

Anon. "Reynolds Heads Iraan Lions Club." *San Angelo Standard-Times*, June 29, 1953.

Anon. "Ladies Feted at Lions Club Meet." *Odessa American*, December 24, 1953.

Anon. "5,000 'Cats' Rock and Roll to Nasal-Twang Refrains." *The Commercial Appeal*, June 2, 1956.

Anon. "The Sun Shines on Rockin' Roy." *Disc Parade*, October 12, 1957.

Anon. "Lifelines of Roy Orbison." Unknown UK source, 1961.

Anon. "Spotlight Albums of the Week." *Billboard*, December 11, 1961.

Anon. "Record Reviews." *Cashbox*, January 26, 1963.

Anon. "Hot Pop Spotlights." *Billboard*, April 4, 1964.

Anon. "'Oh, Pretty Woman' Hits a Million." Unknown US source, October 1964.

Anon. "Roy Orbison, the Rockin' Berries, Cliff Bennett & the Rebel Rousers, Marianne Faithfull: Adelphi, Slough." *Record Mirror*, February 27, 1965.

Anon. "Metro Signs Contract with Roy Orbison." *The Morning Call*, July 7, 1965.

Anon. "Orbison Begins Sessions for MGM, British Decca." *Billboard*, July 17, 1965.

Anon. "Soon: Orbison the Film Star." *Billboard*, October 23, 1965.

Anon. "Blind Date: Stevie Winwood." *Melody Maker*, January 15, 1966.

Anon. "Orbison Carries on in Old Tradition." *Billboard*, April 9, 1966.

Anon. "Orbison, Newbeats on Tour." Unknown US source, 1966.

Anon. "Recording Artist's Wife Crash Victim." *Nashville Banner*, June 7, 1966.

Anon. "Roy Orbison's Wife Dies in Crash." Unknown US source, June 1966.

Anon. "'Pretty Woman' is Killed." *The Daily Record*, June 8, 1966.

Anon. "Rising Star Shining Up in Western Tunes." *The Star-Ledger*, August 8, 1965.

Anon. "Bobby Goldsboro to Sing in Columbus—with Roy Orbison." *Columbus Ledger*, August 28, 1965.

Anon. "Injured Roy Orbison and the Walker Brothers Have the Fans Wild with Hysteria at ABC Cinema." *Cheshire Observer*, April 1, 1966.

Anon. "The Facts of Pop Life." *Rave*, August 1966.

Anon. "12 Girls Collapse at Concert." *The Sydney Morning Herald*, January 22, 1967.

Anon. "Young World: Glitter." *The Sydney Morning Herald*, January 22, 1967.

Anon. "RSL Protest on Pop Hit." *The Sydney Morning Herald*, February 17, 1967.

Anon. "Devon Girls Want a Job with Roy Orbison." *Herald Express*, March 6, 1967.

Anon. "Silver Lining for Jeff in 'Moody' Disc." *Evening Telegraph*, May 13, 1967.

Anon. "Roy Orbison Picks a Nanny." *The Nashville Tennessean*, May 28, 1967.

Anon. "Singer's Sons Lost in Flames." Unknown US source, September 16, 1968.

Anon. "2 of Orbison's Sons Die in Fire in Home." *Billboard*, September 28, 1968.

Anon. "Can Explosion Blamed in Deaths of Singer's Sons." *Knoxville News Sentinel*, September 16, 1968.

Anon. "Roy Arrives—With His Surprise Wife." *Evening Standard*, April 1, 1969.

Anon. "Orbison Disk to '*Zabriskie*.'" *Billboard*, April 11, 1970.

Anon. "Orbison in Decca's Orbit." *Cashbox*, June 26, 1971.

Anon. "Orbison—Sell Out on UK World Tour." *Billboard*, August 19, 1972.

Anon. "The Big O is Still Very Much an Enigma." *The Age*, October 2, 1972.

Anon. "Brown Paper Bag Leads to Gravy Train." *The Age*, February 12, 1974.

Anon. "Big O a Big Hit Behind Wall." *The Age*, February 20, 1975.

Anon. "Mercury Flashes." *Cashbox*, September 28, 1974.

Anon. "Orbison on Tour in Aust, NZ." *Cashbox*, March 8, 1975.

Anon. "Roy Orbison Cancels La Crosse Appearance." *La Crosse Tribune*, May 31, 1975.

Anon. "Roy's Back." *Cashbox*, February 21, 1976.

Anon. Untitled. *Music City News*, March 1976.

Anon. "Roy Orbison Has New Manager, Booking Agent and Record." *Goldmine*, October 25, 1985.

Anon. "Label Hurries Orbison Tribute." *Billboard*, December 17, 1988.

Anon. "*Mystery Girl* press release." Virgin Records, 1989.

Anon. "Roy Again." *Billboard*, December 20, 1997.

Anon. "The Lonely Man of Rock." *Rock*, undated.

Anon. "Where It Came From: Roy Orbison." Unknown source, undated.

Anon. "Forgotten Glasses Started Orbison Popularity Wave." Unknown UK source, 1974.

Anon. "Roy Orbison's Own Rock History." *Rock*, undated.

Anon. "Introducing Will Jennings." *In Dreams* (probably), March 1993.

Anon. "Jackson Browne Says Roy Orbison Inspired Part of 'Take It Easy.'" Nightswithalicecooper.com, February 9, 2022.

Anon. "*Traveling Wilburys Volume 1* review." *The Cincinnati Post*, October 20, 1988.

Arnold, Thomas K. "Roy Orbison, the Man in Black, Riding High on Comeback Trail." *Los Angeles Times*, October 20, 1988.

Arrington, Carl. "Roy Orbison's Got It Made in the Shades." *Detroit Free Press*, November 13, 1976.

Bane, Michael. "Roy Orbison 1936–1988." *Country Music*, March/April 1989.

Barton, David. "The Mystery is Why Orbison Went Unnoticed for So Long." McClatchy News Service, February 1, 1989.

Bell, Andy. "European 'Last' Interview." Unpublished, November 29, 1988.

Bessman, Jim. "Roy Orbison Live Review, New York." *Rolling Stone*, March 1988.

Bickhart, Jim. "Watching Bobby Grow—A Decade of Hits." *Billboard*, October 5, 1974.

Billany, Fred. "Orbison Reaches That £1,000,000 Jackpot." *Lancashire Telegraph*, April 2, 1966.

Booth, Dave and Colin Escott. "Roy Orbison: A Cadillac and a Diamond Ring." *Goldmine*, February 1, 1985.

Brandau, Susan. "Nutcracker Performance Christmas Harbinger." *The Tennessean*, November 28, 1976.

Brown, Peter Stone. "Interview: Carl Perkins." Unpublished, October 31, 1978.

Burbeck, Rodney. "Problems for Orbison, a Challenge for UDE." *Record Retailer*, April 10, 1969.

Campbell, Mary. "Orbison Lost Glasses, Bought Motorcycle." *Wausau Daily Herald*, June 3, 1966.

Campbell, Mary. "Orbison's Music Career Suffered From Tragedies." *The Daily Advertiser*, July 28, 1979.

Campbell, Tom. "Roy's Comeback." *San Francisco Examiner*, March 25, 1972.

Campbell, Tom. "A Runaway Comes Home." *San Francisco Examiner*, May 10, 1975.

Cannon, Geoffrey. "Sun Records: The Ooby Dooby." *The Guardian*, October 30, 1970.

Carol, Jean. "Del and Roy Hope to Tour Here Again—But Together." *Disc*, June 8, 1963.

Carr, Patrick. "Roy Orbison: The Phantom Unmasked." *Country Music*, January–February 1981.

Carr, Roy. "Roy Orbison Makes Big Comeback." *New Musical Express*, September 6, 1975.

Carlton, Bill. "Orbison Returns As Fresh As Ever." *Daily News*, July 9, 1979.

Carlton, Bill. "A Fresh Slice of American Pie." *Daily News*, January 9, 1981.

Carter, Tom. "Ol' Ebony Roy Ain't What He Used To Be." *Tulsa World*, February 6, 1982.

Cook, Richard. "Roy Orbison: *Mystery Girl*." *Sounds*, January 28, 1989.

Cooper, Mark. "Roy Orbison: The Big O 1936–1988." *The Observer*, December 18, 1988.

Crider, Tom. "Two Hits Written in Midland, Melson Reveals." Unknown US source, September 1965.

Cromelin, Richard. "Orbison Sings for the Lonely." *Los Angeles Times*, August 22, 1977.

Daly, Mike. "A Classic From 'The Big O' and Company." *The Age*, March 23, 1989.

David, Melvyn. "The Power Behind Star Roy Orbison." *The Heywood Advertiser*, August 31, 1962.

Dawbarn, Bob. "One Man Who's Not Trying to Get Away From It All." *Melody Maker*, April 26, 1969.

Dees, Bill. "Bill Dees Remembers Roy." Unknown source, undated.

Dees, Bill. "Bill Dees on MGM." Unknown source, undated.

Delehant, Jim. "Roy Orbison's Own Rock History." *Hit Parader*, December 1967/January 1968/February 1968.

Doggett, Peter. "Roy Orbison (on Collecting Orbison)." Unknown UK source, undated.

Doggett, Peter. "Roy Orbison (Peter Doggett Examines the Recording History of the Sixties' Chart-topper)." Unknown UK source, undated.

Dove, Ian. "Janet Martin Describes to Ian Dove Roy Orbison's Home-life." *New Musical Express*, April 12, 1963.

Duffy, Tom. "Orbison Special is a Good Night for Music." *Orlando Sentinel*, January 1, 1988.

Duffy, Tom. "'Mystery Girl': Fitting Farewell to Roy Orbison." *Orlando Sentinel*, February 1, 1989.

Edwards, Joe. "Singer Roy Orbison is Dead at Age 52." Associated Press, December 7, 1988.

Ellis, Bill. "Teen Kings History." Unknown source, undated.

Elson, Howard. *Early Rockers*. Proteus Publications, 1982.

Escott, Colin and Martin Hawkins. "Echoes." *Let It Rock*, October 1973.

Escott, Colin. "Roy Orbison: The Early Years." *Record Collector*, May 1989.

Escott, Colin. "Roy Orbison: The MGM Years." *Record Collector*, May 1989.

Flippo, Chet. "Orbison Estate Sues Sony." *Billboard*, July 25, 1998.

Freund, Nancy. "Beatles' Tailor Pen Pal of Two Wausau Girls." *Wausau Daily Herald*, July 2, 1965.

Fricke, David. "Roy Orbison Remembered." *Rolling Stone*, January 26, 1989.

Goddard, Peter. "Only the Lonely Understand What Roy was Cryin' About." *Toronto Star*, undated.

Goldsmith, Thomas. "Orbison's Roots Include Country, Local Stars Recall." Unknown US source, December 11, 1989.

Goldsmith, Thomas. "Roy Orbison and Friends Debut 'Black and White Night' Sunday." *Nashville Tennessean*, January 1, 1988.

Gray, Michael. "Roy Orbison: 1960's Man of Integrity." *Melody Maker*, March 8, 1974.

Green, Richard. "Roy Orbison, Small Faces: Finsbury Park Astoria, London." *Record Mirror*, March 11, 1967.

Green, Richard. Untitled. *New Musical Express*, May 27, 1972.

Griffiths, David. "Roy Orbison Off the Cuff." *Record Mirror*, May 9, 1964.

Harrington, Richard. "Springsteen: Everybody Knows Nobody Sings Like Roy Orbison." *The Flint Journal*, February 1, 1987.

Harris, June. "Nashville Men Take a Look at London." *Disc*, June 9, 1962.

Harris, June. "Roy Orbison: Hits are Great—But I Miss Those (MODEL) Planes." *Disc*, April 20, 1963.

Harris, June. "Beatles—Roy Orbison Tour is a Sensation." *Disc*, May 25, 1963.

Harris, June. "A Great Tour But Del's Happy to Be Home." *Disc*, June 22, 1963.

Harris, June. "Roy, Brian, Freddie—They're a Knockout!" *Disc*, September 21, 1963.

Harris, June. "Roy Orbison's Moving into his Dream House." *Disc*, February 29, 1964.

Harris, June. "Roy Orbison's Tour May Be His Last." *New Musical Express*, March 11, 1967.

Harris, Peter. "Please Pull Out Electronic Plug, Buck." *Toronto Star*, July 3, 1968.

Hawkins, Martin. "Roy Orbison: The One with the Glasses." *Country Music Extra*, spring 1982.

Heller, Liane. "Orbison Wants 'To Be Remembered.'" Unknown source, undated.

Hilburn, Robert. "The Big O in the Sky." *Los Angeles Times*, December 17, 1988.

Hitch, Slim. "Claudette Orbison Tragedy." Published on Facebook.

Hoskyns, Barney. "The Lonely Blue Dream of Roy Orbison." *Mojo*, January 1999.

Housego, Michael. "Pop Star Roy's Wife Dies in Motorcycle Crash." *Evening Standard*, June 7, 1966.

Howe, Diana. "Malibu Fires Claim Orbison Home." Unknown source, 1994.

Howe, Diana. "Film Director Michael Moore—He Made 'The Fastest Guitar' Come Alive." Unknown source, undated.

Hutchins, Chris. "Claudette Orbison's Death Ends an Era." Unknown source, June 1966.

Hutchinson, Lydia. "Cindy Walker." *Performing Songwriter Be Heard*, July 20, 2012.

Ingham, Jonh. "The Sun Records Revival." *Phonograph Record*, November 1971.

Isler, Scott. "Roy Orbison Gets That Good Feeling." *Rolling Stone*, August 23, 1979.

Isler, Scott. "Roy Orbison *Mystery Girl* Review." *Musician*, February 1989.

Jerome, Jim. "Going Disco is No Sweat After Roy Orbison's Earlier Survival Test: Heart Surgery." *People*, June 1979.

Jerome, Jim. "Bard of the Lonely." *People*, undated.

Johnson, Derek. "C-and-W Stars Pay a Friendly Call on Britain." *New Musical Express*, June 1, 1962.

Johnson, Richard. "Peopletalk." *The Philadelphia Inquirer*, March 1, 1988.

Jones, Peter. "Roy Orbison: One of the Original Sun Greats." Unknown source, no date available.

Jopling, Norman. "Roy Orbison: An Unexpected US Hit for Roy." *Record Mirror*, September 14, 1963.

Jopling, Norman and Peter Jones. "New albums From The Doors, Roy Orbison, Sonny & Cher, et al." *Record Mirror*, April 22, 1967.

Jopling, Norman and Peter Jones. "New albums From Roy Orbison, The Byrds, Jefferson Airplane, et al." *Record Mirror*, April 6, 1968.

Kaufman, Burt. "What If Roy Hadn't Left Monument for MGM?" Unknown source, undated.

Kaufman, Burt. "The MGM Years." Unknown source, undated.

Kent, Nick. Roy Orbison interview. *The Face*, 1989.

Larkin, John. "Orbison Alone, But Not Home, on the Range." *The Age*, January 29, 1970.

Leigh, Spencer. "Bill Dees Speaks." *Record Collector*, December 1990.

Leigh, Spencer. "Questions." *Country Music People*, December 1994.

Lewis, Randy. "Widow of Singer Roy Orbison." *Los Angeles Times*, December 8, 2011.

Lyng, Eoghan. "Inside David Lynch's Decision to Use Roy Orbison's Music During 'Blue Velvet.'" Faroutmagazine.co.uk, January 16, 2022.

MacInnis, Craig. "Reviews." *Toronto Star*, October 21, 1988.

Maher, Jack and Tom Noonan. "Chart Crawls with Beatles." *Billboard*, April 4, 1964.

Marsh, Dave. "Jim Capaldi: *Short Cut Draw Blood*" (album review). *Rolling Stone*, February 10, 1976.

Marsh, Dave. "*Laminar Flow*" (album review). *Rolling Stone*, August 23, 1979.

McAllister, Bill. "Penny Lane Put Composer on Classical Path." *St. Cloud Times*, March 1, 1984.

McKenna, Kristine. "Caruso of Rock Ready to Rescale the Charts." *Los Angeles Times*, May 26, 1979.

McNicoll, David D. "Return to the Rock." *Sydney Morning Herald*, October 8, 1972.

Means, Andrew. "'Golden Oldie' Mines New Lode." *Arizona Republic*, February 1, 1987.

Melson, Joe. Joemelson.com.

Milam, Cathy. "Roy Orbison: The Public Image is Wrong." *Tulsa World*, February 5, 1982.

Miller, Grant. "From Rock Stardom to Bioheads." Stuff.co.nz, June 2, 2010.

Miller, Jim. *I'm Still in Love with You* (album review). *Rolling Stone*, December 18, 1975.

Millman, Joyce. "'Roy Orbison and Friends' One of the TV's Finest Concerts Ever." *San Francisco Examiner*, January 1, 1988.

Mitchell, Greg. "Roy Orbison Rides Again." *Crawdaddy*, undated.

Moody, Carter. "Orbison Files $50m Suit vs Manager Wesley Rose." *Billboard*, August 28, 1982.

Morris, Chris. "Rock Legend Roy Orbison Dies at 52." *Billboard*, December 17, 1988.

Morris, Chris. "Orbison Finds Posthumous Success." *Billboard*, March 11, 1989.

Morris, Edward. "Roy Orbison Estate Sued." *Billboard*, June 10, 1989.

Morse, Steve. "Traveling Wilburys Look Familiar." *Boston Globe*, August 26, 1988.

Neese, Sandy. "Nashville Rocks with Bob Seger." *The Tennessean*, March 2, 1983.

O'Donnell, Red. "Long Tour Scheduled." *The State Journal*, May 7, 1972.

O'Donnell, Red. "Nashville Report." *Record World*, May 12, 1972/November 11, 1972.

Oermann, Robert K. "Roy Orbison Still 'Sings for the Lonely.'" *The Tennessean*, May 17, 1986.

Orbison, Roy. "Orbison Hits Back." *New Musical Express*, October 16, 1971.

Orbison, Roy Jr., Alex Orbison, with Jeff Slate. *The Authorized Roy Orbison*. Center Street, 2017.

Orgill, John. "Orby's Relaxed Way is So Infectious." *Evening Telegraph*, April 2, 1966.

Pareles, Jon. "Roy Orbison, 52, a Singer Famed for Plaintive Pop Anthems, Dies." *New York Times*, December 8, 1988.

Parkinson, Anthony. "Black-clad Orbison with a Big O . . ." *Evening Standard*, May 18, 1972.

Patton, Rex. "Barbara Orbison—Carrying the Torch for Husband Roy." *Goldmine*, July 17, 1998.

Pazzano, Sam. "Death Boosts Orbison Sales." *Toronto Sun*, December 8, 1988.

Pickering, John. Letter to magazine. *In Dreams*, April 19, 1994.

Pidgeon, James. "'Pretty Woman' Makes Clearwater Rock." *Tampa Bay Times*, June 19, 1965.

Pidgeon, James. "Mania Grips Go-Go Girls; Long-Hair Music was Never Like This." *Tampa Bay Times*, June 24, 1965.

Pond, Steve. "Roy Orbison's Triumphs and Tragedies." *Rolling Stone*, January 26, 1989.

Pugh, John. "The Vice." Unknown source, February 1978.

Radel, Cliff. "The Caruso of Rock Has Left One Final Album." *The Ithaca Journal*, February 1, 1989.

Rebillot, M.A. "A Listener Listening – Joe Melson Part 1." *In Dreams* (probably), undated.

Reel, Penny. "25 Years Behind the Shades." *New Musical Express*, December 20, 1980.

Rich, Allen. "The Story of Joe Melson and Roy Orbison." Published online, May 28, 2014.

Robbins, Ira. "Review of Bruce Springsteen's *The River*." *Trouser Press*, January 1981.

Robinson, Lisa. "For the Record: Bowie's Undecided." *The Star-Ledger*, January 6, 1982.

Robinson, Lisa. "Roy Orbison a Survivor, and So are His Records." *The Anniston Star*, April 2, 1988.

Rolling Stone. "Exclusive: The Complete Text of Bruce Springsteen's South by Southwest Address." *Rolling Stone*, March 28, 2012.

Rose, Cynthia. "The Sweetheart Years." *The History of Rock*, 1981.

Saich, Gillian. "Orbison's Massive Family." Unknown UK source, 1970.

Sandall, Robert. "It's Over: Roy Orbison." *Q*, February 1989.

Sandall, Robert. "Outliving a Legend." Unknown source, 1987.

Sandison, David. "Orbison: Svengali with Guitar." *Leicester Chronicle*, April 15, 1966.

Sasfy, Joe. "Sunrise in Memphis." *Musician*, February 1986.

Schreiber, Charles. "Two Versions of Single Tune." *The Buffalo News*, July 17, 1965.

Scorsese, Martin. *George Harrison: Living in the Material World*. HBO, 2011.

Sexton, Paul. "In and Out of Traffic: The Fantastic Career of Jim Capaldi." *Classic Rock*, September 13, 2021.

Sharp, Ken. "Roy Orbison Legacy Well Protected." *Goldmine*, June 14, 2016.

Short, Don. "New Pretty Woman in Orbison's Lonely Life." *Daily Mirror*, March 9, 1967.

Short, Don. "Pop Star Roy is Married Again." *Daily Mirror*, April 2, 1969.

Short, Don and Brian Hitchen. "Two of Roy Orbison's Sons Killed in a Blaze." *Daily Mirror*, September 16, 1968.

Slack, Lyle. "Roy Sings His Own Hit Parade." *The Hamilton Spectator*, November 27, 1976.

Smith, Alan. "The 'Twist and Shout' Battles Hots Up! (and How the *NME* Helped)." *New Musical Express*, July 19, 1963.

Smith, Alan. "Roy Orbison: Talk of the Town, London." *New Musical Express*, August 10, 1968.

Smith, Alan. "Roy's Now Back on the Attack." *New Musical Express*, April 26, 1969.

Smith, Tierney. "DVD Technology Helping to Unearth Roy Orbison Goodies." *Goldmine*, January 9, 2004.

Sperry, Loren. "Orbison Dazzles 1,500 at Armory." *The Sheboygan Press*, November 12, 1976.

Springsteen, Bruce. Transcript of Rock and Roll Hall of Fame speech. January 21, 1987.

Steinblett, Harold. "Roy Orbison 1936–1988." *Guitar World*, March 1989.

Stevens, Guy. "Sun Records: Country Meets Rock." *International Times*, May 23, 1969.

Stierle, Wayne. "Orbison a Victim of 45 Decline." *New Musical Express*, October 2, 1971.

Stierle, Wayne. "Considering the Source: Roy Orbison." *Rock*, undated.

Sullivan, Phil. "Texan Strikes Melodic 'Oil.'" *The Nashville Tennessean*, December 12, 1965.

Sweeting, Adam. "Roy Orbison: Singer of the Lives of the Lonely." *The Guardian*, December 8, 1988.

Tamarkin, Jeff. "A Candid Conversation with . . . Roy Orbison." *Goldmine*, October 1979.

Tamarkin, Jeff. "Barbra Orbison on Roy Orbison." Unknown source, April 1998.

Taylor, Dan. "Orbison Quiets Doubts." *The Press Democrat*, February 7, 1987.

Taylor, Derek. "Derek Taylor's Life with the Beatles." *KRLA Beat*, June 9, 1965.

Thompson, Leon. "Winking Back." Unknown source, undated.

Thompson, Leon. "Roy Orbison Remembered: Anything But Sad." Unknown source, undated.

Triplett, Gene. "Roy Orbison's Performance at Henson's Mesmerizing." *The Daily Oklahoman*, February 6, 1982.

Trollope, Peter. "Pop, Liverpool." *Echo*, July 6, 1979.

Tucker, Ken. "A Rock Knight in Black and White." *Honolulu Star-Advertiser*, January 1, 1988.

Veitch, Jock. "Hits Come Easily to Roy Orbison." *The Sydney Morning Herald*, January 19, 1964.

Walsh, Alan. "Orbison—Friendly American with a Soft Spot for Britain." *Melody Maker*, March 11, 1967.

Walsh, Mike. "Pop Death Toll Mounts." *The Sydney Morning Herald*, January 22, 1967.

Ward, Jeff. "Elvis Said He'd Never Appear on the Same Stage As Me." *Melody Maker*, August 24, 1974.

Welch, Chris. "The Small Faces, Roy Orbison, Paul & Barry Ryan, Jeff Beck: Finsbury Park Astoria, London." *Melody Maker*, March 11, 1967.

Welles, Robin. "Could Have Instant Collectors' Item." *Hi-Desert Star*, January 7, 1983.

Wendeborn, John. "Vocalist Brings '50s into 1977." *The Oregonian*, August 22, 1977.

Westerners, Wink. "Wink Westerners remembers Roy." Unknown source, undated.

Wickman, Forrest. "The Beatles overtake their idols." Slate.com, May 22, 2013.

Widlake, Terry. "Behind the Shades: The Henderson Fire." *In Dreams*, Spring 1993.

Wild, David. "*Traveling Wilburys Vol. 1* review." *Rolling Stone*, October 18, 1988.

Wilde, Jon. "Roy Orbison: The Big O." *Blitz*, February 1989.

Williams, Bill. "Foster Creates a Monument." *Billboard*, December 21, 1968.

Wood, Gerry. "NSAI adds to Hall of Fame." *Billboard*, October 24, 1987.

Wootton, Richard. "Roy Orbison adds rock to the country roots." *Country Music People*, April 1982.

Wynn, Ron. "Orbison monument planned." *The Commercial Appeal*, February 1, 1988.

Young, Jon. "Roy Orbison: The Romeos, Town Hall, New York." *Trouser Press*, February 1981.

Young, Cyndi. "Roy Orbison: He leaves them begging for more and dancing in the aisles at G-F." *Potomac News*, May 10, 1974.

Acknowledgments

Once again, a huge thank-you to James Abbate, Ann Pryor, Jackie Dinas, and all at Kensington Publishing, who are genuine supporters of my work. That means the world to me, so thanks enormously, folks. Here's to many more. And sorry about all the emails.

I also wish to thank, yet again, Dave Booth and the crew at Showtime Music Productions, who have proved to be an invaluable resource with this book and my recent biography of Carl Perkins. If you're ever in the mood to disappear down a research rabbit hole, Showtime is the place. Likewise, Barney Hoskyns and the team at the *Rock's Backpages* website, yet another treasure trove. And special thanks to Glenn A. Baker for the permission to cite his lengthy and revealing 1980 interview with Roy. I'd also like to note how much I appreciate the kind words of Don McLean, Jennifer Warnes, Bob Spitz, and Slim Jim Phantom, who generously offered their time to read this book. Thank you one and all.

I've reached a point in my writing career where I should re-thank the people who've helped me get to where I am today (wherever that is). Accordingly, I extend a big thank-you to Chris Green (RIP), Greg Borrowman, Margaret Cott, Silvia Kwon, Melissa Whitelaw, Chris Charlesworth, Jane Palfreyman, Samantha Kent, Tom Seabrook, Nigel Osborne, Sharon Mullins, Pippa Masson, and Jo Butler, as well as the many others who have contributed, sometimes without full and proper acknowledgment, to what's starting to resemble a legitimate body of work. I am and always will be eternally grateful.

I'm also beginning to realize just how big a supporter my late mother Jean was of my work, likewise my nearest and dearest, Diana, Christian, and Elizabeth. Thanks to each and every one of you. RIP Sheridan Apter—you're sorely missed.

Index